JOHN GLOAG

2000
YEARS OF
England

BRACKEN BOOKS
LONDON

2000 Years of England

First published in 1952 by Cassell & Company Ltd, London.

This edition first published in 1996 by Bracken Books,
an imprint of Random House UK Ltd,
Random House, 20 Vauxhall Bridge Road, London SW1V 2SA

ISBN 1 85170 533 3

Printed and bound in Guernsey by The Guernsey Press Co. Ltd

DEDICATED TO

SIR NEWMAN FLOWER
who thought of
this book
and encouraged me
to write it

CONTENTS

LIST OF ILLUSTRATIONS

LIST OF ILLUSTRATIONS

LIST OF ILLUSTRATIONS

xi

REFERENCES

REFERENCES to authorities, sources of quotations and so forth, are numbered consecutively, and are set out under their appropriate chapters at the end of the book, beginning on page 293. The sources of the illustrations are acknowledged in the captions.

CHAPTER I

THE UNWRITTEN RECORDS

ENGLAND is a living guide-book to over two thousand years of civilisation. It is difficult to travel ten miles in any direction in the country without coming across some aspect of English history, revealed to the observant by the contours of the fields, the direction of the roads, or the survival of some ancient trackway as an overgrown lane, almost impassable because of brambles and nettles, but still known by a name that, like Peddar's Way or Salt Way, recalls a vanished trading route. The shape and nature of the land, as well as the windings of the road, the street plans of the cities, the names of the streets, and, in nearly every parish, the church, preserve the memory of mediaeval civilisation and its pagan forerunners ; and the churches often mark the sites of holy places that are pre-Christian and perhaps pre-Roman.

The furrows and ridges of the fields, the mounds and ditches, as well as the tracks and lanes netted over the countryside, set forth the paragraphs and chapters of English history. That history has been written by poets, scholars, antiquaries, economists and, occasionally, by politicians ; but the heritage of social unity and accomplishment in arts, crafts and industries that has marked and still marks England, is recorded by the face of the land and the character of the villages, towns and cities, and the buildings that adorn or disfigure them, the contents of those buildings, and—most revealing of all—the growth and character of the English home. This book is planned and written to suggest how such records may be read, interpreted and enjoyed. Today, such techniques as open-cast mining, and the reckless use of machines like the bull-

(1)

dozer, could destroy those records with greater thoroughness than merely wicked men, bent on destruction, ever accomplished. Since the first century before Christ, the land that is now called England has been invaded and attacked and harried, and bombarded from the air ; but such disasters, caused by lust for loot or land, or the hatred engendered by war, could seldom do as much damage as short-term industrial exploitation, sanctioned in the name of expediency, or long-term destruction of the evidence of placid and gracious growth, projected in the name of regional planning.

Many changes have been planned in the interests of one or other of the four great myths that have been so strangely honoured in the present century. These myths are likely to be examined with interest, possibly with amusement, by future historians. They disclose much about the moral lameness of our times, for they suggest how those charged with the responsibility of social and economic planning may superficially make their work easier and tidier if they choose to ignore the infinite untidiness that is one of the principal characteristics of mankind. Thus, at various times, during the last fifty years or so, four mythical creatures have secured official recognition or respect, and they are known by these names : 1. The Economic Man. 2. The Average Man. 3. The Man in the Street. 4. The Common Man. Their mythical nature may easily be tested by asking anybody whether they will admit to being one of them. Occasionally, some public man or politician, may, with an ingratiating air, tell an audience that he is speaking to them " as an average man ". That is only a rhetorical assertion ; he would not identify himself with the other three myths—nobody would. But in the name of one or other of these mythical creatures, all kinds of enormities are, in the mid-20th century, advocated and perpetrated against the physical, civic and architectural character of England. Many things that are characteristically English are being discarded ; and with the best and indeed noblest of intentions, some economic and political planners are being more effectively destructive than all the savages and adventurers who, up to 1066, pushed their way into England, and burned crops, villages, towns and cities, and rendered people homeless.

Nobody who is either ignorant or contemptuous of tradition should be allowed to determine the future shape of England. The old shape has survived all the enclosures and rearrangements that have occurred since the Middle Ages ; and it still persists, broken here and there by the lines of railways and canals and motor roads, and obliterated only where the unforeseen growth of some industry has laid waste the countryside.

Every curve of an English road has some significance ; and today the camera and the aeroplane have together revealed just why a road has turned aside, by showing traces of some long abandoned village site, some ancient place of worship, deserted perhaps " Before the Roman came to Rye, or out to Severn strode".

That line from a poem about the English road in G. K. Chesterton's gloriously boisterous tale, *The Flying Inn*, recalls another poem in that book, an unfinished one about a road, by one of the less boisterous characters in the story, Humphrey Pump, the dispossessed innkeeper, who explained that he wrote under a great disadvantage because he knew *why* the road curved about. Most countrymen do know far more about local history than ever finds its way into the guide-books, which usually begin with the church and end with the parish hall, erected by subscription and in the worst architectural taste during the year of Queen Victoria's Diamond Jubilee ; and there is far more to be learned about any stretch of English country from the turns and twists of the road, the fields and woods that flank it, the name and character of the pub, and the memories of the older people who use it, than from any book. Humphrey Pump took his audience a good many miles along the road he knew before he was interrupted as he began the fifty-second line, when one of his companions begged him not to be exhaustive, not to be a scientist, and " lay waste fairyland ". For the innkeeper's method was highly detailed : he included everything : and his verses rambled along like gossip in the cosy bar of an inn, spiced with local allusions and rustic innuendo concerning living or well-remembered people and events.

In six lines he could record the reason for a curve in the road, the independence of a local character who insisted on his rights, the name of a pub, and a change in the course of a stream.

> Then left, a long way round, to skirt
> The good land, where old Doggy Burt
> Was owner of the " Crown and Cup ",
> And would not give his freehold up ;
> Right, missing the old river-bed
> They tried to make him take instead . . .

Roads everywhere in England perpetuate men and memories ; but unless the men were conspicuous enough to find their way into written records, and the memories are connected with acts of war, or social upheavals of some kind, they are likely to be classified contemptuously under the heading of myths and legends. Distrust of any local tradition that could not be supported by chapter and verse in some book or document, became fashionable during the 19th century ; and now, mid-way through the 20th, local lore has been almost obliterated, and the generation that could admire and remember stories heard from parents and grandparents is passing away ; but the roads remain, and so do the fields, and hamlets and villages, towns and cities, and they preserve, in their character and often by their names, a very old England that is not described in any one book, but is revealed, here and there, by poets, and even more vividly by builders. In the suburbs that have spilt over into the countryside from every big city, streets often bear some ancient field name, dating perhaps from pre-Norman times ; and the names of streams persist long after they have disappeared from the surface to flow through conduits and tunnels.

In London, the Fleet River and its tributary, the Hole Bourne, and, east of St. Paul's, and west of the Tower, the Walbrook, have given their names to thoroughfares ; while further west the Tye Bourne, which now flows unseen from Hampstead to the Thames at Westminster, preserved the name of the manor of Tybourn, which became Marybone. The stream itself was once called the Aye-brook or Eye-brook, but was renamed after the manor, and then passed on its name to a once famous place of entertainment, when executions were popular spectacles, and Tyburn Tree drew as many crowds as the cinemas that now shadow the vicinity of its site. The

Tyborne brook was visible as recently as the early 19th century; and a note in Lysons' *Environs of London* gives its course as follows :

" This brook or bourne runs on the south side of Hampstead, and passes near Bellsize to Barrowhill-farm ; thence through Marybone-park to Marybone-lane ; it crosses Oxford-road near Stratford-place, and Piccadilly under a bridge near Hayhill, supposed by some to take its name from this Aye-brook ; which passing through the park near Buckingham-house, and through Tothill-fields, falls into the Thames at a place called King's Scholars' Pond, a little below Chelsea."(1)

The district between Edgware Road and Bayswater is still called Tyburnia, and on its eastern side another stream, the West Bourne, is remembered only by a few street names. It remained visible in Hyde Park as the stretch of ornamental water called the Serpentine, for in 1733 some ponds along its course were drained by Queen Caroline, George II's consort, and the Serpentine was formed ; though a century later the water of the West Bourne became foul with sewage.(2) Fresh water was then supplied by a water company to the Serpentine, and the West Bourne was diverted to a sewer and disappeared from the surface, while the only visible mark of its course today is in Sloane Square Underground Station, which it crosses in a large iron pipe. South of the Thames, the Effra River and the Falcon Brook give their names to Effra Road in Brixton, and Falcon Road in Battersea. Creek Street still marks the place where the Falcon Brook joined the Thames. These are but a few examples of names that have survived ; London is prodigiously rich in such links with the past, and every English village, town and city supplies hundreds of others.

Social and economic changes, the taste of some local magnate, eccentric, fashionable, earnest or frivolous, and the rising and receding tides of prosperity that have affected a place, or the disasters that have depopulated it, are all marked clearly for those who use their natural curiosity to sharpen their powers of observation. If local history was well taught in our schools ; if the significance of the names of streets and places, and the character of buildings, became subjects for familiar study, the urban civilisation of England would be enriched with a sense of continuity and a new, informed knowledge of the value and meaning of tradition. For, whether we like it or not, we are an urbanised civilisation. Every street in every suburb has a story, and some of those stories begin when Britain was a Roman Province, even though the buildings that line the streets speak only of some recent act of greed, idealism, parochial stupidity, or economic planning.

All these unwritten records are described in the Prelude of Palgrave's *Visions of England*, written in 1881 :

> On thy dear countenance, great mother-land,
> Age after age thy sons have set their sign,
> Moulding the features with successive hand
> Not always sedulous of beauty's line :
> And yet Man's art in one harmonious aim
> With Nature's gentle moulding, here has work'd
> A perfect whole to frame. . . .

That sober and realistic admission that the impress of events and actions upon the country is not invariably happy or beautiful is refreshingly different from the uncritical enthusiasm of the " Merrie Englanders ", whose avid praise of " the good old times " is often based upon nothing more substantial than a hearty dislike of the present. Hardly anybody during the last hundred years or so, since William Cobbett and Washington Irving first began to popularise the idea of " the good old times ", has troubled to ask : " How Good ? " or " How Old ? " The substance of some of the chapters that follow may suggest answers to those questions.

CHAPTER II

THE ROMAN BONES

NOSTALGIC longings for "the good old times" evoke popular visions of "the old English home" with "old English fare" and "old English scenes", of the kind usually portrayed on Christmas cards. Those hearty forms of greeting were first introduced during the 'forties of the 19th century, and the custom of slapping your friends on the back in print soon became popular. The cards were designed, perhaps unconsciously, to contrast with the changes that were overtaking English life. The familiar type has plenty of good cheer within and hard weather without—huge fireplaces with glowing logs piled up on the hearth, stage coaches struggling uphill, or a church with lighted windows with a lot of snow in the foreground, enlivened by a solitary robin, tables displaying quantities of food and foaming flagons, subjects indicative of the suppressed longing for something that has passed or is just passing away, indicative also of a preoccupation with the works of man, particularly those arts and crafts that minister to his comfort and pleasure. Apart from the snow and the robins, the backgrounds usually chosen to suggest "the good old times" may be placed somewhere within the last four or five hundred years; the interiors are generally Tudor or Georgian; but the characteristic architecture and furnishing of the English home took many centuries to develop the forms that today gratify a latent affection for tradition, when they are idealised on a Christmas card or caricatured by modern builders and furniture manufacturers.

The "good old times" have probably acquired a sentimental appeal only in periods of change, when most people know or at least suspect that the change is not for the best, or that it implies the irreparable loss of some quality in life. For loyalists in the mid-17th century, the " good old times " would be placed a generation back—before the Puritan dictatorship ; in the middle of the previous century, innumerable men must have looked back with longing to the days before the Reformation and the pillage of the Church ; four hundred years earlier the dispossessed Saxon landlords and their serfs mourned the easy-going days before the Norman Conquest ; and, earlier still, fifteen centuries ago, the Britons whose grandfathers were Roman citizens, saw about them only chaos and decay, and, as they were pushed further and further westwards by the Saxon and Jutish barbarians, thought regretfully of the orderly, settled Roman Province of Britain as a lost golden age, that was already becoming a legend. But even that far distant age has left an enduring mark on England.

A terrifying short story by John Buchan, called " The Wind in the Portico ", begins with some discussion about the disappearance of Roman Britain. One of the characters in the story, an historian, believed that Roman tradition was woven into Saxon culture. " ' Rome only sleeps,' he said, ' she never dies.' " The story is about a remote valley in Shropshire, and suggests that Rome does not always sleep quietly, and that, as another character in the tale said, " 'Sometimes she dreams in her sleep and talks.' "(3) When this happens, it is as disconcerting as conversation would be, coming from the jaws of a skull. We may not care to think about it, but we all carry with us a skeleton that upholds a skull ; though only when life and the flesh have departed, do the bones seem so repellent : the life and the flesh of the Roman Province of Britain vanished over fifteen hundred years ago, but the bony structure remains, and sometimes confronts us intimidatingly.

Roman ruins were for centuries regarded with superstitious dread ; the Saxon invaders avoided them ; for generations the smaller towns were completely deserted, and Geoffrey of Monmouth, writing in the 12th century, bewailed the fact in his *British History*, that once the land was adorned with twenty-eight cities, " of which some are in ruins and desolate ". Four hundred years earlier, Bede had also recorded the former

The façade of the Roman basilica at Leicester, known since mediaeval times as the Jewry Wall. (From Bloxam's *Principles of Gothic Ecclesiastical Architecture*)

existence of " twenty-eight noble cities ". Archaeological research has not yet supplied any examples of Roman buildings underlying Saxon dwelling places, or, according to Collingwood and Myres, " evidence of permanent occupation in the Saxon period ".(4) Church builders were at first the only people bold enough to use bricks and tiles from Roman ruins : and for centuries those ruins remained, while legends multiplied, and odd names became associated with them.

For example, in Leicester, at the east end of the church of St. Nicholas, which is a Norman building with evidence of Saxon work in the nave, there is a place called Holy Bones, and records of that name occur as early as the 14th century, when it is described as " Le Holy Bones ".(5) The name is associated with the site of a Roman temple, dedicated to Janus. This association is conjectural, and that cautious scholar, John Evelyn, when he visited Leicester in 1654, wrote that he " saw the ruins of an old Roman temple, thought to be of Janus ".(6) Holy Bones adjoins a large mass of brickwork pierced by two arches, that has been known for centuries as the Jewry Wall, but was once the façade of the Roman basilica. The basilica occupied approximately the same site as St. Nicholas's church, with the Forum, and later the Public Bath, on its west side. (The Jewry Wall and the excavated site of the Forum backed up by the squat, square tower of St. Nicholas's church are conspicuously visible from the train as it approaches the Great Central Station from London.)

(9)

Leicester was an important town in Roman Britain, built on one of the great arterial roads that ran north-east from Axminster through Bath to Lincoln—the ancient Fosse Way—at a point where it was crossed by another road, running from east to west; it was known as Ratae Coritanorum, and was the tribal centre of the Coritani ; and like most of the Romano-British towns it covered only a small area, in all one hundred and five acres.

Names as unusual as Holy Bones, and the so-called Jewry Wall, have stimulated many speculations about their origin. William Camden in his *Britannia* was as cautious as Evelyn in accepting the suggestion that a temple of Janus once stood upon the site ; but he does specifically state that at the spot called Holy Bones " many bones of oxen have been found, it being the old shambles ".(7)

All over England there are Roman remains that have sometimes influenced place-names, or created local legends ; but our continuity with the Roman Province of Britain is preserved chiefly by the Roman roads. They have been used ever since they were first laid out by Roman military engineers, and they were so well made that large sections of them were in use until the 13th century, with little or no repair.(8) Toynbee suggests that the abandonment of the Roman roads in Western Europe was a consequence of the disintegration of the social system, and not because the technique of road making and maintenance had been forgotten or lost. They became derelict, he contends, " not through a failure of technical skill, but because in Western Europe, between the fifth century of the Christian Era and the eighteenth, the general state of society was such that a road-system of the Roman standard would not have paid its way and would therefore have been a social incubus instead of a social asset ".(9) Technical skill in engineering and building certainly failed and died out in Britain, though it was preserved in some parts of the old Roman Empire, particularly in Gaul, which enjoyed cultural continuity with the Graeco-Roman civilisation and bequeathed its technical achievements to mediaeval France. The glass industry, for example, ceased in Britain after Roman rule ended, but persisted in Gaul and the Rhineland throughout the Dark Ages.(10) In Britain after the 4th century, there was a progressive decay of skill in the arts and crafts : only the roads remained in use as a reminder of the material standards of the Roman province. Those roads are still intact ; and many of them are still in use. Compare the map of Roman Britain which is issued by the Ordnance Survey, with a modern road map of England and Wales, and see how little has been lost, even today. The old lines remain, and even when the road has at some time in English history turned aside, a grass-grown lane or a parish boundary often shows where once the highway ran.

Some of the ports and cities have gone : Lemanis in Kent is now Lympne, and separated from the sea by marshland of post-Roman growth : the old fort of Regulbium, on the north Kentish coast, once an important military station—one of the forts of the Saxon Shore—is now a village with a ruined church, in which Roman material has been used, and is called Reculver. North-west of London, Verulamium has gone, and

Roman gateway at Lincoln. (From Parker's *Introduction to the Study of Gothic Architecture*)

St. Albans Abbey has been largely built with materials taken from the Roman city ; still further north-west, in Shropshire, a city called Viroconium, that, like Leicester, was built at another important road junction, has left a few masses of pink masonry above ground, while the only inhabited places near by are the scattered cottages and farmhouses which form the village of Wroxeter.

Viroconium is one of the four major towns of Roman Britain that have remained uninhabited for fifteen hundred years. The others are Verulamium, Silchester (Calleva Atrebatum), and Caister-next-Norwich (Venta Icenorum). Presumably these were four of the ruined cities to which Geoffrey of Monmouth referred ; but there were many other permanent settlements in the Roman Province, of which some were important industrial centres, that were abandoned during or shortly after the 5th and 6th centuries, and finally forgotten. Of these industrial centres, Dr. M. P. Charlesworth has described what has been called " a third century Birmingham ", now lying beneath some fields south-west of the village of Bromsash in Herefordshire, near Ross-on-Wye. This iron-working centre was known as Ariconium, and the excavated remains indicate " that a great industry was pursued there ; iron was smelted and forged and worked into various implements, and an industrial town had grown up around the iron works. . . ."(11) The glass industry, that was mentioned earlier, also appears to have been well established, and the remains of a Roman glass works have been found at Wilderspool, near Warrington in Lancashire. Excavations there have shown traces of over eight glassmakers' double furnaces and kilns.(12)

At Castor (Durobrivae) in Northamptonshire there were potteries, which produced a characteristic ware that was used all over the Province. The industry was long established in this district, and elaborate and efficient kilns were used ; large, comfortable houses in the neighbourhood accommodated the manufacturers, with smaller residences for their workmen. The industrial districts of Roman Britain did indeed resemble upon a smaller scale those which grew up in the 17th, 18th and 19th centuries ; they represented organised industry, though different in scope and character from the mediaeval craft industries that gave abundant opportunities to individual craftsmen.(13) Like the operatives of Victorian industry, the Romano-British workmen were " hands "—and almost certainly slaves. In the potteries the methods of mass production were anticipated ; and Castor Ware seems to have been made to compete with imported Samian Ware.

Many of the Roman towns and cities survived and some parts of their original names have also survived. We now know far more about the life and character and general structure of Roman Britain than we did fifty years ago ; archaeological research has been continuous and productive ; and the systematic exploration of Romano-British sites suggests that the country south of Yorkshire and east of Wales was thoroughly Romanised. The place-names, roads, towns and villages in that area supply constant reminders of the Roman skeleton that lies just beneath the surface of modern England.

The countryside in the 2nd, 3rd and 4th centuries was probably as orderly and tidy as it was in Georgian England. The land was well cultivated, and adorned with spacious and comfortable villa houses of brick or stone, their outbuildings and servants' quarters tidily disposed, while every prospect revealed a prosperous and settled state. But it was part of a slave state, and was thus vastly different from mediaeval England, and from the post-Reformation England of the squirearchy, which developed into the Golden Age of English civilisation in the 18th century.

As in other Roman provinces, a proportion of the population of Britain consisted of freed men, though what proportion is unknown. The big country estates were probably worked by slave labour, and slave quarters were unlikely to acquire the rich, individual human associations that could grow up in and around a village of free men, or even a village composed of men bound to the land and owing allegiance and giving service to a landlord, whose reciprocal obligation was to protect those who worked for him.

The mediaeval village, consisting of several impermanent cottages, and one permanent building, the church, enjoyed a continuity of character that reflected national peculiarities. The separate cottages indicated a latent independence of spirit and exhibited the desire for privacy which that virtue

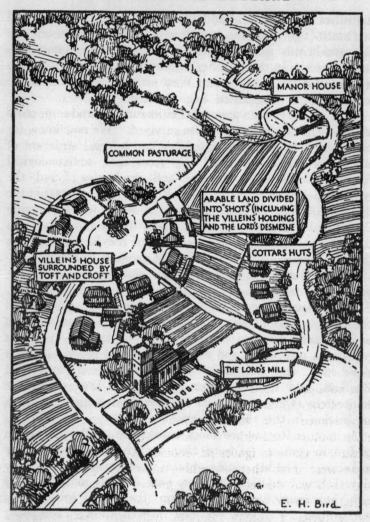

COMMON PASTURAGE

MANOR HOUSE

ARABLE LAND DIVIDED INTO SHOTS (INCLUDING THE VILLEINS' HOLDINGS AND THE LORD'S DESMESNE

VILLEIN'S HOUSE SURROUNDED BY TOFT AND CROFT

COTTARS HUTS

THE LORD'S MILL

E. H. Bird

Pictorial plan of a Feudal Manor, with the perspective distorted to make the lay-out and individual character of the buildings clearer. (The fortified manor house is shown in greater detail on page 148.) The mediaeval village was wholly different in character from the "native" British villages or the slave quarters of a Romano-British villa engenders. The individual buildings might be flimsy, for it was hardly worth the trouble of using stone, as the mediaeval countryside was periodically afflicted with the private wars of turbulent landlords, and part of the landlord's obligation of protection was to give sanctuary to his tenants and work-people within the spacious area enclosed by the walls of his castle. The Earl of Warwick in Shaw's *St. Joan* remarks blandly that " When one has seen whole countrysides burnt over and over again as mere items in military routine, one has to grow a very thick skin."(14) That was probably true. Fire and the sword were hideous and intensely personal realities in the Middle Ages ; though occasionally the clemency and chivalry of those who directed mediaeval warfare interposed, and gave some hope of mercy to potential victims, who also had the strong walls of their lord's castle to secure them. To that extent, they were far better off than the modern populations of the Western world, who are everywhere threatened by the merciless, impersonal efficiency of totalitarian warfare. In feudal England, the village might be destroyed, but the life and skill of the community could be resumed when the tide of war receded.

There were villages in Roman Britain which housed the British natives who formed a free peasantry, apart from the villa population, and were not drawn into the life and labour force of the big landed estates. These native villages showed no advance upon the pre-Roman wattle-and-daub huts. Their builders had either learned nothing from Roman architecture, or chose to ignore its lessons. Round beehive huts of stone were used when something more lasting than wattle-and-daub was desired. Little is known about what may be called the un-Romanised native life that survived throughout the centuries of Roman rule, and little or nothing is known about the land-holding system : certainly not enough to identify the economic place of the native British peasant in the social structure. As usual, architecture has handed on a hint : the remains of British villages and Roman villa houses and their ancillary buildings, suggest that two types of life existed side by side. This gives the appearance of validity to the Romano-British stories in Kipling's *Puck of Pook's Hill*, in which the Roman Province is portrayed as a sort of forerunner of

British India, with the Britons cast for the part of unpredictable and rather unsatisfactory natives, and the Roman soldiers and bureaucrats behaving like the bouncingly healthy polo-playing subalterns, and conscientious and correct Anglo-Indians, that throng the pages of *Plain Tales from the Hills* and *The Day's Work*. Kipling's Roman Britain was thoroughly Romanised south of Yorkshire ; but north of Eboracum (York) and up to the Wall, lay a savage land of moors and forests and untamed Britons.

Although the countryside was so settled and orderly, all the delights of life were to be found in the towns. Bath, for example, was a spa, which as Aquae Sulis was probably as fashionable and luxurious in the 2nd and 3rd centuries as it became in the 18th under the rule of Beau Nash. Architecturally, it may have had a comparable elegance, for Roman Bath and the Georgian city designed by the Woods were built when the classic orders of architecture were honoured and their use understood. But in the Roman city everything was smaller in scale : the total area of Aquae Sulis was only about twenty-three acres.

Romano-British civilisation was largely urban, and as such was ignored, despised or destroyed in the 5th and 6th centuries by the barbarian adventurers who came from Jutland and Germany and Scandinavia, and preferred to make their own village communities, and to build their own houses, without relation to anything that existed. The spacious and often luxurious Roman houses decayed ; and careful excavation has shown that violent destruction seldom overtook them : instead, they fell into ruin. The climate accelerated the process of decay ; the walls sank, and the outlines of hundreds of proud buildings were smudged by vegetation—softened first by grass and field flowers, and then obliterated by bushes and young trees. Anyone today can see how quickly the forest comes striding back—the field flowers and grass and bushes and young trees are already taking over the bombed areas of London and other cities, reproaching man's folly and neglect and hiding his beastly untidiness.

In his book, *The Jungle Tide*, John Still reflects that in this century we probably know more about the history of ancient civilisations than will ever be known again. Writing in

1930, he suggested that another and greater war than that of 1914-1919, or " a period of decay of culture due to some discovery making wealth too easy for our frail natures to stand up to it, or a fungoid disease of paper, any little accident like that might destroy utterly the evidential value of all that has ever been dug up from all the buried cities of the earth. . . ."(15) Reminding us of the frailty both of human memory and paper, he points out that apart from " those two rival frailties, nothing exists to prevent the jungle tide from rising again, and the ruins of London becoming nameless bunkers in golf courses ". Eleven years after those words were published, thin tongues of the jungle tide were lapping at heaps of rubble in London ; as with the same inexorable purpose of undoing man's work and reclaiming for natural life his artificial clearings the jungle tide flowed over Roman Britain fourteen hundred years earlier.

The Ordnance Survey publishes a map of Britain in the Dark Ages, and it is instructive to compare this with the map of Roman Britain. Little survives of the peaceful and flourishing province. The names of a few cities are in process of transition from their Roman form to one that we now recognise. York, for example, has ceased to be Eboracum, and is now Eoferwic : it passes from that form to Ebork, and thus to the modern York. The outlines of now familiar names are set down here and there : Regulbium is Raculf, as a stage on the way to Reculver : Cyningestun on the Thames is Kingston : Tuican Hom, a little further downstream, is Twickenham—but large areas of the country are deserted, marked here and there by cemeteries, and the scarcity of towns makes this map of Britain in the Dark Ages seem like an unexplored, half-savage land, sparsely inhabited.

The barbarian successors to the Roman Province were far inferior as builders and craftsmen to the Romanised Britons ; and wattle-and-daub huts and crude wooden structures everywhere displayed their architectural incapacity. So hardly any ruins exist to record this period, though wherever we go in England today the place-names, or some part of them, remind us of the people who laid the foundations of England. In the spoken and written language we find the roaring, often bawdy, and blustering words of the Saxons, shouting down Latin ;

just as the men who first brought those words into the country, smashed down the Romano-British civilisation, and, generation after generation, pushed what remained of it further and further west till the descendants of the men who had once been Roman citizens found a bleak sanctuary in Wales —the only part of the island that until Norman times had unbroken continuity with the old, lost province of the Western Empire, which was submerged by those twin enemies of civilisation : barbarism and the jungle tide.

CHAPTER III

ARCHITECTS AND SOLDIERS

SINCE the days of Roman Britain, few cities or towns in England have been conceived as new ventures, and their street plans settled before houses and civic buildings were erected. Winchelsea in Sussex, which was one of the Cinque Ports, was laid out upon a grid plan of streets by Edward I, but usually the mediaeval town grew slowly, generation by generation, and in the course of its growth often obliterated all traces of an earlier and more orderly lay-out. Many of the principal English cities and towns are of Roman origin; but their street plans have been lost, and their centres of civic intercourse built over. For example, the basilica of the forum of Roman London is now covered by Leadenhall Market.(16)

After the Roman invasion and conquest of Britain in the 1st century, the first settlements began as camps, and to the end of the Romano-British period many of them remained as military stations. Chester became the permanent head-quarters of the XXth Legion, Valeria Victrix; and from A.D. 75 to about 120, York accommodated the IXth Legion, Hispana, which appears to have been destroyed at that date, and was then replaced by the VIth, Victrix.

As the country became more settled, the towns acquired the amenities and conventional civic grandeur associated with Roman towns in the rest of the Empire. Everything was smaller in scale, and the towns themselves were surprisingly small. Even so, their character was coloured by the Graeco-Roman civilisation which extended eastwards to Armenia, enclosed the Mediterranean, embraced all Europe south of the Rhine and the Danube, and included the North African littoral from Egypt to the Atlantic. By their street plans and

(19)

the placing of the civic buildings, the Romano-British towns reflected in miniature their spacious prototypes that basked in the sunlight round the shores of the Mediterranean ; thus Greece and Rome contributed something to their development.

Military necessity, the needs of a fortress, and strategic considerations, often settled the initial character of a Roman city ; but Greek cities had a very different origin. They were conceived primarily as places that would not only house their citizens, but would give them abundant and diverse opportunities for living full, happy and productive lives. When new Greek cities arose, they were planned with splendid, though sometimes eccentric vision. The influence of Greece still exerts a visible effect upon our surroundings, in England, Europe and America, through the classic orders of architecture (of which more will be said in Chapter XI), and the planning of our cities.

In architecture and town planning, which are both properly the responsibility of the architect, the same problems recur in every civilisation, and the same needs demand satisfaction. Unlike us, the Greeks had an innate sense of civic responsibility that pervaded society, and established the happy conditions when architects and artists and those who plan and build and adorn the environment of their fellow citizens are encouraged and sustained by the understanding and lively sympathy of the public for whom they are working. Creative minds are an accepted and welcome part of such a society : resentment and resistance to the visible work of such minds arise only in artistically insensitive societies, like our own.

In Greek civilisation, a sympathetic partnership existed between art and life. This partnership was constantly demonstrated, by the public buildings of Greek cities, and also by the way their architects used the grid in town planning. Whether the grid plan for streets was or was not a conscious invention has for long been a stimulating though inconclusive controversy. In Greece it may have originated as a result of tidying up the buildings that accumulated on the sides of some main street, or processional way ; at first adopted casually, appreciation of its advantages being a later development. Its liberation from potential inflexibility was an example of Greek lucidity ; for, as Flinders Petrie has said :

" The plan of a town shows much of the mental standpoint of a people."(17) He reinforced that statement by adding : " The Arab is incapable of a town, he can only add together a confusion of huts and houses . . ."

He then described Hotep-Sesostris, an Egyptian town founded by Sesostris II (1906-1887 B.C.) and now called Illahun, that disclosed the social rigidity of the Ancient Egyptian state. There, the privileged bureaucracy lived in fine mansions, some of the higher officials having houses with over fifty rooms and five halls or courts, while the working classes, segregated from their paternal overseers in a different section of the town, enjoyed minimum standards of housing. According to Flinders Petrie ordinary workmen had adequate dwellings, each with an open court and at least three rooms. There were no gardens. Breasted's view was that those houses " so huddled together that the walls were often contiguous " produced conditions which " were not such as would incline towards moral living ".(18)

Apart from the houses and the mean or generous dimensions that denoted their social standing, Hotep-Sesostris was an orderly assembly of socially graded residential areas, set out on a form of grid plan, unimaginative in conception, and deficient in the sense of civic unity that was developed seven centuries later in the Greek city states. Although Haverfield suggests that Greek town planning was inspired by eastern examples, he accepted the view, on the authority of Aristotle, that the first town-planner to use straight, wide streets was Hippodamus of Miletus, who worked for Pericles in the 5th century before the Christian era.(19) In his plan for the harbour town of Piraeus, Hippodamus demonstrated the seductive convenience of the grid, and provided an example that was easy to imitate, and which in the hands of men less gifted and courageously imaginative degenerated into the devitalised pattern of the provincial towns of the Roman Empire and the new towns which arose from the camps and settlements of the pioneers who pushed into the Middle and Far West of the United States during the 19th century.

The Greeks were never intimidated by mere convenience ; to them, the adulation of what we now call functionalism would have seemed an act of repressive immolation performed at the

(21)

expense of imagination. Consequently, Greek architects and town-planners always remained masters of the grid plan ; they were never mastered by it, and they used it as a framework, for the better ordering of their city thoroughfares and great processional ways, and for providing spacious sites for important buildings. The Romans, whose town planning was always a little overcast by military needs—as though every architect's office was haunted by some gloomily practical retired colonel with large and constantly exercised powers of interference— had discovered that the grid plan developed easily if dully from the internal lay-out of a military encampment. They adopted the grid, occasionally varying its rectangular mono- tony by some small irregularity of line or space, usually dictated by some practical need. While Greek architects incorporated natural features, beautified their cities with splendid avenues, and related the whole chess-board street plan to the distinctive and noble character of the principal buildings, Roman towns were pedestrian, tidy and dull, whether they were rich or poor, for they represented the tangible results of a system of planning and government that was devoid of spiritual or intellectual inspiration. If poor, they were grimly utilitarian ; if rich, they were embellished with standardised triumphal arches, temples, and public buildings, while everything worked with exemplary efficiency : the drains, the slaves, the water supply and the innumerable officials. On the Mediterranean littoral they sparkled like the white sugar flowers and ornaments on a wedding cake, and with the same lifelessness, because most of them were the products of a huge, mindless, bureaucratic slave state, and architecture always reflects the ways of men.

Cities of Greek origin were different ; they never succumbed to the tyranny of the grid plan. Even when they were incor- porated in the Roman universal state, they retained an inno- vating independence of character and spirit, irritating enough to administrators, but irrepressible. Most conspicuous among the cities of Greek origin was Alexandria, which in its cosmo- politan character, its grid street plan, its eminence as a port, its wealth and fierce luxuriousness, and its situation upon a narrow strip of land, resembled, more nearly than any other city of antiquity, New York as it is today. Like New York,

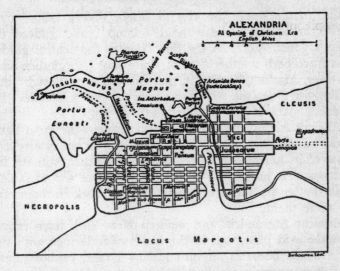

Street plan of ancient Alexandria. (From *The Atlas of Ancient and Classical Geography*, Everyman Library. Reproduced by permission of J. M. Dent and Sons Ltd.)

Alexandria accommodated a polyglot population, and was founded by a nation that did not remain in control of its destiny. The two cities have many common characteristics, and the street plan of Alexandria, squeezed in between the harbour and Lake Mareotis, suggests a miniature, truncated Manhattan. Both ancient Alexandria and modern New York, in vastly different fashions, overcame the tyranny of the grid; but chiefly by the imposing size, the variety, and the brilliancy of the buildings that occupied the rectangular sites formed by the street plan.

In his study of *The Arab Conquest of Egypt*, Dr. Butler has collected various accounts by Arab writers of their impressions of Alexandria after it had been taken by their countrymen.(20) The city that Dinocrates had designed for Alexander the Great was built largely of dazzling white marble; the streets were colonnaded, and in the substructure of the city was a labyrinth of cisterns, descending to the depth of four or five storeys, each upheld by innumerable columns. The intensity of the glare from the white buildings impressed the Arabs; even by night, said one writer, "the moonlight reflected from the

(23)

white marble made the city so bright that a tailor could see to thread his needle without a lamp ".(21) Indeed the avenue which ran from the Sun Gate to the central garden may have been another " great white way ". Another Arab observer, Mas'ûdî, writing in the 10th century, alleged " that awnings of green silk were hung over the streets to relieve the dazzling glare of the marble ".(22)

Ancient Alexandria also had a skyscraper—the great lighthouse on the island of Pharos. Dr. Butler's conservative estimate of its height is 500 feet, although another estimate, less cautious, has put it at 650 feet. The Pharos was as famous in its day as the Statue of Liberty in New York Harbour, and far more useful.

Ancient Alexandria and modern New York have proved how the grid plan, that in the hands of little men with tidy little minds becomes an intimidating tyrant, cannot repress adventurousness in architecture when the spirit of adventure is encouraged by adequate patronage. The palaces, temples and churches of Alexandria were the peculiar glory of the city ; and the patrons of the architects who built them were kings, governors, merchant princes, pagan priests and Christian prelates. In New York, the patronage for architecture has come from commerce and industry ; and its dramatic towers form the architectural monument of free enterprise.

Uninformed by the spirit of adventure, town planning may easily become a form of civic paralysis. The grid entraps the unwary town-planner by its plausible neatness ; for it so obviously eliminates the fortuitous, haphazard groups of buildings that ocurred in a mediaeval city, where the processional avenues of the Greek city were replaced by the winding streets which flowed deviously to the cathedral and the market square. The grid, cutting up the city into orderly rectangular blocks—which look so well on paper—and giving long, apparently endless streets, that continue beyond the built-up areas into the countryside, is never an obvious tyrant ; but it becomes an insistent and implacable tyrant if it is allowed to develop into an instrument for imposing a pattern of life upon a city and its citizens, and it could become the quintessence of inhumanism, if in the words of M. le Corbusier, it " is a direct consequence of purely geometric considerations ".(23)

A society run in a purely utilitarian fashion might consider imagination to be an unnecessary extravagance ; but it would not be a civilised society, nor could it leave to future ages any spiritual legacy. In the Greek world imagination, however eccentric, was honoured ; in the Roman Empire it was subdued and often crushed out by utilitarian considerations and administrative systems. An instance of the opportunities that awaited enterprising architects with unusual ideas is provided by Dinocrates, the Macedonian designer of Alexandria.

Dinocrates was a man whose flamboyant imagination would have attracted attention in any age ; for his approach to architecture and city planning was boldly unusual and occasionally fantastic, and he possessed the blatant vigour of a super-salesman. His first town-planning proposal to Alexander combined staggering ostentation with the whimsicality of a Heath Robinson : his method of securing an interview at which to propound the scheme was also ostentatious and whimsical. Vitruvius, relating the story in the second of his ten books on Architecture, tells us that Dinocrates was a tall, good-looking man who grew tired of waiting for his letters of introduction to be presented to Alexander, and decided to exploit his natural advantages in seeking an interview. So he discarded his ordinary clothes, anointed himself with oil, put a wreath of poplar on his head, slung a lion's skin over his left shoulder, and, armed with a large club, visited the royal tribunal, where the young king sat in judgment.

It was impossible to ignore such a figure, and when Alexander saw him he became as curious about him as the people attending the tribunal. The crowd was ordered to make way, and the remarkable stranger was questioned personally by the king. Explaining that he was a Macedonian architect, Dinocrates described a scheme for carving Mount Athos into a colossal statue of a man, holding in his left hand a spacious city, and in his right a vast cup, into which all the mountain streams would flow, and from thence be poured into the sea. Such a proposal would not have seemed particularly out of place in the ancient world ; it had such a regal air that Dinocrates, the born salesman, had no hesitation in putting it before the one man who was likely to become an indulgent and courageous client. Though Alexander had too much hard, practical sense to plant a city at the end of a bleak peninsula, where the soil could not furnish food for the inhabitants who would have to depend upon sea-born supplies, he was sufficiently impressed by Dinocrates to appoint him as his consulting architect. ("Though your plan might be carried into execution, yet I think it impolitic. I nevertheless request your attendance on me, that I may otherwise avail myself of your ingenuity." Thus Alexander, according to Gwilt's translation of Vitruvius.) So Dinocrates secured his client in a most unconventional, not to say unprofessional way ; and in the end his salesmanship brought him a commission to design a city that became one of the most famous in the world.

Marcus Vitruvius Pollio, the Roman architect who lived three centuries later, also cultivated the goodwill of a monarch, but was more cautious. He wrote ten books to establish his mastery of architecture and building ; a technical testimonial, humbly, almost abjectly, dedicated to his emperor. His idea

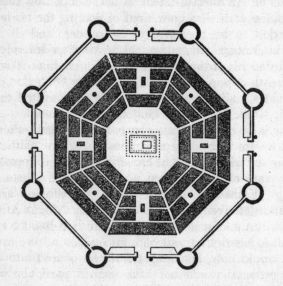

The plan of a city, "so set out as to afford shelter from the noxious winds". (From Plate II of Joseph Gwilt's translation of *The Architecture of Marcus Vitruvius Pollio*. London : 1826)

of a city lacked the intoxicating novelty of the Mount Athos project : cautious, practical and pedantic, he plodded on with his utilitarian specification, to which he devoted the last four chapters of his first book, dealing in turn with the site, the walls and towers, the internal lay-out, and the disposition of the principal buildings. For purely military reasons he recommended a polygonal plan. Within the circuit of the walls, the streets formed an orderly web, which corresponded to the eight facets of the walls, those running parallel with the facets being crossed by eight streets, leading inwards from the walls to the forum in the centre of the city, thus forming eight wedge-shaped blocks. This arrangement was devised as a method of reducing the force of winds, and Vitruvius had some hard things to say about cities where such protection was ignored. He instanced the town of Mitylene, which was superbly designed, well built, but ill placed. " When the south wind prevails in it, the inhabitants fall sick ; the north-west wind affects them with coughs ; and the north wind restores them to health : but the intensity of the cold therein is so great, that no one can stand about in the streets and lanes."(24)

This certainly suggests condemnation of the grid plan, though Haverfield deduces from the criticism that Mitylene had a fan-shaped rather than a square or rectangular outline.(25) The street plan that Vitruvius recommended differed in form and conception from the grid, included no provision for processional ways or magnificent approaches to the centre of the city, and became rigidly geometric as a result of military and utilitarian considerations. What effect these proposals had upon the plans of Roman provincial cities is difficult to assess. In Britain, Silchester (Calleva Atrebatum) unhappily combined a grid plan with an irregular eight-sided circuit of walls ; but Vitruvius was merely setting forth his idea of a safe, comfortable, healthy city, to be built on a new site, carefully chosen. Such a city was incapable of growth within the walls, once it had been built up ; it could be changed, but only by demolition and rebuilding. The walls limited expansion, for only a few special and sacred edifices were deliberately placed in the adjoining countryside. Vitruvius recommended that the temple of Mars should be out of the city, also the temple of Ceres.(26)   In the cities of ancient Greece the wall was a late addition, and was not, as Professor Wycherley points out, " a primary or essential element in the architectural form of the city ".(27)   In making it clear that Greek town-planners and architects were not intimidated by the need for defence, he says : " The wall was loosely flung around the city ; it was not the frame into which the rest was fitted, and it was not normally a dominant factor in the plan.   This is particularly true of the earlier towns ; in those which were founded comparatively late, when walls had become usual and were considered a necessity, a circuit might be marked out and built up at an early phase, for the sake of immediate security ; but still the outline was irregular and did not conform to a type."(28)

The Greeks were never specialists in the architecture of fear : the purpose of the city was never obscured by the transient dangers that occasionally beset the state.   Professor Wycherley contrasts the minor part played by walls in the structure of a Greek city, with Egyptian, oriental, and even Italian cities.   " Italian town-planning ", he reminds us, " had strong military and religious associations ; the town was related to the camp, in which a regular *vallum* with its gates placed in the axis of the two main streets defined the whole plan and fixed the type."(29)

When the Vitruvian formula for town planning is dissected, the absence of any daring or imagination and the honouring of safety, comfort, health and utility—all crassly material considerations—suggest that its author was a cautious forerunner of the modern functionalist.   Vitruvius was already living in a world from which imagination was being gradually drained off ; a world that Augustus was transforming into a vast bureaucratic machine (it is conjectured that the emperor to whom Vitruvius dedicated his work was Augustus) ; a world wherein there was a place for everything except fantasy or experiments, and, eventually, a rule or regulation for the conduct and occupation of every individual.   (That happened a few centuries later under Diocletian.)   It was a world in which a sprightly innovator like Dinocrates would have been both out of place and unoccupied ; sprightliness was not encouraged by patronage in the Roman Empire, as Apollodorus

(28)

of Damascus discovered when he criticised the Emperor Hadrian's plans for a temple. As an architect, he realised that if the statues of goddesses seated in the temple area could stand erect, their heads would go through the roof. Unfortunately, he mentioned this, and lost his client and subsequently his life, for Roman Emperors, surrounded by subservient bureaucrats, were impatient of independent specialists.

So little did imagination inspire the planning of cities in the provinces of the Empire, that few of them impressed a pattern upon their mediaeval successors. In Britain, as we have seen, the Roman street plans of cities are lost. New growth refashioned the cities, when England emerged from the Dark Ages and the Roman Province was forgotten. This fact is sometimes used to support the argument that after the collapse and conquest of Roman Britain the cities were deserted, and even London had no continuity of occupation ; but the discarding of Roman street plans and the disuse of Roman buildings might indicate only a different conception of city life, different habits and beliefs, and certainly different and much lower standards of health and comfort, though an equal regard for safety. The line of the walls survived. In London, the northern limit of the Roman city wall, that was also the wall of mediaeval London, is still marked by existing streets : London Wall, and eastwards, Wormwood Street, Camomile Street, Bevis Marks and Duke Street. From the point where Duke Street joins Fenchurch Street—which is the site of Aldgate—the line of the Roman wall runs south, under the east side of Jewry Street, and then proceeds in a straight line to the Tower.

The walled city was the only kind that could possibly survive in England between the decline of the peaceful Roman Province and the 15th century. Under the *Pax Romana*, the land we now call England enjoyed three centuries of freedom from fear. From the end of the 3rd century onwards, fortification curbed growth as surely as it did in the plans recommended by Vitruvius for the building of safe and comfortable cities.

The soldier and the architect are bad mixers ; but for over two thousand years they have been forced into uncomfortable partnership in Western civilisation.

CHAPTER IV

THE LAND AND THE "NATIVES"

BEFORE the growth of the town is traced from its Roman foundations to its present incoherent and architecturally unruly condition, the sort of country in which our towns were first built should be considered. Many of the sites chosen for the Roman camps and strong points which subsequently became towns were already British settlements, though often such settlements were little more than groups and clusters of huts, dome-shaped structures, built sometimes of stone, but more often of wattle and daub. The stone houses were built of dry masonry, constructed like the walls that separate the fields of Yorkshire, Derbyshire and the Cotswolds. Such dome-shaped houses were still built and inhabited up to the middle years of the 19th century in the Hebrides, and were generally known as beehive houses, the Gaelic name being *bo'h* or *bothan*.(30) The beehive form was given by laying large, undressed stones in courses that overlapped each other and curved inwards until only a small hole was left at the top of the dome. This was one of the oldest forms of masonry, and it may originally have led to the discovery of the arch, though in the beehive houses of Lewis and Harris the arch principle was not used.

To such accomplished builders as the Romans, the domestic architecture of the Britons must have seemed crudely primitive. The architectural inferiority of Britain was dramatically admitted by the captured chieftain, Caractacus, when he saw Rome for the first time and asked : " When you had all this, did you covet our hovels ? " (That question is attributed to him by Joannes Zonaras, the 12th-century Byzantine historian.) (31) A British village and a Roman city must have

furnished as vivid and startling a contrast as would a Zulu
kraal with modern London or New York. Even Stonehenge,
and the much bigger and more important temple of Ave-
bury, which excite our admiration today, would hardly have
impressed Roman soldiers and officials ; for although such
structures represented not inconsiderable feats of erection,
they could appear only as barbarian fumbling compared with
the triumphal arches and temples that bedecked Rome and
every settled province of the Empire. The Romans were
possibly more interested in Silbury Hill, which may at that
time have been as it is now the largest artificial mound in
Europe ; its use as a shadow hill, or clock of the seasons,
for measuring the progress of the year by the sun had probably
been long discontinued and perhaps forgotten, so its original
purpose was unknown to the Roman engineers, who respected its
bulk sufficiently to turn aside the road that runs westwards from
Silchester through Speen to Bath. Estimates of the date these
monuments were built have varied between 2000 and 400 B.C.,
but it seems likely that they were five or six centuries old when
the Romans took over the country.(32) And what a strange
country it was—a land of marsh and forest, with great uncouth
temples squatting on the open downland or in secluded valleys,
with straight green roads of springy turf following the ridges
of the uplands, and, like a huge net over the country, innumer-

Beehive houses built of rough, undressed stones. Houses of
this kind were inhabited as late as 1859 in Uig, Lewis. (From
a drawing by Captain Thomas, included in Dr. Arthur
Mitchell's book, *The Past in the Present*. Edinburgh : 1880)

able straight trackways, sighted on mark stones and mounds, linking up villages and camps, storehouses and assembly places, which the natives knew by heart and could use unerringly by day or night. That cliché, the " trackless forest ", was inapplicable to the dense woods of ancient Britain. Everywhere the trackways gave evidence of traffic and trade and an ordered and established system of communication. It is still possible to follow many of these sighted tracks, and to pick up the marks on which they are aligned, both by sight and on a large-scale Ordnance Survey map. In his book on the subject, *The Old Straight Track*, Mr. Alfred Watkins has adopted the term " leys " for these alignments through the mark-points ; and he contends that these ancient, straight trackways determined the site of almost every branch of communal life.(33)

The main roads of pre-Roman Britain have been mapped and described in that comprehensive work by Hippisley Cox, *The Green Roads of England* ; and their course along the high ground suggests not only the great extent of marshland that they were designed to avoid, but the existence of coastlines and estuaries, long since silted up or drained.(34) The excellent map of Neolithic Wessex, published by the Ordnance Survey,(35) shows the coast of Somerset as a smudged meeting place of marshland and sandbanks, between the Quantocks and the Mendips, the marsh running far inland, over the Bridgwater and Glastonbury Levels, penetrated here and there by thin fingers of forest lying along the strips of land that stood above sea level. Inlets along the coast of East Anglia allowed the Roman galleys and, a few centuries later, the long ships of the Saxons and Danish Vikings to penetrate far inland ; in Kent, old ports have become inconspicuous towns or villages, their harbours and quays covered by fields ; and in the north too the land has been raised by twenty feet or more,(36) which gives substance to the theory that part of Scotland was once an island, separated from the south by the Forth and Clyde, which were joined in Stirling.(37) In a map made about the middle of the 13th century by Matthew of Paris, the English chronicler, who was a monk at St. Alban's Abbey, this separation is shown, the Clyde and Forth are connected, and the northern island is called Scocia Ultra Marina. The map by Richard de Haldingham and de Lafford, which

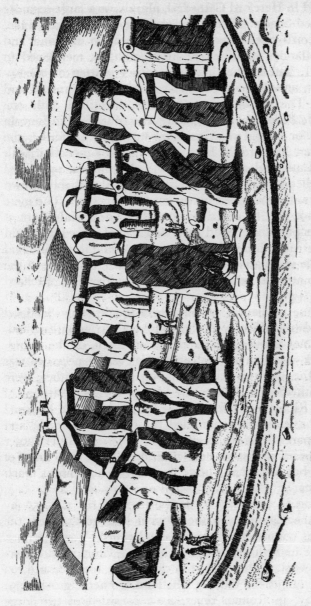

Stonehenge, copied from the engraving in Gough's edition of Camden's *Britannia* (1789). This is based on a much older engraving, dated 1575, which is probably the earliest pictorial record of the monument. (From *Stonehenge and its Barrows*, by William Long. Devizes: 1876)

is preserved in Hereford Cathedral, also shows a large separate island called Scocia. This map was drawn about A.D. 1280, and it records twenty-six cities and towns in England and six in Scotland. (Geoffrey of Monmouth, as mentioned in Chapter II, had in the previous century written of twenty-eight cities, an unspecified number of which were ruined and derelict.) The cartographer has been identified with one Ricardus de Bello, who held the Prebend of Lafford in Lincoln Cathedral for several years previous to 1283. Lafford is the old name of Sleaford in Lincolnshire. His connection with Hereford Cathedral dates from 1305, when he was appointed to the Prebend of Norton. "The map was probably drawn before the author resigned his prebend at Lincoln. The mere circumstance that he describes himself as ' de Haldingham et Lafford ' implies this. Had he drawn it at Hereford he would surely have called himself ' de Norton ' ; while in the interval between his resignation of the one and his acceptance of the other appointment, he would have signed himself as ' Richard de Bello '."(38)

That these mediaeval cartographers should show Scotland as an island is significant, for they were both living in England, and were not drawing maps of remote parts of the world. Their work was not largely conjectural, as by necessity was much of the work of earlier map-makers when they were dealing with the far West of the known world : Matthew of Paris and Richard of Haldingham lived within five hundred miles of the strait that connected the Clyde and Forth, and did not apparently doubt its existence. In the twelfth chapter of his *Ecclesiastical History*, Bede mentions these " two inlets of the sea ", but says that " they do not reach so as to touch one another ".

According to the map of the world made in A.D 150 by Ptolemy, the Egyptian mathematician and geographer, the British Isles consisted of a large island called Albion, with a smaller one immediately north of it called Thule, with Hibernia on the west. Thule was too close to be Iceland, and too large to be one of the Orkney, Shetland or Faeroe groups.(39) Britain may, in Roman times, have consisted of two large islands ; Ptolemy may have based his map of the Empire's western extremities upon far more information than the

mediaeval cartographers possessed ; and the strait between
England and Scotland, if one ever existed, may well have been
much wider when Ptolemy showed it as a space between Albion
and Thule, than it was in the days of Matthew of Paris and
Richard of Haldingham. The Romans were disappointingly
incurious about the geography of the West ; they were
intrigued by the mystery of the Nile's source—Nero sent an
exploring expedition to find it—but they ignored the mystery
of the Atlantic. Roman mariners probably knew far more
about the Atlantic than scholars and geographers. A fragment of grey Roman earthenware has been dredged up by a
trawler in 150 fathoms of water, near the Porcupine sandbank,
which is one hundred and fifty miles west of Ireland. On the
bottom is a crudely scratched drawing of an animal that looks
like a bear, and above this a graffito which appears to read :

C   PISCI
FAGI

This fragment is now in the National Museum of Wales.(40)
It is a tantalising find ; both stimulating and unsatisfying to
the imagination.

Whatever knowledge the Romans may have had of the seas
that surrounded the British Isles, they had a detailed and well-
recorded knowledge of the country south of the Forth and
Clyde. The land was thickly wooded ; the clay soils supported
the common oak, with hazel, blackthorn and a tangled undergrowth of briars and brambles ; the better-drained soils were
covered by birch, ash, beech and yew, with little undergrowth,
and interspersed with heaths and grassland.(41) The oak is
one of the oldest inhabitants of Britain ; it is found in what
used to be called " Noah's Woods ", the submerged forests of
which traces may be seen at low tide on many parts of the
coast, and which flourished in Neolithic times. Since then,
there has been a change of sea level of 80 feet, possibly
more.(42) Sir Cyril Fox suggests that the sea level has remained unchanged since about 700 B.C., and that the climate is
much the same now as it was when the Romans took over the
country.(43) In those dense woods there were bears, wolves,
boars and wild cats. As late as the 12th century, wild boars
and wild oxen swarmed in the woods north of London.(44)

The Romans began to clear those woods in places, and to pierce them with their spear-straight roads, felling the trees for seventy yards on each side of the roadway to protect traffic and to discourage the predatory inclinations of the more conservative British natives, who remained stubbornly unimpressed and untamed by Roman civilisation. This enormous labour, far more formidable than the clearing of African jungles with modern mechanical appliances, was occasionally avoided by swinging the roads away from natural obstacles.(45) Many of the Roman towns and settlements were situated in great, artificial clearings ; but when Britain ceased to be a Roman province, the woodlands reoccupied them, and marched back over deserted forts and stations, cities, villages and ruined villa houses. The clearings were absorbed in the forest, and four hundred years of order in administration and technical skill in engineering and architecture and town planning were forgotten. The rain and the wet winds from the south-west restored the rule of Nature ; and for five hundred years the forests were reprieved, for few inroads were made upon them by the fragmentary civilisations that preceded the Norman Conquest.

As for the natives, they became squatters in the ruined country houses of the Romano-British gentry ; life of a kind probably flickered on in some of the towns, but the Saxon settlers and raiders who began to invade the country long before Roman rule had finally collapsed were not townsmen. They were adventurers who wanted land to own and farm, and cities to loot. In their blithe, uninhibited fashion, they fought for what they wanted, killed or enslaved the men and raped the women. Housman has condensed the story of those days of rapine and re-settlement into a couplet in his poem, *The Welsh Marches* :

> Couched upon her brother's grave,
> The Saxon got me on the slave.

The Saxons rejected town life ; and the growth of the town which had continued with various fluctuations from the 1st to the end of the 3rd century in Britain was arrested, like the destruction of the forests. The modern Englishman's love of the country, his unconscious rejection of town life and his desire to escape from it, even if he can only symbolise that desire by devotion to a patch of garden or a window-box, is perhaps rooted in that old and unrecorded England, when the town-scorning Saxons settled down to make their homes in the countryside. There was no easy and civilised transition from Roman province to barbarian kingdom, as in France, where the Roman provincials and their conquerors, Goths, Burgundians and Franks, worked out a reasonably satisfactory scheme of partnership in land and produce, and the cities retained their Roman form of self-government. This transition has given France direct continuity with the Western Roman Empire : the lack of it in Britain has given the three countries, England, Scotland and Wales, independent traditions in every department of life, and particularly in architecture and the arts and crafts.

CHAPTER V

THE LAST OF THE GREEN WOOD

WHILE some native squatters were lighting fires and doing their cooking upon the tessellated pavements of the fine houses in the dying towns of Roman Britain, others took to the woods, not always for fear of Saxon raiders, but because good government and the security it provides had broken down in the province.(46) That breakdown had occurred in Britain before the critical and disastrous 5th century, when Roman civilisation was everywhere fighting a rearguard action against barbarism, until in the year 476 its defeat was proclaimed to the world by the barbarian king, Odoacer, who informed Constantinople that there was no longer an Emperor in the West.

The woods were the refuge of tribesmen who had remained obstinately native, of runaway slaves, and other unruly characters who preferred the free life of the hunter to the law and order of the town or the hard routine of farming. Game was abundant, and the woodlanders could live well; for generations they were the undisputed lords of the forest, and there they established a tradition of woodcraft and skill in the chase, and wove it into the rich texture of mediaeval life. Their gaudy freedom always annoyed kings and great landlords, who after the Norman Conquest regarded the outlaws of the forest much as the English colonists of North America had regarded the native Red Indians. Life was easy enough for them when England was a collection of disunited warring states, half pagan, half Christian, lit briefly in the 7th and 8th centuries by the literary and artistic achievements of Northumbria; but after the Normans came the outlaws were consistently harried and tracked down; landlords established savage traditions of persecution; oppressive game laws with

ferocious penalties for offenders were made ; and those traditions survived and found expression in the merciless attitude
of the 18th- and 19th-century squires towards poachers. As
the woodlands began to diminish after the 11th century,
the men of the forest were, generation after generation, confined to narrower areas, and it became easier to attack them.

It was only when the country was united by a strong government that towns began to grow again, and church building as
well as shipbuilding expanded, thus increasing demands upon
the forest trees. Because the face of England has changed,
for worse rather than for better, during the last two hundred
years, and most current denunciations of the Industrial Revolution are concerned with the damage it has done in destroying
large areas of productive agricultural land, in creating foul
slums, and in scattering up and down the country untidy
and ugly industrial buildings and plant, we have forgotten
the effects of an earlier and much slower form of destruction.
But four centuries ago it was disturbing the minds of far-
sighted Englishman quite as much as the effects of the Industrial Revolution disturb them today. The forests were
sentenced to death after 1066—slowly but inexorably that
sentence was executed in mediaeval England.

The biggest demand for timber was for fuel—not only for
heating and cooking, but for the iron industry. The Forest
of Dean had provided fuel for the forges of the 3rd-century
Birmingham at Ariconium in the Wye valley ; that great
forest also supplied English smiths in pre-Norman times, and
the Abbey of Flaxley, founded in 1140, organised iron production in many districts in that part of Gloucestershire, and
those centres remained active until the 17th century. Several
of the great abbeys had their own iron-producing plants, for
making agricultural implements.(47) In the Middle Ages,
the chief English iron-working centres were Kent, Sussex, the
Forest of Dean area of Gloucestershire, and Rockingham Forest
in Northamptonshire ; all areas that were rich in woodlands.
Sussex and part of Kent were covered by the great forest
known to the Saxons as Andredes Leag. This extended from
Lympne, the Roman port of Lemanis, on the east, to the
western borders of what is now Sussex, and on the north it
merged with the woodlands of Surrey.

Other industries gradually became large users of wood fuel, notably the glass industry; and by the mid-16th century, England was experiencing a serious timber shortage. In 1543 an Act was passed that regulated the cutting of wood and coppices, though Surrey, Sussex and Kent were excluded. With the increasing importance of shipbuilding a timber shortage was a nightmare to England's rulers during the 16th century, and in 1558 another Act was passed, that forbade the use as fuel of any timber growing within fourteen miles of the coast or navigable river; though from this Act the woodlands of the Weald were again excluded.

The Kent and Sussex iron trade was active during the Elizabethan period, although in 1576 the casting of cannon in the Weald was prohibited, because the country's supply was supposed to be adequate; but a " black market " in guns continued, and gun-running to the Continent was a flourishing though officially " invisible " export trade. During this period glass works were also devouring wood fuel in Surrey, Sussex and Kent; but early in the 17th century coal began to replace wood for glass-making. Meanwhile the iron industry continued the work of destroying the great Forest of Anderida, the Andredes Leag, of which now hardly any trace remains. Only when the work of destruction was nearly complete did the Wealden iron industry disappear, as iron-working was transferred to areas that could supply coal for fuel.

Tudor statesmen and monarchs alike could perceive the destruction wrought by an essential industry; they deplored the passing of the woodlands, but they thought largely in terms of prohibition and restriction—curbing the development of industry and trying, vainly, to set limits to the expansion of the town. The woodlands were vanishing, and already they were a subject of romantic regret; the Elizabethans could think of them with the anxious longing with which we now think of the whole of rural England. Shakespeare praised all those old, copious freedoms of the woodlanders' life when he wrote :

Who doth ambition shun,
And loves to live i' the sun,
Seeking the food he eats,
And pleased with what he gets,

Come hither, come hither, come hither :
Here shall he see
No enemy
But winter and rough weather.

The woods had already become peopled with legendary
heroes ; but side by side with Robin Hood and Little John
were darker figures, witches and magicians, and an army of
sprightly and less sinister little folk who were mischievous and
only occasionally malevolent. Strange things went on in the
woods ; and pagan rites were still practised in the 17th century.
An Old Religion, older than England, older than Rome, and
rooted in pre-Roman Britain, stubbornly persisted. Shelter
for the dark practices of witchcraft, asylum for the outcast and
the type of man who, because he was at heart a hunter, could
never fit into the increasingly precise pattern of contemporary
civilisation, and a home for landless men who loved liberty
above all else, could always be found " under the greenwood
tree ". When they thought of their doomed woodlands, the
Elizabethans, despite their robust confidence in themselves,
their country and its future, may have thought of old times
as good times. Their rulers tried to arrest the destruction of
the forests ; but it was not until the latter part of the 17th century that a constructive and creative approach to the problem
was fostered by that great Englishman, John Evelyn. His
treatise, *Sylva*, which he described as " a Discourse of Forest-
Trees and the Propagation of Timber in His Majesties Dom-
inions ", became a best-seller, and was reprinted, not only in
Evelyn's lifetime, but during the 18th century. In his introduction to that work, which was first published in 1664, Evelyn
recorded reasons other than industrial for the progressive
diminution of the woodlands. He said : " For it has not been
the late increase of shipping alone, the multiplication of glass-
works, Iron-Furnaces, and the like, from whence this impolitick
diminution of our Timber has proceeded ; but from the disproportionate spreading of Tillage, caused through that prodigious havock made by such as lately professing themselves
against Root and Branch (either to be re-imburs'd their Holy
purchases, or for some other sordid resect) were tempted, not
only to fell and cut down, but utterly to extirpate, demolish,
and raze, as it were, all those many goodly Woods, and Forests,

which our more prudent Ancestors left standing, for the Ornament and service of their Country. And this devastation is now become so Epidemical, that unless some favourable expedient offer itself, and a way be seriously, and speedily resolv'd upon, for a future store, one of the most glorious, and considerable Bulwarks of this Nation, will, within a short time, be totally wanting to it."(48)

Evelyn's proposals for planting, both as a duty and a pleasure, greatly influenced the English landscape during the 18th century ; though much of the damage that was repaired by the planting undertaken during the Georgian period was to be repeated by another Industrial Revolution, quicker and far more devastating than the slow destruction of English forests during the Middle Ages. Since the end of the 1914–19 war, some of the ravages of the Industrial Revolution have been and are being repaired by the slow, but well-planned and far-sighted work of the Forestry Commission. By A.D. 2000, England may again have more woodlands, and a more abundant timber supply, than she has had since the Middle Ages.

To think about the " good old times " in terms of the forests that once nearly covered the country, is to admit that the magic of those old stories of Robin Hood and his band is still potent. Legends about a righter of wrongs, acting outside the law, sound as many responsive chords today as they did seven or eight hundred years ago, as proved by Edgar Wallace's popular tales of *The Four Just Men*, and the best-selling *Saint* stories by Leslie Charteris. Robin Hood must almost certainly have been a real person ; so was John Naylor, " Little John ", his gigantic lieutenant, whose long grave may still be seen in the churchyard of the little stone-built village of Hathersage, that is built up the side of a steep hill in Derbyshire.

In that 20th-century classic, *The Sword in the Stone*, T. H. White has suggested that the common forests of mediaeval England resembled a jungle on the Amazon, and were " almost impenetrable ".(49) That wild, uncontrolled, natural wastefulness of growth is now utterly forgotten. The " good old woodlands " of the " good old days " were vastly different from the orderly planting advocated and described by John Evelyn in the late 17th century, and by William Cobbett, with less grace but quite as much practical common sense, in the early 19th,(50) and far less orderly and commercially profitable than the work of the Forestry Commission in our own century. It is now recognised that timber is a crop ; but recognition of that fact was long delayed in England, and because of that, our towns and industries have grown partly at the expense of the natural wealth represented by the great forests that once covered so much of the land.

CHAPTER VI

PROGRESS AND THE GROWTH OF
THE TOWN

ALTHOUGH the importance of preserving the countryside
and planting woodlands is now appreciated, the fact
that England has for some time become a land of streets
is not recognised. Many of us behave as though an inex-
haustible area of countryside still surrounded our towns, and
when steps are taken to secure green belts of agricultural
land, we usually inveigh against planning, or else accept the
plan, praise it, and ignore or flout it, as the mediaeval Londoners ignored or flouted the building act made by their first
Mayor, Fitz-Ailwyne, which prohibited the use of thatch and
made stone party walls compulsory. South of the Yorkshire
and Lancashire towns and industrial regions, a web of urban
development has looped and wriggled its way over large tracts
of the countryside. This urban growth has been accelerated
during the last fifty years, but it has been going on unchecked
for well over a hundred, and maps of residential areas in and
around the great cities—London in particular—made during
the 19th century resemble ink spotted on blotting paper, the
spots spreading and gradually joining up, as village ran into
village, and new, built-up streets branched off all the main
roads that led from the city.

The significance of such urban development, and the nature
of the problems that it was likely to cause in the future, were
noted by a few writers like H. G. Wells at the beginning of this
century ; but few authors fully understood the new conditions
of life that were being created around them, or if they did,
they wrote about them either in the spirit of the upper classes
doing a bit of " slumming " as a matter of duty, or, as mis-

(44)

sionaries indignantly eager to attack social injustice. Arthur Morrison's *A Child of the Jago*, first published in 1896, was a potent piece of such missionary writing, for it dealt with that wretched by-product of industrialism and greed, the slum. Most writers ignored the change of outlook and taste that followed a new way of life, for the people who lived in slums and suburbs were wholly different from the townsmen of the Middle Ages and the 17th, 18th, and early 19th centuries ; they had an urban outlook, but little or no civic pride. That outlook was affected by the sort of place they lived in. The little terraces of houses, or the small detached or semi-detached house, the garden and the party wall and the separate front door still preserved the illusion of the " Englishman's Castle ", and thus encouraged individualism, though the corresponding quality of variety could be expressed only by the exterior paint-work of a house, its front door knocker, and its window curtains and interior furnishing. (Neighbourliness was diminished in these suburban streets in a way that would have astonished and probably shocked the mediaeval townsman.) The tall tenements that were built during the second half of the 19th and during the present century encouraged their inhabitants to have a far less individual outlook, and separated them from all contact with the soil, for the man who had the use of the smallest patch of garden was still akin to the older type of townsman, who when towns were still small and adjacent to the fields and woods was not very different from the country-man in character : but the families who lived in tenements were so conditioned by their environment that they might have been living in another country whose physical features were quite unlike those of England. It has been suggested, and with reason, that the great plains of Central Europe, which stretch eastwards to the Urals, impose upon their inhabitants a mental and moral readiness to accept uniformity and all that it implies in regimentation and tidy social systems. The diversity of the English countryside, its refreshing irregularities and varied scenery, stimulate and sustain an independent and intensely individualistic approach to life. Only the artificial uniformity created by industrial slums and huge, impersonal tenements encourage their inhabitants to accept Continental ideas of regimentation.

The effect of architecture and the growth of the towns upon social characteristics has been largely ignored or at least unobserved by many writers of novels and stories, and even in this second half of the 20th century few English authors write about the life of the streets with the intimate, racy knowledge with which Damon Runyon and O. Henry wrote about the street life of New York and other American cities. So many writers in England appear to survey the world with conscious or unconscious detachment from some well-appointed flat or house in a town, without belonging to that town, as Arnold Bennett belonged to the Five Towns, or else they live in some surviving part of rural England, where they act as petty squires, or are earnest, artistic " colonists "—in the country but not of it. Few writers mix with the people in a place as Chaucer mixed with his fellow countrymen, so that they can write, as Damon Runyon habitually wrote, as " one of the crowd ".

How has England become a land of streets, and why have the social implications of this change in our national environment been interpreted, and often misinterpreted, largely by economists, sociologists and architects ? All these specialists advocate or actually make plans that affect life ; and many writers apparently accept their findings at second-hand and take them on board, using academic theories instead of the rich stuff of experience to supply their fiction with the semblance of life; while their thinking is infected by that current abstraction " the people " when they write about their fellow men. The use of that arrogant abstraction leads unconsciously to a lot of casual inhumanity. For many honest and intelligent people it excuses plans that attempt to trim the lives of others into unfamiliar and possibly uncongenial patterns. Of all the specialists qualified to interpret the social characteristics and changes that reflect, or arise from, the growth of a town and the nature of its buildings, the architect is the one whose work is most intimately connected with the daily life of people ; and unlike other specialists, when the architect thinks of social science he is concerned less with the implications of the word science than with the rich, human variations and unpredictable eccentricities covered by the word social. Architects are the trustees of the English tradition in design ; if

(46)

they are good architects they preserve continuity with tradition, and never ignore the basic needs of ordinary people. How those needs have been met are told by the streets of any town or city ; and no highly technical knowledge is necessary in order to read such records in brick and stone and timber.

In the opening chapter, it was said that every street in every suburb has a story, sometimes reaching far back into the history of our island ; but some of the recent examples of rapid growth have a comparable interest, showing as they often do the fate of good intentions and the lack of any sustained civic sense during the last century. Not only in England, but all over the world, towns have been growing in an exuberant but haphazard fashion during the last hundred and fifty years. A town that has grown slowly enjoys an organic unity which rapid growth seldom confers, and careful planning occasionally excludes. Many towns began as villages ; as we have said, those villages are often swamped by residential development as the suburbs of a town overflow into the country, and join village to village and hamlet to farmstead for many miles. This has happened with nearly all the big English industrial towns ; while London supplies the most conspicuous example of such devouring growth. Slow growth often creates picturesque agglomerations of architecture and tangles of crooked streets, that are labelled lovingly as " cunning " by American visitors, though English motorists describe them differently.

By the second half of the 19th century the disadvantages of rapid growth became dismally spectacular. People who cared about their visible surroundings deplored the times they were living in. William Morris advised his contemporaries to " Forget the spreading of the hideous town ; think rather of the pack-horse on the down. . . ." This unhelpful though soothing advice was not likely to make people think constructively at a time when transport was passing out of the horse-and-cart age. Such attempts to focus admiring attention upon mediaeval civilisation caused far too many influential and intelligent Victorians to forget that there had been such a thing as town planning in the previous century, and that even some of the new industrial towns had begun well, and were planned with vision, although the plans were subsequently muddled and maimed by expediency, lack of money (or too much of it) and by those old enemies of civilisation—greed and stupidity.

A cautionary tale of rapid growth is told by what is now the County Borough of Birkenhead on the Mersey side of the peninsula of Wirral in Cheshire. Birkenhead is not mentioned as a place in the early maps of Cheshire. The chief town in Wirral was Parkgate, on the Dee side of the peninsula, which was a port, where the road from London through Chester ended and from whence the Dublin packets sailed. The nearest place to Birkenhead that is mentioned, even as late as 1803, on Butters' map of Cheshire, is Bebbington.

Birkenhead was a tongue of land jutting into the Mersey opposite Liverpool, and it is supposed to have derived its name from the birch trees that covered its gentle slopes. This little peninsula had long been known as Woodside. Birkenhead is mentioned in an early 19th-century guide-book called *The Stranger in Liverpool*; but only in connection with the ruins of the Benedictine Priory. That book describes Woodside as " the most ancient of all the ferries " across the Mersey, and also records that accommodation at the Ferry House was good and that the Priory ruins lay a quarter of a mile to the south.(51)

The clearest and best-documented history of the growth of Birkenhead is to be found in *The Outline Plan for the County Borough of Birkenhead*, prepared for the Council by Professor Sir Charles Reilly and N. J. Aslan, and published in 1947 with commendable enterprise by the County Borough of Birkenhead.(52) In this copiously illustrated work, five maps trace the expansion of Birkenhead from 1824, when it was an isolated rural community, to 1945, when it was an overgrown, almost unmanageable wilderness of slums, industrial and residential areas, and bombed buildings. In 1824 the place was sparsely inhabited, with one or two great houses—including a large, early 17th-century house called Tranmere Hall—and a few farms and hamlets. Northwards, it was bordered by Wallasey Pool ; westwards there was heath, interspersed with agricultural land, rising to the wooded hills of Bidston and Storeton. The first stimulant to the growth of Birkenhead was the establishment in 1825 of a shipyard by a

Woodside Boat House, Birkenhead, at the beginning of the 19th century. (Reproduced from the fifth edition of *The Stranger in Liverpool*, published in 1816)

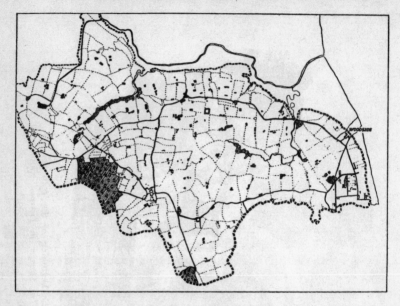

Birkenhead was a thinly populated farming community in 1824, with the ruins of a Benedictine Priory near Woodside Ferry. Here is the area covered by Birkenhead and Claughton. Compare this with the map on the opposite page. (The plans of Birkenhead on these two pages are drawn from two highly detailed historical plans published in the *Outline Plan for the County Borough of Birkenhead*, by Sir Charles Reilly and N. J. Aslan, which was issued by the County Borough in 1947)

Greenock shipbuilder, named Laird. A year later a town plan, with wide, straight streets, was made, and if that original lay-out had been followed Birkenhead would now be a proud place. The only part of the plan that was completed as it was originally conceived was Hamilton Square, designed by Gillespie Graham, an Edinburgh architect. Hamilton Square was the beginning of a fine interpretation of that street plan, and it still retains its classical urbanity. The fact that the town had its ups and downs of prosperity, while men of small vision with mean minds have lined many of those fine broad streets with two-storey cottages which soon become slums, does not dim the initial splendour of conception that impelled a town with less than 3,000 inhabitants to make provision for

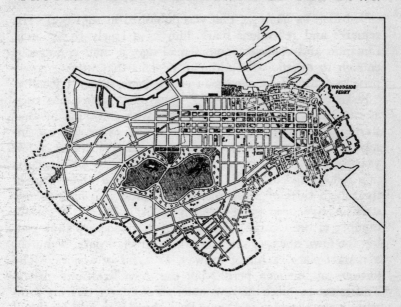

Birkenhead in 1858. It acquired a fine street plan in 1826, and a large park, laid out by Joseph Paxton, in 1843, and opened in 1847. Railways were cutting across the street plan, and shipyards had destroyed the old river front. (See opposite page)

future growth with a sense of spaciousness and with confidence in the prospect of prosperity.

Another example of the vision that consistently inspired the rulers of this growing place was the laying out of Birkenhead Park in 1843, when the town had 10,000 inhabitants. Designed by Joseph Paxton, the Duke of Devonshire's gardener, and the designer of the great glass house at Chatsworth, and later of the Crystal Palace, the Park was opened in 1847. Meanwhile, docks were being constructed and industrial prosperity increased, though in an intermittent and unforeseen way. Fortunately we have, mid-way in the 19th century, the views of an independent critic, who looked dispassionately and disapprovingly upon all this turbulent enterprise and inconclusive though determined growth. At the beginning of the eighteen-fifties an observant writer with a minatory pen, named Samuel Sidney, recorded his impressions of Birkenhead in a little book called *Rides on Railways*, that was published in 1851.(53) His remarks and reflections mark him as a lonely realist in a romantic and confident commercial age, a man courageous enough to question the ultimate benefits that private enterprise and industrial expansion could confer upon a locality. "Birkenhead is a great town," he wrote, "which has risen as rapidly as an American city, and with the same fits and starts. Magical prosperity is succeeded by a general insolvency among builders and land speculators ; after a few years of fallow another start takes place, and so on—speculation follows speculation. Birkenhead has had about four of these high tides of prosperous speculations, in which *millions* sterling have been gained and lost. At each ebb a certain number of the George Hudsons * of the place are swamped, but the town always gains a square, a street, a park, a church, a market-place, a bit of railway, or a bit of a dock. The fortunes of the men perish, but the town lives and thrives. Thus piece by piece the raw materials of a large thriving community are provided, and now Birkenhead is as well-furnished with means for accommodating a large population as any place in England, and has been laid out on so good a plan that it will be one of the healthiest as well as one of the neatest modern towns. It has also the tools of commerce in a splendid free dock, not executed so wisely as it would have been if Mr. Rendel, the original engineer (the first man of the day as a marine engineer), had not been over-ruled by the pennywise pound-foolish people, but still a very fine dock. Warehouses much better planned than anything in Liverpool ; railways giving communication with the manufacturing districts ; in fact, all the tools of commerce—gas, water, a park, and sanitary regulations, have not been neglected.

"Some people think Birkenhead will be the rival of Liverpool, we think not : it will be a dependency or suburb of the greater capital. 'Where the carcase is, there the eagles will be gathered together.' Birkenhead is too near to be a rival ; shipping must eventually come to Birkenhead, but the business will still continue to be done in Liverpool or Manchester, where are vested interests and established capital.

* George Hudson, 1800–1871, was the "Railway King" of the mid-19th century. His financial schemes ultimately collapsed in ruins.

"An hour or two will be enough to see everything worth seeing at Birkenhead. To those who enjoy the sight of the river and shipping, it is not a bad plan to stop at one of the hotels there, as boats cross every five minutes, landing at a splendid iron pontoon, or floating stage, on the Liverpool side, of large dimensions, constructed with great skill by Mr. W. Cubitt, C.E., to avoid the nuisance of landing carriages at all times, and passengers at low tides in boats."

He gave some attention to other places on the Wirral shore of the Mersey and referred to New Brighton as "the best settlement", noting that it enjoyed "a share of the open Irish sea, with its keen breezes". He added, as he loved to knock the gilt off every piece of gingerbread in sight, "it must be bracing, healthy, dreary and dull ".(54) (Before the end of the 19th century local enterprise had attempted to alleviate the dullness by turning New Brighton into a place of entertainment, complete with pleasure and fair grounds, a pier, a rather rowdy promenade lined with restaurants and cafés called "the Ham and Egg Parade", and a huge iron tower that could be seen over most of Wirral.)

Samuel Sidney devoted rather more than a page to Liskeard which he described as "a ferry on the Cheshire side ", but was chiefly interested in a model dairy farm that had been established by Mr. Harold Littledale, whom he described as "a member of one of the first firms in Liverpool ". He also mentions Eastham and records that the neighbouring country "is the prettiest part of the Mersey ". At the time he wrote, the residential character of Wirral had become recognised, for he could state that "the Cheshire side of the Mersey forms a suburb of Liverpool, to which steamers are plying every ten minutes from the villages of Rock Ferry, Tranmere, Birkenhead, Monk's Ferry, Seacombe, Liskeard, Egremont, and New Brighton ". He follows that statement by a reference to the amenities of Seacombe. "The best idea of the extent of the Liverpool Docks may be obtained from The Seacombe Hotel, an old-fashioned tavern, with a bowling green, where turtle soup, cold punch, and claret are to be had of good quality at moderate charges."(55)

Sidney may have deplored the sporadic and uncertain growth of Birkenhead ; but he certainly managed to suggest

(53)

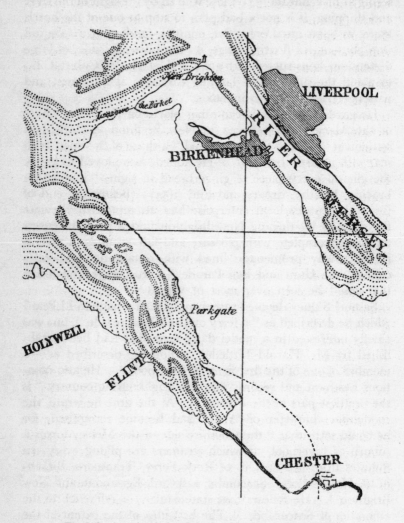

The Wirral peninsula in 1878, showing the relative areas of
Birkenhead and Liverpool, and the disused port of Parkgate
on the Dee. (From *The Mersey, Ancient and Modern*, by
Benjamin Blower. Liverpool : 1878)

that there was something about the locality that attracted enterprising people and sharpened their commercial perceptions. This fact was dramatically emphasised nine years after the publication of his book, when George Francis Train, an American citizen, with a flair for publicity and an urge for public speaking that would take no denial, persuaded the municipal authorities of Birkenhead to allow him to lay down a trial tramway from the Park to Woodside. It was the first tramway in Europe ; and Birkenhead was the only place in Britain with sufficient enterprise to sanction such an experiment. It was opened on August 30th, 1860.

Today, in the mid-20th century, Birkenhead is a comprehensive mess. It lacks unity, beauty and convenience, and is crippled by a cancerous growth of slums that demands a bold surgical operation. The Reilly-Aslan *Outline Plan* shows very clearly the major disaster that occurred when the inhabitants of Birkenhead were cut off from the river. Woodside is now occupied by the ferry and a coal storage dump. The ferry buildings prevent anybody from having a glimpse of the landing stage beyond, or a sight of the broad Mersey with its shipping. The foreshore, between Laird's yards and Rock Ferry, is a dismal sea of mud. That mud has been there a long time : probably since Tranmere Hall, whose wooded grounds once descended to the waterside and surrounded the ruins of Birkenhead Priory with a lawn, was pulled down by a speculative builder about 1850. At the beginning of the 19th century the hall was used as a farm-house, and was then known as Tranmore, after the ancient family of Tranmore or Tranmols, who had owned it during the Middle Ages.(56)

A much later and far more complacent writer than Samuel Sidney, after quoting a detailed description of the past glories of Tranmere Hall, reflected that " Change is inevitable in a progressive country, but it must always be remembered that in beauty it is possible to change a progressive district for the worse. What would Bernard de Tranemoll, its local lord in 1267, think of all the change, could he once more revisit the glimpses of the moon ? "(57) That question was asked in 1909, by Harold Edgar Young, author of *A Perambulation of the Hundred of Wirral*. He would have disliked the views a 13th-century landlord might have expressed as much as the mediaeval gentleman would have disliked his complacency about progress.

The particular wilderness of streets that is called Birkenhead is the result of short bursts of rapid growth between 1825 and 1900. We are again enjoying a period of conscious town planning, and the Reilly-Aslan plan of 1947 for Birkenhead has much to commend it, though in its utopian, 20th-century way, it is as grandiose as the plan of 1826 which left only a fine structure of streets, and the respectable architectural achievement of Hamilton Square. At least the new plan would enable growth to be guided, or so it seems on paper. As an example of town-tidying it is interesting and in places highly desirable ; for it recognises the social significance of the way buildings are grouped, though the so-called " neighbourhood units " it advocates might be better named as " nosey parker plots ". The neighbourliness that was lost or reduced by the unplanned suburban development of the 19th century is unlikely to be restored by such artificial devices, handicapped by such a name as " neighbourhood unit " with its suggestion of synthetic bonhomie, and the far more sinister suggestion of the planned imposition of a way of life.

Birkenhead may get as much from this 1947 plan during the next fifty years as it got during the last one hundred and twenty-five, from the assorted industrialists, merchants and speculators, who contributed to the prosperity of the place and whose generosity endowed it with a fine park, and started off the splendid though unrealised plan of 1826, but marred its execution by a regrettable indifference to tidiness and a tendency to inopportune bankruptcy.

Cities and towns that are planned for future growth by far-seeing or ambitious people seldom grow in the way their planners have imagined, as the short history of Birkenhead has demonstrated. Sometimes places have stopped growing and have disappeared after existing only for a few years, like the mining towns of California and Nevada in the pioneer days, or for a few centuries, like the towns of Roman Britain. During the last hundred and seventy years, the impetus given by the industrial revolution to the increase and redistribution of populations in Europe and North America has fostered the belief that growth is inevitable, so that any town planning done since the end of the 18th century has nearly always been based on the assumption that growth would continue ; thus plans have been made with the object of guiding the process of growth along and adjacent to the lines of existing roads. There was little else that the planners could do ; and the measure of their boldness and optimism and their occasional misunderstanding of the likes and dislikes of their fellow men are revealed by the character and scale of their plans ; though the direction and subsequent growth of building development would almost certainly cause the creators of any town plan to experience dismayed astonishment. The tidy, if uninspired, Roman town-planners would have been horrified by the picturesque congestion of the mediaeval city, with its open sewers and doubtful water supply ; to the mediaeval citizen the squalid hideousness of the modern industrial city would have been far more horrifying ; and the great architects of the late 17th and 18th centuries would have been as critically disgusted with what happened to English, Scottish and American cities during the Victorian period as they were with the maze of streets that they had inherited from the Middle Ages, when cities were tightly girdled by their forbidding but necessary walls.

For example, the federal capital of the United States has grown along the lines originally laid down by its designer, Major Pierre Charles L'Enfant, whose work was supervised by George Washington and Thomas Jefferson ; but to those three gifted men, Washington as it is today would seem a rather lop-sided city. The White House and the Capitol and the Avenues that radiate from those two focal points and the cluster of great white buildings that, from the air, suggest a gargantuan edition of some Greek city, would satisfy the orderly ideas of 18th-century gentlemen with an informed taste for classical architecture ; but the alternate patches of magnificence and meanness that characterise the building development of Washington would outrage those ideas. L'Enfant could certainly be comforted by the survival of his ingenious geometrical inter-play of avenues and streets, that suggests the lay-out of some stupendous estate, with paths and drives, pleasure gardens, parkland and great houses and little summer retreats, and even a folly (with the Smithsonian

Institute cast for that part) : but he would be appalled by many of the buildings and by the general untidiness which mar his majestic plan.

New York was laid out on a grid street plan as far as 145th Street as long ago as 1811 ; but it was then impossible to foresee the vertical irregularity that would darken so many of the projected streets and avenues, extravagantly broad though they may have seemed in the horse-and-cart age. New York grew like any other 19th-century city, without any violent variation of its skyline, until the ten-storey Tower Building began the race upwards in 1889, and bigger and better lifts encouraged the ideas of architects to soar as they had done five hundred years earlier, when structural skill under spiritual impulsion had reared throughout Europe a glorious array of towers, spires and pinnacles. Modern cities, like Washington that was consciously conceived as a new city, and New York which has packed most of its spectacular, unprecedented growth into half a century, are familiar examples ; and such demonstrations of expansion reinforce but fail to justify the belief that the growth of cities is an inevitable though not necessarily a continuous or regular process.

CHAPTER VII

TOWANS OF ARRESTED DEVELOPMENT

WHEN civilisation passes into a period of apparent security, when the exhaustion that follows either victory or defeat in war makes men temporarily weary of weapons, or when fortification seems needless and cities are unconfined by walls, a belief in the inevitability of expansion is disclosed by the plans that are made for the future growth of those cities. The destructiveness of war and the bitter chaos that follows revolution are easily forgotten by people who are separated only by two or three generations from such afflictions, and far more easily when two or three hundred years have passed. Bede, writing in the fourth decade of the 8th century, could refer to " the peaceable and calm disposition of the times ", for he was living in the high noon of the brief and brilliant civilisation of Northumbria ; the collapse of an ordered society and the obliteration of the arts of architecture and civic life that followed the disintegration of Roman Britain seemed remote, while the disaster of the Danish raids still lay darkly beyond the horizon of the future. Meanwhile the sun shone and men went about their church building and sculpture and painting, ignoring the ruins of cities whose street plans and public buildings illustrated a way of life that had little meaning for those who dwelt in the disunited kingdoms of 8th-century England. Bede stated that " The island was formerly embellished with twenty-eight noble cities, besides innumerable castles, which were all strongly secured with walls, towers, gates and locks."(58) Art and culture had long been disassociated from city life, and civilisation was now centred in the great monastic establishments, like the new monastery at Jarrow, built by Benedict Biscop, where Bede wrote his *Ecclesiastical History*.

The ruins of the Romano-British towns remained visible for a long time. Geoffrey of Monmouth's reference to them has been quoted in Chapter II, and before the end of the 12th century when Monmouth wrote his *British History*, Gerald de Barri had written a detailed description of the deserted Roman city of Caerleon, that was still standing with its temples, theatres, palaces and baths. The empty towns slowly disappeared. The mediaeval builders learned nothing from them, though they used them as quarries for materials.

From the street plans of some of the Romano-British cities that have remained uninhabited for over fifteen hundred years, we may learn a salutory lesson. Some of them may be best described as cases of arrested development ; others indicate an attitude of negligent acquiescence to damage caused by fire or war. For instance, the forum and basilica at Viroconium (Wroxeter) in Shropshire were burnt down shortly after A.D. 155, and were then rebuilt on much the same plan. But one hundred and twenty years later, at some time between A.D. 275 and 300, they were again destroyed by fire, together with a portion of the public baths. The forum and basilica were never rebuilt.(59) While this sort of thing would have surprised us some years ago, it is not quite so astonishing in the mid-20th century, to think of the life of a city going on amid burnt and blackened ruins, since in London and other English cities we have, in the years following the Second World War, behaved in much the same way as the Roman citizens of Britain in Viroconium and other cities sixteen hundred years ago. For the last century of its life as a city, Viroconium was in a condition of economic and political decay.(60)

The excavations at Verulamium, undertaken during the early nineteen-thirties, have revealed the fluctuations in that city's development, and the results are recorded in exhaustive detail in the reports of the Research Committee of the Society of Antiquaries of London.(61) We know now that during the second quarter of the 2nd century, fifty years of intensive development began, and the outline of Verulamium was re-planned to include a fresh area ; new defences were designed and many buildings reconstructed in permanent materials. In the summary of the report on Verulamium by R. E. M.

Wheeler and T. V. Wheeler, it is stated that " The plan of the new city allowed optimistically for a further expansion which never wholly materialised."(62)   During the 3rd century the city decayed ; after 296 it was largely rebuilt under Constantius ; but " a century later this renewed attempt to naturalise Roman urban life in Britain had failed in turn, and the city was once more languishing into decay ".   The authors of the report record that " All material evidence ceases at Verulamium by the end of the fourth century ; and, when in 429 Germanus visited the city, he found, as his biographer indicates, a tradition of Roman citizenship but, as archaeology equally indicates, very little of the actuality of Roman culture."

Another Romano-British town that was planned for growth which never took place was Silchester.   The whole town plan has been recovered, and reveals that in the 100 acres which the walls enclosed, only 80 houses were built.   There were four temples and a Christian church ; a basilica, a forum and a public bath.   The street plan was a simple grid with the forum roughly in the centre of the town ; but the grid was unrelated to the walls, which with their eight facets of unequal length imposed an irregular shape upon the town.   Collingwood and Myres have recorded that at Silchester, Caerwent and Verulamium there were large areas on the outskirts of the town which were never built upon.   " The walls were evidently laid out on a generous scale to make room for large increases of population, and more land was included than was ever required."(63)

Dr. R. E. M. Wheeler, in discussing the Silchester excavations, had reminded us that in 1890 none of our Romano-British towns had been excavated, and that " we knew almost nothing of their plans and buildings, of their material and sociological make-up.   We could not, in fact, begin to discuss the economy and sociology of Roman Britain.   What was wanted, and within a measurable space of time, was just such a picture as the excavators of Silchester proceeded to give us."(64)

There is an almost contemporary note of unfulfilled planning about Silchester, which, like that example of 19th-century growth, Birkenhead, could not live up to its original plan. This may have occurred because the populations of the

Romano-British cities did not live up to the standards of planning that had been set for them by diligent architects, following the precepts of Vitruvius. The "attempt to naturalise Roman urban life in Britain" may have failed because too many natives preferred the freedom of the woods, or the unsupervised squalor of their own native villages of primitive huts. The excavations that have revealed the half-empty town of Silchester, the neglected public buildings of Viroconium, and the arrested expansion of Verulamium, suggest that stubborn native inclinations may defeat the ambitious paternalism of administrators and technicians who make plans, particularly when the intention to change a way of life is implicit in their character. The towns of Roman Britain with their tidy streets and orderly spaciousness, their commodious public buildings and luxurious baths, never grew with the exuberant spontaneity of mediaeval English towns. Nearly all those that survived were fundamentally changed in character when they emerged from the ruinous dark ages and were salvaged and patched up, revived and gradually rebuilt during the Middle Ages.

Are the plans that are being made today for new towns and old ones as optimistic, on a larger scale, as those made by the Roman architects of Silchester and Verulamium? Like those long-dead town-planning specialists, perhaps we are assuming a continuance of growth and a readiness on the part of the native population to accept an alien tidiness. Because of such assumptions, we may be attempting to "naturalise" strange foreign social habits and ideas in a country where for nearly a thousand years people have enjoyed increasing privacy and independence and have thereby attained a cheerful mastery of the art of living.

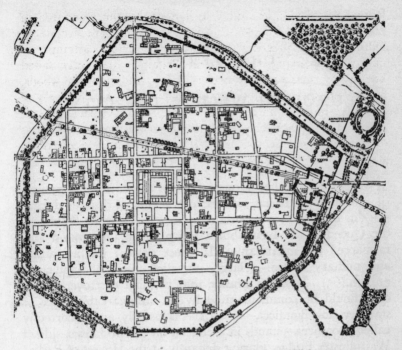

Plan of the Roman town of Calleva Atrebatum at Silchester, Hampshire. This is a reduced reproduction of the plan included in the *Short Guide to the Silchester Collection,* and is reproduced by permission of the Reading Public Museum and Art Gallery

CHAPTER VIII

GROWTH WITHIN THE CITY

LONDON furnishes a long record of the fluctuating growth of a city. It has suffered every kind of disaster during its history, the first occurring in A.D. 61, when Boudicca, the Queen of the Iceni, burnt the place to the ground and massacred the inhabitants. In those days it was a trading and military centre—a large, unwalled town, of haphazard growth.(65) It seems strange that the first destroyer of the city should be commemorated by an unremarkable piece of statuary, for Boudicca—or as she is usually and incorrectly called, Boadicea—stands in a chariot on the Middlesex side of Westminster Bridge, glaring defiantly at the Houses of Parliament. Since that first disaster, there are records of ten large and devastating fires, some of them the result of conquest or attempted conquest by an enemy; though long before the end of Roman Britain that uneasy association of the architect and soldier had begun, which was for many centuries to limit the growth of the town.

When western civilisation sank into the Dark Ages in the 5th and 6th centuries, the wall became the dominating structure in cities all over Europe, as it had been before Rome established the universal state that preserved—and petrified—the Hellenic way of life. Whatever else was neglected, the city wall had to be kept in repair : its significance had become as great as that of a sea wall, for the barbarians, bursting their way into placid provinces and testing the failing strength of the Western Empire, were as ruthless as angry water. There is evidence of haste in the construction of the Roman walls of London. All sorts of odds and ends of masonry, fragments of statuary, bits of capitals and columns, were incorporated ;

for example, in the Camomile Street bastion there were " large blocks of re-used pink cement and masonry ", also " fluted pilasters, shafts of half columns, portions of canopies, cornices, door jambs, etc.—together with the sculptured figures of a soldier and a lion, and a human head of colossal size. . . ."(66)

Preparations to protect cities from barbarian raiders must often have been undertaken with the same anxious speed that characterised the planning and execution of air-raid precautions in European cities sixteen hundred years later. Walls had been used in the Roman provincial cities, but their significance had not been apparent in the settled centuries of the *Pax Romana*, when only frontier incidents—trouble in North Britain, on the eastern borders of Gaul, or in the uneasy province of Dacia—disturbed the extremities of the Empire.

Directly men had to seek protection behind walls, life became narrow, crowded and inconvenient ; the old partnership between city and countryside was lost ; country estates and their houses became unsafe ; and even the burial grounds outside city walls lost their immunity from disturbance, for barbarian bands respected nothing in their search for loot. Weapons change, but the anti-creative spirit remains, latent in every civilisation—including our own, though before 1914 many people thought it had been extirpated. Heartened by recurrent opportunities for destruction, that anti-creative spirit has always been unconsciously at war with architecture and town planning, and its most repressive achievement was the wall—a master stroke against the open, happy life that men might so easily lead everywhere.

London had been rebuilt inside the walls, century after century ; and with great frequency in Saxon and Norman times and for good reasons. The first of those ten large and devastating fires occurred in 961, the last nearly a thousand years later, in 1940 : and eight of them took place in a period of just over three centuries, between 961 and 1264. It is conceivable that they altered the internal arrangement of the city, though changes of lay-out would affect only the less important streets : the sites of churches, civic buildings and commercial centres would guarantee the retention of the main street plan, and in Saxon London and the early troubled

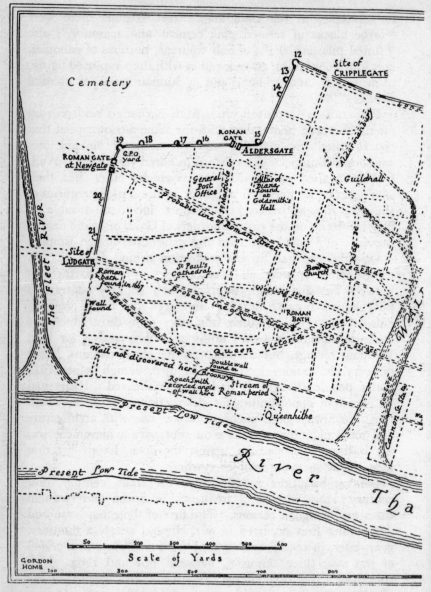

A PLAN OF

The landward wall that surrounded the city is shown with double lines from Ludgate to
the Tower : where it still exists the space between the lines is shown in solid black.   The
Walbrook, then a stream of some size, divided the area of 326 acres into two unequal
parts.   The Walbrook and its tributaries, like the Fleet River, have since become sewers.

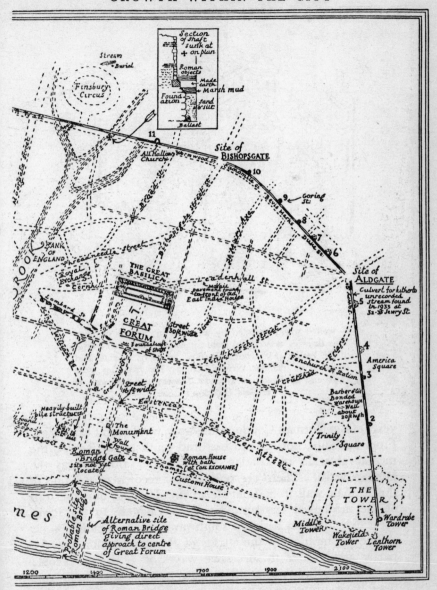

ROMAN LONDON

The eastern part of the city contained the Basilica, the Forum and probably most of the temples and public buildings. This conjectural plan, shown on these two pages, is by Mr. Gordon Home, F.S.A. (Scot.) and is reproduced from the 1948 edition of his book, *Roman London*, with his permission and by courtesy of the publishers, Eyre and Spottiswoode

A walled town, depicted by an artist in the 9th century.
This drawing was copied from an Anglo-Saxon manuscript
of the Psalms (MS. Harl., No. 603) by F. W. Fairholt and
included in Thomas Wright's books, *The Homes of Other
Days* and *A History of Domestic Manners and Sentiments in
England* (London : 1862)

years of the Norman Conquest the walls would limit expansion.
From Ludgate, north, then east and south to the Tower, the
mediaeval walls of London followed the same line as the
Roman walls.   There are only scanty records of the line of
the Roman wall from Ludgate to the Thames, and the wall
of the mediaeval city turned west at Ludgate to the River
Fleet,(67) and ran beside it southwards to the Thames.

The obliteration of the streets of Roman London may be
partly attributable to successive waves of disastrous events :
though eight fires crowded into three hundred and three years
may have stimulated changes in building technique rather
than in town planning.   Over a century before the first great
fire, London had endured a devastating raid by Vikings.
Chesterton's lines aptly describe those white savages :

(68)

Their souls were drifting as the sea,
And all good towns and lands
They only saw with heavy eyes,
And broke with heavy hands.

They sacked London in 851 ; an event that may have
wiped out the remains of the Roman city so completely that
no mediaeval or modern London street follows the course of
any Roman predecessor.(68)   That is the simplest explanation,
and it is significant that W. R. Lethaby, who had the advantage
of being both an archaeologist and an architect, rejected its
attractive plausibility.   He suggested that when Alfred recovered London, some thirty-five years after its sack by the
Vikings, the city was not merely a heap of rubble enclosed

The pilgrims leaving Canterbury, with the mediaeval city
in the background. Drawn by F. W. Fairholt from an
illustration in a manuscript of John Lydgate's poem, *The
Story of Thebes* (MS. Reg. 18 D.ii.), and included in Thomas
Wright's books, *The Homes of Other Days* and *A History of
Domestic Manners and Sentiments in England* (London : 1862)

by a ruined wall, but that the Roman city still existed, and that the inhabitants maintained the streets and lived in the patched-up remains of Roman houses side by side with their new, rather flimsy wattle-and-daub houses that were little better than glorified huts, just as Londoners after the Second World War lived in patched-up buildings, and flimsy, temporary structures.(69)   He also suggested that the assumption that Roman London was symmetrically planned was not necessarily true, as streams like the Walbrook and the persistence of old road lines would have interfered with a chessboard grid plan.(70)   This conclusion is modified by the happy, illogical streak in human nature, that often allows traditional associations to interfere with the tidiest of plans. For instance, the old trail across Manhattan Island from the Battery to Yonkers still survives as Broadway, and cuts across the grid-iron plan made for New York city in 1811 and since carried out.   City streets shift their lines in the course of centuries, though not necessarily at the dictation of disaster. Even old routes may disappear after they have lost their original significance.   The example of Broadway in New York city is less than one hundred and fifty years old, and for that comparatively short period a traditional track has remained, though the temptation to regularise it, to fit it into the orderly grid of streets that were being laid out and built up, must have been great.   New York city itself was merely a group of huts on the southern tip of Manhattan Island less than three and a half centuries ago.   Roman London was lost in the dark ages eleven hundred years before that.

We have a tendency to imagine that traces of Roman streets survive in our cities, possibly because the roads which lead to them have survived.   Roads live on for centuries, while city streets alter, generation after generation, and may be lost or utterly changed in a growing city.   They are perpetuated usually by their convenience, their religious or civic associations or their financial significance.   Since the beginning of the present century London west of the city has changed parts of its street plan.   Kingsway has been slashed through a tangle of grubby and ancient lanes and alleys ;   Aldwych has altered the character of the east end of the Strand ;   further west, Curzon Street now joins Park Lane and has ceased to be the secluded backwater of the Mayfair that Mr. Michael Arlen described in the nineteen-twenties. There are other changes, though not in the city itself. Though rebuilding has been continuous and so lofty that some of the narrower thoroughfares begin to suggest the shadowed gulfs by Wall Street in New York, within the area once encircled by the city walls the old street plan has remained unaltered. The colossal value of the sites makes the rearrangement of blocks or street widening out of the question, financially. Thus a modern city becomes the prisoner of its prosperity, confined to existing inconveniences by site values, just as the mediaeval city was through military necessity a prisoner within its walls.

Because England is netted over with roads and tracks that still mark the military needs of the Roman Province of Britain, or the habits of pre-Roman commercial travellers, it seems logical that those roads should continue their way into and through the cities, particularly when the cities have a rectangular plan and the streets within them cross in a Carfax. Dr. Haverfield has condemned the tendency of antiquaries to attribute a Roman origin to such streets, and cites evidence that even in Italian towns that have been continuously inhabited since Roman times, the Roman streets and town plans have seldom survived, and that even in Rome there is hardly a street in use today which was used in the ancient city.(71)

The natural process of growth, the accidents of fire or the effects of war, change city streets : but far more potent and even violent factors are modern traffic and modern industry. Notwithstanding our tidy and logical acts for planning towns and the countryside, the casual habits of the late 18th and 19th centuries are still with us ; and we overshadow or destroy ancient serenities, and condemn old streets with new ruthlessness in the spurious interests of power, production and speed.

The rediscovery of the street as an architectural and social entity during the Renaissance has been forgotten, for modern streets are in danger of becoming speedways or parking places, and the man who now has power over the destiny of the street, power without responsibility, is not the soldier, the policeman, the great king or lord or prelate, but the manufacturer of motor vehicles. His reign may be short : before the end of the 20th century the helicopter may free our streets, so that people may walk in them with pleasure and safety. So far, in this century, we have changed our streets almost wholly in the interests of traffic, and we have called the operation, " relieving congestion ". No city, yet designed, has prevented congestion ; no city in existence is yet within measurable distance of curing it. Only some ruinous disaster can free a modern commercial city from its acquiescent tolerance of an ancient and outmoded plan. In London the city fathers may prove as incapable now of using the freedom to replan and rebuild, which the German air raids conferred, as they were after the Great Fire of 1666. Plans may be made : indeed, plans have been on both disastrous occasions ; but in the 17th century the will was lacking, and history may repeat itself, though after the Second World War money and labour are as scarce as will power.

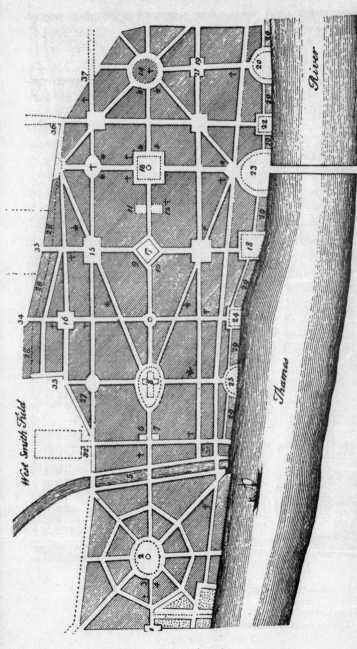

John Evelyn's plan for the rebuilding of London after the Great Fire of 1666. The site of St. Paul's is at 8, the Lord Mayor's house at 17, and a new channel for the Fleet is shown at 5. From a contemporary engraving. Compare this with Wren's plan on the three pages that follow

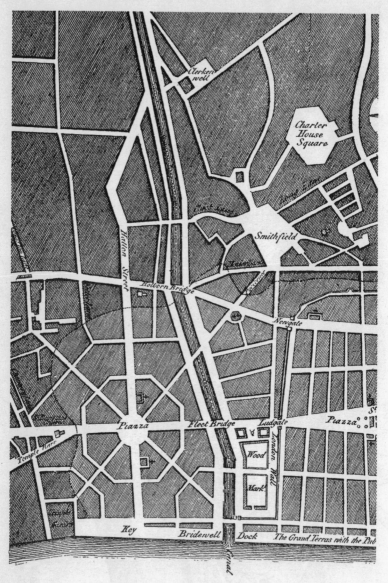

Sir Christopher Wren's plan for London, made after the
Great Fire of 1666. Here are his proposals for the street
lay-out west of the City wall, from Ludgate to Temple Bar.
The continuation eastwards of the plan is shown on the two
pages that follow

Continuation eastwards of Wren's plan, from Ludgate to
Dowgate, showing Piazza at St. Paul's. (See opposite and
the page following)

(75)

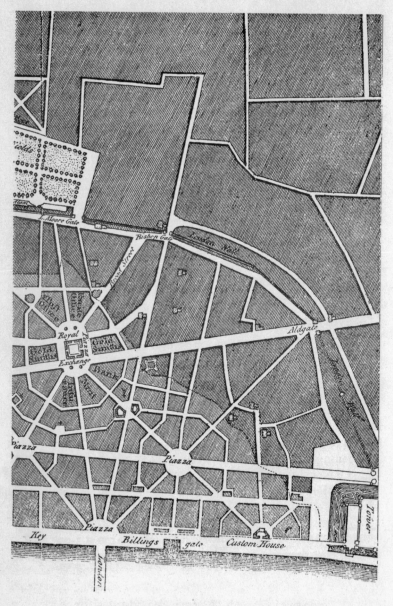

The eastern part of Wren's plan, from the Royal Exchange
to the Tower. (See previous pages for the plan from Temple
Bar to Dowgate)

CHAPTER IX

GROWTH ALONG THE RIVER

REEDOM from the limits imposed by city walls was impossible in a lawless land ; but directly strong and stable government promised security, building beyond the walls began, and often the proximity of a river encouraged the builders. Exceptional towns, such as those which grew up about a great university, soon won immunity from military needs. As early as the 14th century, the college builders in Cambridge were using as a quarry for their materials the castle constructed by William the Conqueror. Throughout England, except in the north, where as in Roman times, there was always the threat of raiding savages, the reaction to more settled conditions was for towns to spread into the country outside their walls ; and towns that were bisected or begirt by navigable rivers were the first to be liberated from the atmosphere of cowering isolation that walls engendered. Though walls were staunch armour against foreign enemies or domestic tyrants, they were also tyrants—gaolers whose comforting assurance to citizens that " nobody can get in " was disheartening to those who wanted to get out and build and adorn the adjacent countryside with houses and churches. But in London their advantages were too great for them to be abolished, although they were allowed to decay. They might repress the ambitions of architects, but they strengthened the power of civic authorities ; and London was able at will to defy kings, or befriend them on favourable terms, while the walls existed, even though they were in a state of disrepair in many places.

When the Dark Age of lawless confusion passed, European civilisation grew into new and vigorous patterns ; and men once more began to invest their surplus energy and wealth in splendid, creative adventures. Like the builders of modern

New York, directly the structural skill was developed architects escaped upwards from the limits imposed by confined space. The cathedrals and great churches climbed into the sky ; towers and spires rose far above the summits of the walls, and in the more settled countries of Europe, and particularly in mediaeval England, cities burst once more from their walls, and where there were rivers they were soon bordered by suburbs and fine houses and gardens.

In London the Thames had conquered the south, riverside wall of the city by the reign of Henry II. William Fitzstephen, the friend and biographer of Thomas à Becket, whose descriptions of London in the late 12th century are quoted by Stow in his *Survey*, said : " The wall is high and great, well towered on the north side, with due distance between the towers. On the south side also the city was walled and towered, but the fishful river of Thames, with its ebbing and flowing, hath long since subverted them."

John Stow, writing his survey of London in 1598, carefully recorded the structural history of the walls, but his quotations from Fitzstephen suggest that although the walls were repaired periodically after the 12th century, the city was released from their bondage long before that time. A continuous suburb linked London with Westminster, for the river coaxed builders westwards, and an array of noble palaces standing in ample gardens diversified the north bank. Within the walls the city might be piled up on the flanks of crooked streets and sunless alleys, but the suburbs were spacious and pleasant. There was plenty of room, and people took advantage of it. According to Fitzstephen's description : " On all sides, without the houses of the suburbs, are the citizens' gardens and orchards, planted with trees, both large, sightly and adjoining together. On the north side, are pastures and plain meadows, with brooks running through them, turning water-mills with a pleasant noise. Not far off is a great forest, a well wooded chase, having good covert for harts, bucks, does, boars, and wild bulls. The corn fields are not of a hungry sandy mould, but as the fruitful fields of Asia, yielding plentiful increase, and filling the barns with corn. There are near London, on the north side, especial wells in the suburbs, sweet, wholesome, and clear. Amongst which, Holywell, Clarkenwell, and St. Clement's well, are most famous, and most frequented by scholars and youths of the city in summer evenings, when they walk forth to take the air."

Stow's *Survey*, which was published in 1603, shows how the principal extensions of London beyond the walls were east and west, following the course of the Thames. The river was a highway, busy with craft, and providing the most rapid and pleasant route from the suburbs to the City. It remained a highway for centuries, and there were numerous landing places, stairs as they were called, where steps led down to the water-side, and hundreds of watermen plied for hire. In his *Description of England (1577–1587)*, William Harrison gives details of the river traffic and mentions " two thousand wherries and small boats, wherby three thousand poore watermen are main-teined ", also " huge tide-boats, tiltbotes, and barges, which either carrie passengers, or bring necessarie provision from all quarters of Oxfordshire, Barkeshire, Buckinghamshire, Bed-fordshire, Herfordshire, Midlesex, Essex, Surrie, and Kent, vnto the citie of London ". This gives a good picture of teeming waterways, serving a great city, and bringing from the banks of the Thames and its tributaries the produce of the countryside ; while the river and the streams that flowed into it nourished the life of innumerable towns and villages.

Great cities and small have nearly always grown up near water. It was the early and rapid development of inland waterways that enabled civilisation to expand westwards at such speed in North America after the War of Independence. H. G. Wells once wrote a scientific romance called *The World Set Free*, about the effect the release of atomic energy might have upon the history of man. Writing in 1914, before the First World War, and looking into the future which is now our immediate past, he said : " A population map of the world in 1950 would have followed seashore and river course so closely in its darker shading as to give an impression that *homo sapiens* was an amphibious animal."(72) London owes its growth to the beckoning stream of the Thames, as well as its prosperity as a great port, even as Liverpool and Birkenhead owe their very existence to the Mersey ; and when a river fails, the city or port it has served is eclipsed, like Chester, since the Dee has silted up, or shrinks to picturesque insignificance,

THE SAVOY PALACE
Its appearance during the mid-18th century

like Parkgate, now parted by sandbanks from the narrow navigable channel of that same faithless river.

London's ribbon development along the Thames westwards was pleasant enough ; and for nearly two centuries after Stow's *Survey* was published, the river was a most agreeable place from which to see London and its stately buildings. Gradually, village was linked with village, though plenty of open space remained—large pleasure gardens, like Vauxhall, the grounds of great mansions, and fields and orchards coming down to the water. Late in the 18th century, a new form of growth began along the river banks, apparently unnoticed, or if observed, the only emotion that was recorded—usually in the pages of a guide-book—was respectful approval of the

(80)

FROM THE RIVER THAMES
An engraving reduced from a view by G. Vertue, 1736

wonders of the age. The character and pace of this new form
of development are revealing.

In 1761, a work entitled *London and its Environs Described* was
published in six volumes by R. & J. Dodsley of Pall Mall, and
claimed to be " An account of whatever is most remarkable for grandeur, elegance, curiosity or use in the city and in
the country twenty miles round it." It was illustrated with
indifferent engravings of buildings and monuments, but from
its concise, alphabetically arranged description of localities in
the area, a good idea of the state of residential and suburban
development may be gained. It is instructive to compare the
descriptions of the Thames-side villages between Westminster
and Richmond with those recorded half a century later.

(81)

Buildings to the west of old Somerset House

(82)

Part of old Somerset House, as it appeared in 1700

(83)

The Grand Orchestra at
Vauxhall in the early
19th century (From Kidd's
*New Guide to the " Lions "
of London,* 1832)

Mr. Simpson, the Master of
Ceremonies at Vauxhall who,
according to Kidd's Guide,
made " a regular tour of the
Gardens at least once in every
five minutes, and when once
seen can *never* be forgotten ".

Within fifty years, something sinister and ugly had happened ;
but the encroachment of this sinister and ugly influence did
not apparently alarm anybody ; nor was its real significance
appreciated.

Vauxhall, which was described as a hamlet in the parish
of Lambeth, was the subject of two and a half pages of restrained
enthusiasm—restrained because the whole work was written
with the rather self-conscious dignity that characterised such
publications. The description concluded with a statement
that everything was provided in the gardens " in the most
elegant manner for the company who chuse to sup ".

When we move on to 1814, and dip into Priscilla Wakefield's
Perambulations in London and its Environs,(73) we discover a
critical note, for of Vauxhall we learn that : " Refreshments
are provided for those who choose to partake of them ; with
every alurement that could gratify the senses, or please the

(84)

fancy. The price of admission is low, which often draws company of a very inferior description." This was the genteel, early 19th-century way of saying : " Oh ! it *has* gone down ! "

The reputation of Vauxhall, already shaky, was soon to be lost altogether ; and by 1859, the gardens were closed. Ten years before that date, John Fisher Murray, in his *Picturesque Tour of the River Thames in its Western Course*,(74) had noted that the celebrated gardens had " passed into other hands ", and that nothing remained of the buildings that had once adorned them. Mr. Murray did not seem to regard this as a matter for regret, and mentions with brisk cheerfulness that the buildings had been levelled with the ground, and " the trees cut down, the walks cut up, and the ground advertised to be let for ' building ' ".

From Vauxhall to Richmond, the Surrey bank of the Thames was still rural and undisturbed in the mid-18th century. Westwards from Vauxhall, there was the little village of Nine Elms ; then came Battersea Fields, and the magnificent mansion of Lord Bolingbroke, who died there in 1751. The house was bought for Earl Spencer in 1763 ; most of it was demolished in 1778, and a mill and a malt distillery were erected on the site. Battersea was noted for its market gardens, and particularly for cabbages and asparagus. Between Battersea and Putney the Wandle flowed into the Thames at Wandsworth, where, in 1761, there were " several handsome houses belonging to the gentry and citizens of London ". Early in the next century Wandsworth was being changed by the new form of development that was in time to spread along the Thames. There were some long established industries at Wandsworth ; Huguenot refugees late in the 17th century had set up cloth works ; but in *The Ambulator*, that ran into many editions in the early years of the 19th century, the extensive growth of industrial Wandsworth is reported. Many " considerable manufactures " are mentioned, including iron furnaces and mills, where shot, shells and cannons were cast, also calico-printing works, linseed oil and white lead mills, and a large vinegar works. Also, the first public railway, the Surrey Iron Railway, ran from Croydon to Wandsworth, where goods were unloaded. All this development was blandly accepted as evidence of the progressive tendencies of the age ; and later on, John Fisher Murray, in his *Picturesque Tour*, ignored this disruptive growth altogether, merely quoting Pope's reference to the Wandle, " the blue, transparent Vandalis ", mentioning the pursuit of manufactures " with spirit and success " by the Huguenot refugees, and finishing with Wandsworth by stating that the first Presbyterian congregation in England was established there. He omitted to observe that the place had been devastated.

Industrial development came gradually at first : factories and foundries, breweries and distilleries, mills, wharves, warehouses, all gradually crowded their way along the banks of the Thames, elbowing out the parks and gardens, fouling the air and polluting the water. Nobody appeared to notice what was happening ; and very few people criticised the untidy muddle that was growing up around and about London, but particularly along the westward suburbs that followed the course of the river.

During the 18th century, various London areas had been built up in a piecemeal fashion, though each separate development was in its way well planned and became a complete and satisfying entity. Squares were laid out north and west ; those enterprising Scotsmen, the brothers Adam, developed the Adelphi site by the river, although they ran out of money before it was finished, and had to get permission for a public lottery to raise the funds necessary to complete the work. Presently, John Nash was laying out other unrelated but spacious schemes : Upper and Lower Regent Street, Carlton House Terrace, Portland Place, and Regent's Park. Much further west, elegant little housing developments, like Edwardes Square and Pembroke Square in Kensington, were planned and built.

After the first third of the 19th century, development got out of hand. Great architects like Robert and James Adam and John Nash had a sense of civic and social responsibility ; but they had innumerable imitators, men whose plans were made to bring in the maximum amount of profit, who, not content with a reasonable return on the money they invested, built badly and greedily—for overcrowded building development is the most permanent and visible form of greed. There were some exceptions. One of them was Thomas Cubitt, who inherited the spacious ideas of the great 18th-century architects,

The Red House, the famous
pleasure resort at Battersea, as it appeared in the
early 19th century

and who developed the Clapham Park district, upon fields
some 200 acres in extent, south-west of Clapham Common. An
interesting and detailed account of the early life and work of
Thomas Cubitt is given in *Man and Boy*, the autobiography of
Sir Stephen Tallents,(75) who is the great-grandson of that
master builder. It is to Thomas Cubitt that we owe the
existence of Battersea Park, for this tract of swampy ground
which produced such succulent asparagus and excellent cabbages had been leased by Cubitt from the Marquess of Westminster. He submitted a scheme to the Metropolitan Im-
provement Commissioners, for a public park on this ground.
The government approved, but Disraeli, then Chancellor of
the Exchequer, opposed it. Cubitt, by offering to buy the
land for what it had cost, helped to turn the scale in favour
of the scheme.

Cubitt was an exceptional man. Unfortunately most people
concerned with industrial and residential development in the

19th century were unexceptional : that is to say they were ordinary, selfish, commonplace people, concerned only with their own interests, and exercising the right of free Englishmen to make the largest possible muddle in the smallest possible space. Today we live with the results of their ordinary, commonplace selfishness.

As the 19th century grew older, the former landmarks of pleasure and leisure were effaced from the banks of the Thames. The Red House at Battersea, almost opposite Chelsea Hospital and surrounded by Battersea fields and their market gardens, was a favourite resort of water parties, though the recreation for which it was famous was condemned in Kidd's *Picturesque Pocket Companion to Richmond and its Vicinity* as " the cruel and silly amusement of pigeon shooting ".(76) This sententious little work was published in 1833, and already disapproval of the sports and pastimes that had delighted the previous century was beginning to harden into the intolerance and specious refinement that became ingredients of Victorian respectability. Though moral sensitivity increased, the eyes of the English were closed to the hideous accompaniments of unplanned urban growth, and what happened to the Thames and to south-west London in the 19th century reinforces the belief that at some time between 1820 and 1850 the national sense of sight was lost.

For over fifty years this thoughtless destruction of riverside amenities continued. The fields and gardens that adorned Battersea Rise were built over ; the green valley of the Wandle was obliterated by industrial and residential development ; the villas and gardens went the way of the pleasure grounds, and by 1820 the Thames ceased to be a salmon river.(77) Even the eels deserted the stream, for at one time large numbers of young eels ascended the Thames from the sea, and there used to be an " eel fair " at Richmond. Above Richmond, Twickenham Ait was famous as Eel Pie Island, and when Kidd's *Picturesque Pocket Companion* was published the place was still " celebrated for its excellent eel pies ".

How much has been lost since the Thames was polluted and its banks invaded by industry may be gathered from Captain Marryat's *Jacob Faithful*, which was published in 1834, and describes the river as it was in the opening years of the century.

Marryat writes about the traffic and life of the river, of isolated cottages amid the marshy expanse of Battersea Fields, of the innumerable villas of the nobility and gentry whose gardens fringed the stream ; but the mixture of fine residences, wharves and warehouses never strikes him as incongruous. Perhaps it seemed no more unusual to the late Georgians and early Victorians for human activities to be so intermingled by the riverside, than it was for merchants to have their offices and homes in the City ; though the segregation of residence and place of business was slowly proceeding.

If anything, the coming of railways slightly retarded the pace of development, for when the London and Southampton line, which became the London and South Western Railway, ran from Nine Elms, its original terminus, through Battersea, Clapham and Wandsworth Common, it took people out into the country. For the moment, the coalescence of villages on the south side of the Thames was halted ; but not for long. In 1846, a suburban branch line was opened to Richmond, leaving the main line at Clapham for stations at Wandsworth, Putney, Barnes and Mortlake. In 1848, the terminus was moved north-east from Nine Elms to Waterloo. The city gent and the city clerk could now settle down anywhere they liked south-west of the river. Suburban development, that had been accepted beyond the walls of London centuries earlier, and which had followed the course of the river, now began to follow the new railways.

In 1849, John Fisher Murray in his *Picturesque Tour of the River Thames in its Western Course*, could give directions for " a constitutional holiday walk, not unmixed with intellectual entertainment ", from Wandsworth through Wimbledon and Richmond Park, to Putney. At Wandsworth, the reader was advised to enquire for the thoroughfare through Earl Spencer's park. Then, " a pleasant stroll, over hill and dale, through corn-clad fields and alleys green, will bring him in a couple of miles, upon Wimbledon Common ". After that he could walk down, through the woods, which is still possible, to the Robin Hood Gate of Richmond Park, which, if you survive crossing the traffic on the Kingston by-pass, you may still enter ; and then across the Park to the Richmond Gate, or, by the Roehampton Gate, " taking water at Putney ".(78)

The full extent of the wreckage caused by unplanned industrial growth may be appreciated by all who sail from Westminster to Putney. Some open spaces still remain : Battersea Park, the little patch of green by Battersea Church, an elegant brick structure with a porch of Tuscan columns and a candle-extinguisher spire, but between Battersea Bridge and Putney, what remains ? On the north bank, power stations and desolation, broken only by the open space of Hurlingham ; on the south bank, factories, breweries, warehouses and gas-works, ending abruptly at Wandsworth Park, and beyond that a few gardens which come down to the river's lip, just before the District Railway Bridge. A once beautiful reach of the river has been destroyed.

Early in the present century, the most confident predictions used to be made about London ; how one day it would spread north, south, east and west, until at last it stretched from Brighton to St. Albans and from Reading to Southend. Although the Victorians never invented the phrase " bigger and better ", they might have taken it as the first line of their hymn to progress. Glorying as they did in the triumph of man over nature, they occasionally committed to verse such boastful chunks of arrogance as Tennyson's *Mechanophilus* :

> Dash back that ocean with a pier,
> Strow yonder mountain flat,
> A railway there, a tunnel here,
> Mix me this Zone with that !

Nothing that Tennyson wrote suggested that God had given him a sense of humour, so we may presume that those atrocious lines were intended to express approval of the visual consequences of mixing " this Zone with that ". Tennyson was praising that most recklessly anti-social technician, the mid-Victorian engineer, who, aided and abetted by his employer, the manufacturer, dumped down industrial plants in the most inappropriate places ; and nobody cared whether his work was related to existing residential or rural amenities or not. He produced isolated pockets of efficient industrial development, and left it at that : his job was to make things work in a given area. As for the architect, he had abandoned his once universal responsibility for design, and had become a fastidious artist, dealing with fancy elevations, with hardly a thought for town-planning. The results of this segregation of technical interests were almost as disagreeable as the effects of total war.

Nearly everything that the Victorians built, and every fresh section of the countryside that they developed, suggested that " bigger and better " was the idea which inspired the builder, who was always chasing bigger and better profits, and in that relentless pursuit was making bigger and better muddles.

A few places defied engulfment, resisting the torrent of suburban building that swept outwards from London, and followed the river and the railways. It washed against them, but not over them ; and they preserved their individuality, never becoming a part of another place. Some permanently open space, steeply rising ground, or a traditional respect for local character, have been as protective as a wall, and thankfully appreciated by those lucky enough to live within the area of immunity. When villages and hamlets overran their parish boundaries and joined up one with another ; when, south-westwards, from the industrial chaos at Nine Elms, Clapham, Battersea, Wandsworth and Putney became a continuous mass of building, relieved only by the open spaces of Battersea and Wandsworth Parks, and the commons of Clapham, Wandsworth, Putney and Barnes, Richmond retained its independence, retained too something of an ancient and placid dignity.

The changes that have taken place in Richmond during the last two centuries are considerable ; but it has not, like other places near London, changed beyond all recognition. The Green is still there ; so is the Hill ; so is the great expanse of Richmond Park, that the practical selfishness of Charles I has bequeathed to generations of Londoners. The river still flows through gardens, open spaces abound, and ancient inns and houses survive. Anybody from the 18th century, visiting Richmond today, would miss a few important places ; they would miss the Wells, for a spring, with an adjoining assembly room, was once an attraction of the little town ; there was also a theatre, probably near the rise of the hill, which was opened in the year 1736. Another one on the Green, an elegant structure, was built under the direction of Garrick, in 1766 ; and although there is still a theatre on the Green, nobody could describe its architecture as elegant. Like many buildings in Richmond, it is a hangover from the Victorian period.

Richmond is spacious ; the Green and the big houses about it, the beautiful façade of Maids of Honour Row, the fragment of the old Palace gateway, and the innumerable Georgian houses, give the place a settled air of serenity. It was always a fashionable little town ; catering for pleasure parties from London in the past, as it does today, though on a larger scale ; and close by was that strangest of all places near London, the village of Petersham, which is no village, but a little curving street of great mansions, to which modish people retired for long week-ends to recover from the exertions of social life in Georgian London. Richmond has its own green belt, which has proclaimed : " Thus far and no farther ", so that the town cannot spread beyond its existing confines, nor can other places, less distinguished, join up with it save along the Upper Richmond Road. To the south and east is the Park, Pesthouse Common, and Sheen Common : to the north there is the old Deer Park, with Kew Gardens beyond, and westwards is the river, while building on the Hill is limited by the Terrace Gardens and Petersham Woods. So, about its narrow knot of streets, Richmond has changed little in a hundred years, and up to a short time ago the fine stone bridge, which was designed by James Paine and opened in 1777, was still sufficient for the hundreds and thousands of tons of traffic that were hurled across it, undreamt of by its architect, and only recently acknowledged by judicious widening. The Twickenham bridge, that is approached through the old Deer Park, has drained away the through traffic from Richmond, which can now concentrate on the business of entertainment, instead of becoming the quiet backwater that many of its residents had desired.

A town that is built around and about a hill always has an advantage. Even little towns like Halton-on-the-Hill, near Runcorn in Cheshire, can attain distinction, though deficient in outstanding architectural character ; but Richmond, despite the conglomeration of 19th-century and modern houses, still has enough architectural distinction for the emptiness of contemporary architecture, and the ugliness of Victorian building, to be, if not forgotten, at least overshadowed. For generations,

Richmond, Surrey, seen from the Hill.   (From a mid-18th-century engraving)

Richmond has attracted the attention of the publishers and writers of guide-books ; and various authors, famous, erudite, obscure, ignorant and amateur, have attempted to record its history and to set down their variegated views about its character. What is there about the place that has attracted so many writers, and so many distinguished residents ? It consists of a Green, three or four principal streets, and a Hill with a magnificent view over the Thames valley. It has been called, indifferently, a town or a village, and one John Evans, LL.D., who wrote a little guide called *Richmond and its Vicinity*, the second edition of which was published in 1825, began his work of genteel praise with these words :

> Richmond is only a village, but one of the pleasantest villages in his majesty's dominions. It stretches itself along the borders of the noble river Thames, which here by its picturesque windings heightens the beauty of the surrounding scenery. It is nine miles distant from Hyde Park Corner ; containing about one thousand houses, and above six thousand inhabitants. The town consists of one long street, with smaller ones branching from it in various directions.

Having disclosed his indecision by calling it a village in his opening sentence, and a town in his fourth, Dr. Evans describes in loving detail its history and amenities, and its capacity for providing entertainment and refreshment. Richmond is an example of unplanned but gracious growth. Like many other English towns, its life has always flowed along and about a few streets, and it has had the supreme advantage of a river front, unspoilt, a Green unenclosed, a Park through which rights of way have existed for many generations, access being denied only when great wars have destroyed old liberties, and bureaucracy has maintained restrictions.

How has Richmond grown ? A bird's-eye view of the town, in 1730, shows much open space, generous gardens and villas, orderly housing development on the Green, and the main pleasure traffic, for which some excellent inns catered, coming by water. William Hickey, that refreshingly uninhibited 18th-century diarist, describes some stupendous debauches at the Castle Tavern. There are few mean streets in Richmond ; and nearly every house has a garden. Though growth has

Two views of Richmond Parish Church, showing 18th-century additions to a Gothic structure. Compare this natural growth of a building with the artificial " Gothic Revival " church of St. Matthias on page 97

been untidy and unplanned, the place has something about it which no new town ever succeeds in acquiring—rich, serene humanity, ten generations deep. It possesses something that only gentle and unhurried growth can confer ; no kind of town planning, with grandiose schemes for social and community centres, and broad vistas, slashed ruthlessly through the accretions of earlier ages, can ever give the intimacy and comfort, and tranquil charm that a place like Richmond enjoys. The town has grown gently up the Hill ; its builders have never been too ambitious or too greedy ; and it has something infinitely better than those artificial modern focal points of social life, community centres—its public houses are well ordered and inviting.

In England, the natural community centre is the public house ; the other great centre for an English town or village, its spiritual mainspring, has been the church. Richmond has

(95)

many churches ; the old parish church being an unpretentious Georgian building, congested a little inside with the extravagant monuments of the nobility and gentry, whose virtues are set forth in ornate but dignified language that matches the scrollwork and the floreated carving on their tombs, so that you feel their virtues, like their last resting places, were slightly rococo.

Another church, St. Matthias, designed by Sir Gilbert Scott, the architect of the Albert Memorial, is a Victorian Gothic structure with a noble spire, the tower swollen on its north-east side by an ungainly tourelle ; but for a mock Gothic building, it is not unpleasing. That tower and spire dominate the surrounding countryside. It is probably the most conspicuous church in the south-west of London. There are several other churches, and from the towing path by Petersham Fields, Richmond has a slightly Continental air, with houses crowning the hill, and spires and towers dominating the houses.

Richmond demonstrates that when a little English town has limits set to its growth, and growth takes place slowly over two or three centuries, the results can be as satisfactory as the most carefully planned development ; perhaps more enduringly satisfying because such a town has so obviously been made for men.

St. Matthias, on Richmond Hill, Surrey. A Gothic Revival
church, designed by Sir Gilbert Scott, the architect of the
Albert Memorial. From a drawing published in *The Builder*,
August 7th, 1858. (See Chapter XIX, pages 260 to 276)

CHAPTER X

GROWTH ALONG THE RAILWAY IN ENGLAND AND AMERICA

ROADS and rivers which had been the chief and most potent factors in the founding and growth of towns all over Europe, and indeed, all over the world, since men took to living in settled communities, ceased to be so when railways gradually spread westwards across the United States of America. In England and Europe, railways merely linked up existing towns ; they provided a new, speedy, comfortable method of travel, and although their convenience was appreciated, their proximity was not. Some towns rejected their disruptive modernity, and occasionally the city fathers drew aside the hem of their garments, so to speak, in order to preserve an isolation that has been well and truly cursed by their descendants. Cambridge and its railway station, remote from the town, is a typical example of such fastidious exclusiveness. Because the railway has passed them by, some English towns have sunk into what restlessly efficient people call decay, and more placid folk repose. These serene and pleasant places were excluded from the ebullient triumphs of the Industrial Revolution. Like the old, gracious towns of the Southern states in America, they have done with growth ; but, unlike those towns, built by the old tide-water aristocracy of Colonial days, they have mellowed, for they are of staunch brick and stone and were built to resist English weather in all seasons. In South Carolina and Georgia the buildings have an air of out-at-elbows magnificence : but wherever they are, in England or America, towns that have escaped development in the 19th century are agreeable reminders that once we had a civilisation with standards that we no longer possess, and are now attempting to revive on paper, forgetting that such standards when expressed in architecture and civic planning can be sustained only by a known and respected sense of values.

The first industrial revolution, based on iron, coal and steam power, was also a revolution in values, and what railways did for the growth of the town showed how greatly values had changed from all those accepted in the previous civilisation, that had depended on wind and water power, animal traction, and handicrafts. In the Midlands during the second half of the 18th century, the linking up of Birmingham with the colliery district round about Wolverhampton by means of a canal began the process that was to end in the comprehensive destruction of a complete area of England. By the time the railways came, the district between Birmingham and Wolverhampton was darkly occupied by industrial development. The foundries, mills and factories that used coal and bulky raw materials, which had been established on the canal banks, were now encouraged to a fresh spurt of growth by the railway; and the results remain. The most depressing and discouraging view in England today is from the train between Birmingham and Wolverhampton, for it reveals the depth and breadth of the desolation that comes from the shortsightedness of industrial man.

In England, the chief contribution of the railways to growth was the expansion of existing industrial areas, the development of new ones, and the steady extension of residential areas all over the country. As the previous chapter recorded, urban building spread along the railways unnoticed; and it was long before the public became conscious of the evils of this form of residential development. Railways that enter a city are nearly always flanked by industrial plant, or the back gardens of small houses. These forms of growth could not have occurred unless at some period between the late 18th and the middle of the 19th centuries, the English, as a nation, had become deaf as well as blind. Unplanned industrial areas intermingled with residential and civic areas in a city are an offence to the eye; noisy railways bordered with residential development are an assault on the ear. Only where the railway actually penetrated an existing city were areas cleared or tunnels made for its entry : but in England, Scotland and Wales, nearly all the railways passed through areas that were not developed, either residentially or industrially, and their presence promoted both forms of development indiscriminately.

In England the railway was subjected to some forms of civic discipline. The public were protected, for the track was fenced. There were penalties for trespassing upon bridges and embankments and cuttings. Level crossings were reduced to the minimum, and bridges, mostly of cast iron, brought into existence a new and comely form of architecture, characteristic of the industrial period, and generally designed by those unacknowledged industrial designers and architects of the early 19th century, the great railway engineers, like the Stephensons, father and son.

In the United States, the railway brought the town into existence ; it was the new road, often the only road ; and, characteristically, it was always known as the railroad in America. It made the main street of the village. Stores and saloons, a few shacks, a pinewood hotel, grew up on either side of its track. The depôt, a mere shanty without a platform or a roof over the heads of the waiting passengers, was often the beginning of a fortuitous concurrence of buildings. Such haphazard hamlets, for they were little more, created by some industrial or agricultural interest of which they became the focal point, often grew at a rapid pace. Soon the railroad depôt and the half-dozen shacks, the saloon, the store, and a church, became the core of a huge, modern American city. And it was the railroad that fed the vitality of these incipient cities during the great westward wave of development, that in the 19th century finally expropriated the original owners of North American soil, the Red Indian tribes, and carried the Stars and Stripes to the Pacific coast and south to the Mexican border.

In the towns that owed their birth and growth to the railroad, the line of Main Street was usually established by the track, and they were then laid out on a grid plan. The town lots were snapped up by speculators or far-sighted citizens, and developed with febrile rapidity. The first check to this growth of towns was caused in the sixties, by the Civil War (1861–65) ; but that was only a temporary check, though it meant the dissolution and ruination of the old-established towns of the South, and a new, breathless, hurried expansion of cities in the Middle and Far West.

The pace of growth and replacement in these new cities was terrific, and was accelerated by the indigenous architecture of wood which exists in America, for houses, public buildings, offices and churches were all timber-built, so they could easily be removed and replaced either intentionally or unintentionally. The great fire of 1871, which destroyed most of Chicago, wiped out the whole of the early growth that must have represented an astonishing conglomeration of structures. The rise of Chicago shows the impetus that railways gave to cities, particularly when they became junctions. Chicago, that began its existence as Fort Dearborn, a post established by the Federal Government in 1804, was destined to become the biggest railroad junction in the United States. A few years after its founding, Fort Dearborn was surrounded by a settlement consisting of fourteen houses : even in 1830, the population of the place was below 100 ; but within ten years, it rose to nearly 4,500, and by 1870, the year before the fire, 306,000 people lived and worked there. This vast expansion was due largely to the railroad. After the great fire of 1871, Chicago was rebuilt. (In England, funds were raised to the value of half a million dollars to relieve the distress of the thousands of people made homeless by the disaster.) Unfortunately, the city was rebuilt in the worst period of architectural taste ; but the pace of growth and the architectural impatience of America have demolished nearly all those 19th-century buildings, and they are replaced by tall, beautifully sited and often elegant buildings, that adorn the lakeside and give this most strident of all modern American cities a skyline almost comparable in daring and beauty with that of New York. Despite its grid plan, and one or two magnificent boulevards, Chicago is so badly planned that in the Loop district the hopeless traffic situation is openly proclaimed by the displayed posters of the overhead railway, which, on every bridge and station, urges Chicago's citizens to " ride above congestion ".

The swift-growing American towns generated an intense local patriotism, that was sustained by their citizens' capacity for making lots of money. Few other values were accepted, or apparently suspected. Opinions about manners and customs expressed by professional writers are not nearly so valuable an indication of the places they write about as their chance recorded observations of town planning and building. Rudyard Kipling, when he was a young journalist, left India for a West-to-East tour of the U.S.A., and between 1887 and 1889 he wrote a series of articles and letters for the *Civil and Military Gazette* and the *Pioneer*. His observations on America in those articles are collected in the second volume of *From Sea to Sea*.(79) Even today the views of that knowing young Victorian are stimulating and instructive ; particularly when he reveals the casualness that was a by-product of American impatience. In their eagerness to make everything bigger, the most elementary matters were ignored or forgotten by those who built cities.

Kipling noted that in Portland, Oregon, the paving of streets and the disposal of sewage were neglected. He saw some foundations being dug, and the soil was saturated with twenty-year-old sewage ; the stuff that was being shovelled out had, he observed, " a familiar and Oriental look . . ."(80)

But America was so large, so bountifully supplied with raw materials and natural power, that throughout the 19th century development went on without thought for the morrow. Cities that began as camps, or as a group of shacks by the railroad, grew and changed every few years, expanding laterally until after 1889, when the ten-storey Tower Building went up in New York. Since then, gradually at first, but now as an accepted practice, American cities grow not only horizontally, but vertically—into the clean and often smoke-free air, and also below ground. Here again the railroad has initiated a new form of growth, and from New York's buried stations, Grand Central and the Pennsylvania, underground ways radiate, lined with shops.

This development has not stopped with the New York railroad stations and such contiguous buildings as the Pennsylvania Hotel ; for the Rockefeller Centre is a busy place of shops and offices, far below the street level of Fifth Avenue. All this is on a scale far bolder and bigger than such neat, compact developments below ground as we have in Piccadilly Circus and Leicester Square Tube stations in London. But even in London, such development came from the enterprise of railways.

The growth of American towns and cities has been stimulated primarily by two instruments of locomotion : one horizontal, the other vertical : the railway engine and the lift—or, in American, the railroad locomotive and the elevator. Though many of the communities that grew up in North America during the 19th century were nourished by the railroad or by some adjacent industry, few derived much architectural inspiration from such sustenance. The grid plan, adopted for its obvious convenience, was occasionally orientated by the line of the railroad that had originated the community, and ran down Main Street, or else the railroad, immovably established, cut across and disrupted any plan that was subsequently adopted.

There were some discerning attempts to make communities connected with some industry into well-planned, pleasant places. As early as the eighteen-sixties, George Mortimer Pullman, who invented Pullman cars, tried to create a model town for his workpeople in Cook County, Illinois. The Pullman Palace Car Company was a long way ahead of its time ; and its model town was eventually absorbed by Chicago. It was not until the present century that towns, starting clean, as it were, ceased to be regarded as semi-benevolent by-products of industrial development, though occasionally they became political exercises in terms of architecture for intellectuals with an appetite for collectivism. Some of the towns that have been built as part of the regional planning schemes of the Tennessee Valley Authority, have authentic social riches as communities, arising from the satisfaction of human needs and not from political theory ; expressed architecturally by men who build for people, and not for that lifeless, theoretical entity, " the people ".

The siting and building of new towns in the United States are not hampered by limitations of space ; there is not the urgent need for compression that has inflated the cost of land in England, Scotland and Wales, and, with increasing demands upon its surface, has made us realise uneasily the smallness of our island. Our fields and towns, villages and hamlets, are being squeezed together, always by fresh demands, either from industry, claiming new areas for development, or from that glutton for land—the airport.

Richard Sheppard, in his book *Building for the People*, has pointed out that " Comparisons between conditions in one country and another are always misleading and are nowhere more likely to be misinterpreted than in building. Standards of living and purchasing power, national habits and industrial traditions, all have an effect upon the finished form of a building. We have been called upon to admire, at various times, different things from different countries, flats in Vienna, prefabricated houses in America, and housing schemes in Sweden, and from all these there is much to be learnt—and much that depends upon different, unassimilable conditions."(81)

Mr. Sheppard followed up that piece of hard common sense by admitting that while we have all sorts of things to learn about building, " we have a good deal to teach ". We have indeed ; such as our national capacity for creating homes ; a capacity that is derived from the properties of the English character, and our national love of liberty, privacy and comfort, in that order. Because the American nation shares, unconsciously, so many qualities that have made the English spirit great, the approach of those who build homes and plan towns in the United States is similar to ours ; only they would put liberty, comfort and privacy, in that order, with privacy last. (There is a lot of fraternity in America, and occasionally it deprives people of privacy.) But the American home is still influenced, albeit remotely, by the English tradition of design ; and the origins and growth of that tradition in relation to the English home are traced in the chapters that follow.

CHAPTER XI

ARCHITECTURE AND HOME LIFE

EVERY city in England, Europe or America has some building or buildings whose architectural lineage may be traced back to Graeco-Roman civilisation or to the mediaeval civilisation that succeeded it, apart altogether from examples that have survived from those periods. In England, during the 16th and 19th centuries, there were deliberate revivals of the characteristic architecture of former ages, that interrupted and ultimately destroyed existing traditions of design. The potency of Greek architectural influence has been mentioned in the second chapter, and that influence has been prolonged by a system of design, expressed by what are called the classic orders of architecture. These orders originated in Greece, and are known as Doric, Ionic and Corinthian. The earliest was the Doric, which appeared about the 9th century B.C., and it followed and was probably derived from Minoan architecture that had evolved in the island of Crete, where Minoan civilisation had flourished. The Ionic and Corinthian orders appeared some two or three centuries later ; and all three orders represented a system of control over horizontal and vertical elements, whose relationship and proportions were harmoniously determined by known rules. Each order consisted of upright columns, supporting an entablature that was composed of three main members—the architrave, frieze and cornice. Each column diminished in diameter upwards from the base, and the capital that terminated the upper part varied in each order ; a plain moulded capital was used in the Doric ; ornamented spirals called volutes appeared on the Ionic ; and the Corinthian

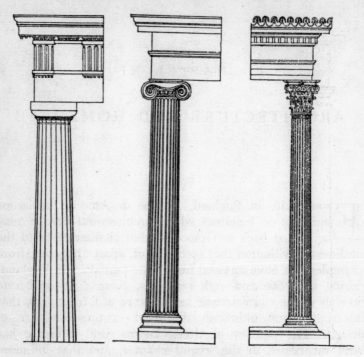

The Greek Orders of Architecture. *Left :* Doric, with a plain capital. *Centre :* Ionic, with volutes on the capital. *Right :* Corinthian, with a capital decorated by formalised acanthus leaves with small volutes above. Compare these with the Roman adaptations on pages 107 and 108. (Reproduced from Plate II of Thomas Rickman's *Architecture in England.* London : 1835)

sprouted a band of formalised acanthus leaves, surmounted by small volutes.

Columns and capitals were not invented in Greece, though they gained their most refined forms at the hands of Greek architects : they were used in Egypt, and, like the arch, were invented at least three thousand years before Christ. Probably the earliest example of the arch in masonry is in a tomb at Bet Khallâf, dating from the 30th century B.C., according to Breasted.(82) The Egyptians did not use the arch in architectural composition ; nor did the Greeks, though they almost certainly knew of it ; like the Egyptians they used post and

(106)

Three Roman Orders of Architecture. *Left:* Doric.
Centre: Tuscan, a Roman variation of the Doric order.
Right: Ionic. The Doric and the Ionic Roman orders
were based on the Greek prototypes shown on page 106.
(Reproduced from Plate III of Thomas Rickman's *Archi-
tecture in England.* London : 1835)

lintel construction, which is called trabeated architecture.
The Greek orders gave a majestic coherence to this form of
architecture, and the Romans adopted and adapted the Doric,
Ionic and Corinthian, and invented a new order, based on the
Doric, which they called the Tuscan. They also invented a
vulgarised elaboration of the Corinthian, which they called the
Composite order.

The Romans used the arch, but regarded it largely as a
structural convenience, and it was seldom aesthetically inter-
related with any of the orders. If arches were used in a
Roman building, then one or other of the orders would appear

Left : The Roman Composite Order, an ornate development of the Corinthian. *Right :* The Roman Corinthian Order. (The illustrations showing detail of capitals and entablatures are from Parker's *Concise Glossary of Architecture.* Oxford : 1875 : those showing the complete orders are from Plate III of Rickman's *Architecture in England.* London : 1835)

as an ornamental embellishment to the façade, without making any structural contribution.

This system of architectural design remained in use as long as the Western Empire of Rome lasted : in England it disappeared during the Dark Ages, but was re-introduced in the 16th century, by which time the buildings of Roman Britain had been utterly forgotten, their materials incorporated in castles, town walls and churches, and the dignity of the public edifices and the comfort of the fine town and country houses only by chance recorded in chronicles like those of Gerald de Barri (Giraldus Cambrensis), who described the ruins of Caerleon on the Usk after he had visited them in 1188, when he accompanied Bishop Baldwin through Wales to preach the Third Crusade.

The towns of Roman Britain and the houses on the country estates would have had an architectural family likeness, arising from the general use of the classic orders throughout the Empire. Roman remains in England preserve the standardised mouldings and ornaments of one or other of the orders. (At Viroconium the bases of fourteen of the columns that once upheld the entablature of the forum are still visible : in the adjacent village of Wroxeter two dwarf columns flank the gateway to St. Andrew's Church, and the font is formed from the upturned base of a column, of greater diameter than the columns of the forum.)

The type of house adapted to the needs and circumstances of the occupant was to some extent standardised, and in the

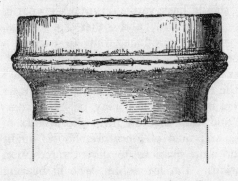

The upturned base of a column from the Roman town of Viroconium, that has been hollowed out and used as a baptismal font in St. Andrew's Church, in the adjacent village of Wroxeter. (From *The Roman City of Uriconium*, by J. Corbet Anderson. London : 1867)

sixth of his ten books on architecture, Marcus Vitruvius Pollio devotes Chapters VIII and IX to " The forms of houses suited to different ranks of persons ", and " The proportions of houses in the country ". From these descriptions of the architectural environment of life, which applied even to the far western Province of Britain, we gain an impression of an orderly, regulated type of home ; conventionally appointed, efficiently equipped ; wholly different from the richly in-dividual English home that began to acquire its characteristics in Saxon England, and after a thousand years of development during which it passed through a communal phase, when the great hall dominated the design of the house, had by the end of the Middle Ages attained a distinctive and satisfying national style in domestic architecture and furnishing. The Roman house was deliberately designed to reflect the social circum-stances of the owner, and had private rooms for the master of the house, rooms for general use, and guest rooms. The private rooms—such as bedrooms and baths—were entered only by invitation. Anybody could enter the common rooms, such as the vestibule and the cavaedium (which was a vacant space or court within the body of a house), and Vitruvius states that " for a person of middling condition in life, mag-nificent vestibules are not necessary ", explaining that such persons sought favours which were granted by the higher ranks of society, and were presumably unlikely to have impor-tant people waiting on them to ask for favours, so were not obliged to impress their visitors. He suggests that house-holders " who have to lay up stores that are the produce of the country, should have stalls and shops in their vestibules : under their houses they should have vaults (cryptae), granaries (horrea), store rooms (apothecae), and other apartments, suited rather to preserve such produce, than to exhibit a magnificent appearance ".

He continues his directions for reflecting the occupation and rank of the owner by the nature of the design. " The houses of bankers and receivers of the revenue may be more com-modious and elegant, and well secured from the attacks of thieves. For advocates and men of literature, houses ought to be still handsomer and more spacious, to allow the reception of persons on consultations. But for nobles, who in bearing honours, and discharging the duties of the magistracy, must have much intercourse with the citizens, princely vestibules must be provided, lofty atria, and spacious peristylia, groves and extensive walks, finished in a magnificent style."(83) (The atrium was the court or hall of a Roman nobleman's house, oblong in plan, supported on three sides by columns, and open to the sky. The peristylium was a continuous row or series of rows of columns, surrounding a court or a building.)

Vitruvius emphasises that the rules he sets down " are no less applicable to country than to town dwellings, except that in town the atria must be close to the gates, whereas, in the country villa, the peristylium is near the entrance. . . ."(84)

The size of the country houses " should be dependent on the extent of the land attached to them, and its produce ". Minute directions are given for the siting and dimensions of the various apartments, which reveal the character of those well-run villa houses, staffed by docile slaves, that were built in Britain to Roman specifications from the 1st century to the end of Roman rule. " The courts and their dimensions will be determined by the number of cattle, and the yokes of oxen employed. The kitchen is to be placed in the warmest part of the court ; adjoining to this are placed the stalls for oxen, with the mangers at the same time towards the fire and towards the east, for oxen with their faces to the light and fire do not become rough-coated. Hence it is that husband-men, who are altogether ignorant of the nature of aspects, think that oxen should look towards no other region than that of the east. The width of the stalls should not be less than ten feet, nor more than fifteen ; lengthwise, each yoke is to be at least seven feet. The baths should be contiguous to the kitchen, for they will be then serviceable also for agricultural purposes. The press-room should also be near the kitchen, for the convenience of expressing the oil from the olive ; and near that the cellar, lighted from the north, for if it have any opening through which the heat of the sun can penetrate, the wine affected by the heat becomes vapid. The oil room is to be lighted from the southern and warmer parts of the heaven, that the oil may not be congealed, but be preserved liquid by means of a gentle heat. Its size must be propor-tioned to the quantity of fruit, yielded on the estate, and the

Conjectural appearance of a Romano-British villa house, with a corridor built round an open courtyard, and a second storey constructed of timber framing. Drawn by A. S. Cook

number of vessels, which, if of twenty amphorae (cullearia), are about four feet diameter. The press, if worked by levers instead of screws, should occupy an apartment not less than forty feet long, so as to allow room for the revolution of the levers. Its width must not be less than sixteen feet, which will give ample room to turn and expedite the work. If two presses are employed, the width must be twenty-four feet. The sheep and goat houses are to be constructed so that not less than an area of four feet and a half, nor more than six feet, be allotted to each animal. The granaries are raised, and must be towards the north or east, so that the grain may not heat, but be preserved by the coolness of air; if towards other aspects, the weevil, and other insects injurious to corn, will be generated. The stable, especially in the villa, should be in the warmest place, and not with an aspect towards the fire, for if horses are stalled near a fire, their coats soon become rough. Hence those stalls are excellent which are away from the kitchen in the open space towards the east; for when the weather is clear in the winter season, the cattle brought thither in the morning to feed, may be then rubbed down. The barn, hay-room, meal-room, and mill, may be without the boundaries of the villa, which will be thereby rendered more secure from fire." If a villa house was intended to be more magnificent than usual, it had to conform with the proportions laid down for town houses, " but with the precautions necessary to prevent the purposes of a country house being interfered with ".(85)

For the well-to-do classes, the landowners, military staff and bureaucrats of the higher grade, Roman Britain afforded standards of living that would have satisfied even the exacting demands of the Victorians in matters of comfort. Their well-planned houses were mostly of the corridor type, built round an open courtyard, usually of one storey, comfortably furnished, and warmed by a central heating system that was probably more satisfactory than any methods in use today. Externally, the houses presented a pink-hued wall surface, save in those parts of the country where stone was used for building; their small windows were glazed with panes of translucent, greenish-blue glass; and there were red tiles on the sloping roof. A second storey was probably added to some of the villa houses in the country, and may have been constructed of timber framing. Within, the walls would be plastered and decorated with painted patterns, and mosaic pavements would ornament the floors.

The furniture consisted of low couches and chairs, rather low tables, of metal and wood, sometimes of stone, and there is evidence that woven cane chairs were used, not unlike Victorian basket chairs. There would be plenty of fabrics, hangings, and probably rugs.

There was excellent plumbing, and if the house was large enough it would include a bath, though usually the public baths in some adjacent town were patronised. There was abundant food : Britain raised splendid crops, and exported corn to the Continent. As the Province was part of the huge free trading area formed by the Western Empire, foreign wines and other luxuries would be imported at comparatively low cost. Beer would be brewed locally, and wine of a sort was produced in the southern part of the Province. But one thing an Englishman would have missed—whether he had lived in the reigns of Henry VIII, Elizabeth, the Georges or Victoria— and that was the fireplace. The Romano-British householder would have considered the habit of gathering round an open fire both barbaric and uncomfortable. There was no fireplace in his luxurious home. Instead, some of the floors would have hot air circulating below them, which rose through hollow tiles in the walls, and escaped by means of vents or cowls through the eaves of the roof. The heating chamber below the centre of a floor was known as a hypocaust, and was two or three feet high, the floor above being supported by rows of brick pillars, set close together. This was a heat-distributing chamber ; burning fuel was admitted to it through a duct from the external stoke hole, and this duct became a furnace. The heat thus generated was carried through several rooms. Gerald de Barri in his 12th-century description of Caerleon writes of " stoves contrived with wonderful art, to transmit the heat insensibly through narrow tubes passing up the side walls ".(86)

Writing eleven or twelve hundred years after the hypocaust heating system had ceased to be used anywhere in Britain, Sir Henry Wotton in his paraphrase of Vitruvius, that he

A hypocaust, shown in the foreground of this drawing of the ruins of Viroconium. (From *The Roman City of Uriconium*, by J. Corbet Anderson. London : 1867.)

THE OPEN HEARTH

The central fireplace was a raised hearth with iron dogs, andirons or cobirons as they were sometimes called, to support the logs. The smoke escaped through vents in the roof. This is a comparatively late example, from the Great Hall of Penshurst Place, Kent, a typical manor house built in A.D. 1341. See pages 150 and 151. (From a drawing by F. W. Fairholt in Thomas Wright's *History of Domestic Manners and Sentiments in England*. London : 1862)

called *The Elements of Architecture* (published in 1624), quotes a note from Palladio " who observeth that the *Ancients* did warm their Rooms with certain secret *Pipes* that came through the Walls, transporting heat (as I conceive it) to sundry parts of the House from one common *Furnace* ; I am ready to baptize them *Cali-ducts*, as well as they are termed *Venti-ducts*, and *Aquae-ducts*, that convey Wind and Water ; which whether it were a custom or a delicacy, was surely both for thrift, and for use, far beyond the German *Stoves* ; and I should prefer it likewise before our own fashion, if the very sight of a fire did not adde to the *Room* a kind of *Reputation*. . . ."(87)

The forms of heating used in the houses of Saxon England were extremely primitive by comparison with the hypocaust system. Fires heaped up upon a central hearth in the single large room—that forerunner of the great hall—gave out heat

THE EVOLUTION OF THE FIREPLACE: NORMAN

When the fireplace was moved against a wall, a recess accommodated the hearth, and a flue in the thickness of the wall dispersed the smoke, when the wind was favourable. This early Norman fireplace, from Rochester Castle, *circa* 1130, is simply an arched opening

The next stage shows the use of a sloping fireback and a canopy supported by columns. From Conisborough Castle, *circa* 1170. (Both examples are from Parker's *Glossary of Terms used in Grecian, Roman, Italian and Gothic Architecture.* Oxford: 1865)

of a sort, and the smoke, after begriming everything under the roof including the inhabitants, their clothes and their food, escaped through a vent in the roof. Some hundreds of years passed before this isolated central hearth was moved up against the wall and a canopy and a flue built above it to

Above and below, left : Fireplaces from Aydon Castle, North-umberland, *circa* 1270. The mantel shelf makes its appearance above the canopy. *Below, right :* Fireplace from Edlingham Castle, Northumberland, *circa* 1330. (From Parker's *Glossary*)

THE EVOLUTION OF THE FIREPLACE
13th and 14th centuries

draw up the smoke, and much of the heat with it ; but the hearth, whether it occupied the centre of the hall, or was part of a vast fireplace, restored a primitive habit, that was unknown to the civilisations that had grown up round the warm sunny shores of the Mediterranean—it restored the old sociable circle of people warming themselves round a visible fire, and it stimulated all those sociable habits—the exchanging of stories, the singing of ballads, the reciting of sagas—which such comfortable and cosy association with one's fellows promoted. The English love of the visible fire, as deep-rooted as the English love of the countryside, is an ancient love : going back to the first crude wooden halls of Saxon England. The fireplace has become a symbol of home, and about it cluster innumerable legends and memories. Since the 15th century it has been the focal point of furnishing. A completely different conception of home life must have existed in the centrally heated houses of Roman Britain. Their inhabitants might enjoy the antique refinements of life with their plumbing and their *cali-ducts* (so aptly named by Wotton) ; but the Englishman wanted the visible heat of a fire on the hearth, which did add to the room " a kind of *Reputation* ", and this understanding of the significance of the fireplace was the result of centuries of progressive achievements in the art of homemaking.

THE EVOLUTION OF THE FIREPLACE

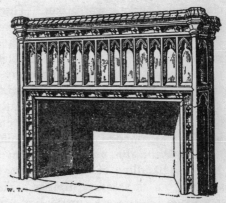

The last phase of Gothic design : a fireplace from Sherborne Abbey, Dorsetshire, *circa* 1470. (From Parker's *Glossary*)

CHAPTER XII

ORIGINS OF THE ENGLISH HOME

DURING the centuries when the town was growing, spilling its suburbs into the countryside as it increased in size, and attracting the more industrious and enterprising elements of the population, the home was acquiring the characteristics of comfort, welcome, and privacy that are associated with houses wherever the English tradition has become established. The history of the English home begins in the Post-Roman period, with the houses of the Saxon settlers, whose rejection of town life—mentioned in Chapter IV—gave a new, if barbaric, significance to their country houses. Those houses were not only in but of the country ; they were primarily farm-houses, unlike the villa-houses of the Roman landed proprietors, which were little oases of luxury in the countryside, reproducing the amenities of town life, and catering for a class whose outlook was urban. The precise and commodious planning of the Romano-British town and country houses, their convenient equipment, and the accomplished structural methods by which they were erected, were not transmitted to the homes of 6th- and 7th-century Saxon England, because they made no appeal to the barbarian settlers.

For many generations the creative impulse was denied opportunity for expression in domestic architecture : Saxon landlords demanded from their builders a sturdy structure : utility was the aim, and it was achieved with the use of timber. Now the handling of wood encourages skill, not only in converting, but in selecting timber. The structural members of a wooden house were curved limbs from trees ; part of their length provided vertical uprights, and the bent portion supplied the rafters. A sufficient number of such limbs would form the structural bones of the single room of which most houses consisted—the hall that was to become the centre of English social life for centuries.

Walls of wattle and daub and roofs of thatch were weather-proof; but those timber houses were easily and no doubt frequently destroyed by fire. Bede has described how easily such accidents occurred in relating what befell a traveller (A.D. 642) who came at nightfall to a village. He " entered a house where the neighbours were feasting at supper ; being received by the owners of the house, he sat down with them at the entertainment. . . . They sat long at supper and drank hard, with a great fire in the middle of the room ; it happened that the sparks flew up and caught the top of the house, which being made of wattles and thatch, was presently in a flame ; the guests ran out in a fright, without being able to put a stop to the fire. The house was consequently burnt down. . . ."(88)

Those timber-framed houses with their clay-daubed wattle walls were always in danger of being burnt down : no examples have survived, and their builders, ignoring or accepting this frailty, made no attempt to insulate or guard the open hearth with its pyre of hot wood ash upon which fresh spark-spitting logs were thrown when the fire was made up. All that those builders bequeathed to posterity was a tradition of skill in woodworking, which was supplemented and amplified by the skill developed in shipbuilding. Both crafts gave experience to wood-workers, and Saxon England, despite the fluctuations of its civilisation, had attained, long before the Norman Conquest, notable ability in the handling of wood and other materials. Masonry was reserved for the churches and abbeys that were built during and after the 7th century, as the pagan kingdoms which had occupied much of the old Roman Province were reclaimed by Christianity. The building of churches and the planning and adornment of the great religious houses not only revived architecture, but gave it new inspiration and direction.

In those pre-Norman centuries the foundations of English craftsmanship were firmly laid ; and mediaeval masons and carpenters drew upon the cumulative skill of many generations of craftsmen, when they began to build the great naves and

Saxon church of St. Lawrence, at Bradford-on-Avon, Wiltshire, *circa* A.D. 700. (From Parker's *Introduction to Gothic Architecture.* Oxford : 1849)

transepts and towers of abbeys and priories, and to rear the forbidding and immensely strong castles and keeps of the Norman ruling class.

Domestic architecture in Norman England was repressed by the claims of fortification : safety first was an inevitable requirement in a land wherein a dispossessed population had to be held down by force. We still suffer a little today from the anti-Saxon propaganda of the conquering classes ; and it is unfortunate that very few pre-Norman buildings now exist, for they would help to abate the impression, sedulously propagated during the 11th century, that Saxon England was barbaric, crude and incapable of architectural expression. Some of the little, exquisite Saxon churches that have survived refute the charge of crudity ; and the great civilisation of Northumbria, that produced an historian of the calibre of Bede, is not to be dismissed as barbarous, nor can its standards of life and culture be compared with the early, hardly-won settlements of the Saxon invaders, who finally occupied the Roman Province of Britain. Dr. Adamson, in his book, *The Illiterate Anglo-Saxon*, has pointed out that " the pre-Conquest English were not the nation of universally illiterate, sottish boors, such as they are pictured by Norman monks and by the popular historians of a much later day. The process of belittling Anglo-Saxon England to justify Norman aggression began early and in a way which has become all too familiar to the present generation. Paul, the first Norman abbot of St. Albans (1077–93), destroyed the tombs of his predecessors in office since, as he alleged, they were rude and unlearned although, unlike himself, of royal or noble lineage. Their language was ' barbarous ', ' alien ', declared another ecclesiastic of Norman times, the Italian Faritius, abbot of Abingdon, who died in the year 1115."(89)

The Anglo-Saxon states, although they suffered occasionally from the depredations of Viking raiders, were immune from the miseries endured by Europe during the barbarian wars, and the Arab invasion, that surged up through Spain and into France, where the Moslem army was defeated at Poitiers by Charles Martel. In a comparatively peaceful atmosphere, the English Church was able to foster learning and the arts, which between the arrival of Theodore (669) and the death of Bede (735) attained levels that were unsurpassed until the Middle Ages. Mr. T. D. Kendrick has suggested that this " Golden Age of the English Church " placed England during the 9th century in a remarkable position of leadership, when the country " was not merely a convert to the classical tradition, but actually its guardian and foremost promotor ". Enlarging upon this view, he says : " If from our distant standpoint we seek the lineage of Anglo-Saxon renaissance drawing and sculpture, we have to look either back or forward in the direct pedigree of the great classical tradition. The work stands alone in Europe, not the contemporary version of a continental art, but a sudden and unique revelation of the mainstream itself. It is perhaps one of the most remarkable events in the whole art-history of England. For a brief moment this country, rousing itself from its obsession with barbaric ornament, stands out bravely and is illumined in the sight of all Europe as the principal custodian of that immense and potent tradition that had found expression in Greek and Roman and Late Antique art and was to become in the western world Carolingian and Ottonian art."(90)

Despite this passing brilliance—for it was soon eclipsed by the shadow of wars—some of the building crafts and in-

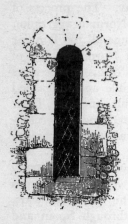
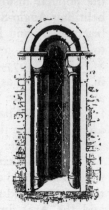

Early Norman windows. *Left:* Gillingham, Norfolk. *Right:* Ryton, Warwickshire. Even in church architecture the window remained a narrow, arched opening : at the end of the 11th century it was still obviously the " wind-eye " or " wind-hole ", seldom glazed. (After Bloxam)

dustries that had existed in Roman Britain had gone. Brick-making was a lost art ; skilled masons were rare ; glass was unknown and Bede records that in the year 675, the Abbot of Wearmouth, Benedict Biscop, had to import from Gaul " some masons to build him a church in the Roman style ", also glass-makers, as they were " at this time unknown in Britain ", in order to glaze the windows of his church, also the cloisters and dining-rooms.(91)

This revival of glass-making in the 7th century had no permanent effect on building. The knowledge of glass-making, imparted by the French to the English craftsmen who were building the monastery at Wearmouth, was apparently lost, for eighty-three years later, in 758, Cuthbert, Abbot of Jarrow, asked the Archbishop of Mainz to send some artisans who could make glass for windows and vessels, explaining that the English were " ignorant and helpless ".(92)

Centuries elapsed before anything comparable with the comfort of glazed windows, even as poor as those used in Romano-British houses, was again common in England. The windows of the Roman houses had been mean in size, and were not transparent ; but they were weatherproof and they did admit daylight. The very name window, derived from the old Norwegian word *vindauga*, means " wind-eye ". It was for centuries a small " wind-eye " or " wind-hole ", for its size was determined by the need to keep out intruders and missiles. In Saxon and Norman England windows were narrow slits, high up in the wall, protected by wooden shutters. In town houses windows were larger than in the castles and fortified manor houses of the countryside, and oiled linen, or parchment, let in a little light and shielded rooms from weather : how such fragile substances were fastened to the window is unknown ; but they must have been renewed frequently. The technique of glazing probably began with the use of panes of horn, ground very thin and framed in channelled strips of lead. This glazing was done by lead workers—an association that has persisted, for today plumbers are still glaziers.(93)

Experiments in the use of building materials were made occasionally in 7th-century England, and Bede describes a church on the Isle of Lindisfarne in 652, that was built of oak and walled with reeds—presumably some form of thatching. This thatch was removed by Bishop Eadbert, who covered the walls and roof with lead plates. This happens to be recorded : there may well have been other examples of innovation and experiment in church building, for it was from the church only that patronage and inspiration for architecture were forthcoming. The towns no longer afforded opportunities for builders apart from the patching up of

Early Norman window at Beaudesert, Warwickshire. The proportions are more generous than those of the windows shown opposite, and the rounded arch has been ornamented. Compare this elaboration of the arched form with the Saxon church on page 122, and the doorways on pages 138 and 141. (After Bloxam)

existing buildings, and the maintenance of their walls. Town life revived very slowly in the Saxon states, and though there is some reason for assuming that London—the Saxon Lundenwic—had unbroken continuity with the Roman Londonium Augusta, it was probably a very dilapidated city.

The independence of London, which was part of the Kingdom of Kent, is suggested by the action of its citizens early in the 7th century, when they rejected Mellitus, the Christian Bishop, against the wishes of their sovereign, King Eadbald of Kent. Bede states that " the Londoners would not receive Bishop Mellitus, choosing rather to be under their idolatrous high priests ; for King Eadbald had not so much authority in the kingdom as his father, nor was he able to restore the bishop to his church against the will and consent of the pagans ".(94) This defiance of a king suspected of weakness has been repeated more than once in the long history of the city, and from this early act of aggressive independence it has been concluded by some authorities that London preserved at this time " some of the attributes of the ancient city-state . . ."(95) Such independence must have been based upon more than the security of walls in a good state of repair, and citizens who were ready to defend them. Trade must have continued to supply the means for independence, and to nourish the spirit that sustained it ; and as an active trading port, London would have maintained warehouses and offices and market places. We have no knowledge of what 7th-century London looked like, or what sort of town houses the traders and artisans lived in : Lethaby's view that even in Alfred's time much of the original Roman city still existed has been mentioned in Chapter VIII ; but before the disasters it suffered at the hands of the Vikings during and after the 9th century—between the years 994 and 1016 the city was besieged three times by those raiders—it must have been fairly intact, and far from ruinous. Mr. Gilbert Sheldon believes that it was " most unlikely that it was ever stormed or sacked ", although the citizens had probably been compelled " to admit a body of Teutonic settlers as co-inmates ".(96)

Although we know nothing of the character of the Saxon town house, we know that the country house, beginning as a single chamber, developed into the hall, with separate bed

The Saxon bed was an enclosed bunk, curtained or shuttered. This drawing, copied from a contemporary manuscript, Alfric's version of Genesis, by F. W. Fairholt, is included in Thomas Wright's books, *The Homes of Other Days* and *A History of Domestic Manners and Sentiments in England.* (London : 1862)

chambers or bowers adjoining it ; though in its earliest form the benches of the hall served as beds, with a few enclosed bunks, or shut-beds, lining the walls, with curtains that could be drawn across at night or wooden shutters that could be fastened, so the bunk or bed became a secret and stuffy little cabin. There may have been occasions when some Saxon nobleman used the shell of a Roman villa-house, and adapted it to his own use ; but, as mentioned in Chapter II, Collingwood and Myres state categorically that " not a single villa in the country has been found underlying a Saxon dwelling, or has yielded evidence of permanent occupation in the Saxon period ".(97)

Evidence of the form and character of Saxon dwellings found in contemporary, or nearly contemporary manuscripts, is unsatisfactory and often misleading. For example, an illustration in the Harleian Manuscript, No. 603, which is probably as early as the 9th century, shows a conglomeration of buildings which has been described by various writers, who reproduce copies of the drawing, as an Anglo-Saxon mansion. There appears to be a central hall, roofed with pantiles, and approached by three arches that spring from Tuscan or Doric columns : other buildings flank this central structure, with walls of masonry, and rising behind the hall is a circular building, crowned by a cupola. The drawing illustrates the giving of alms to beggars by the just and righteous chieftain: it may have been copied from other existing representations of Roman houses, but though it certainly shows an example of domestic architecture that has Roman characteristics, the locality of the model that served the artist may not have been Anglo-Saxon England.

The civilisation of the 7th and 8th centuries that produced a domestic architecture of timber, and the stone-built churches of which so very few have remained, and flowered with such artistic splendour in Northumbria, arose from the successful welding of two races ; for although the descendants of the Romano-Britons still thought of themselves as Romans and called the Saxon settlers barbarians, the two stocks had to share the country, after the final defeat of the independent British at the Battle of Dyrham in 577, and the fall of Bath, Gloucester and Cirencester. This fusion of the two races, like that of the Saxons and Normans which took place seven centuries later, gave a fresh and vigorous impetus to life, and although the new civilisation had few material amenities, it had a copious vitality that before the end of the 7th century was fruitfully directed by the English church.

Materialism, which has been worshipped under a variety of names, has for the last century or so put so much emphasis on physical comfort that the importance of its continuity has seemed to many historians and students of history the supreme test of a progressive civilisation. The bewailing of the collapse of Roman Britain, and the dark years of inconclusive conquest and increasing settlement by barbarians, is usually prompted because those who weep are weeping for the lost comforts of the well-appointed villa-house, are mourning for the heating appliances that no longer work, and the baths that have parted from their plumbing, and all those circumstances of luxury which depend upon an abundant and constant supply of hot water.

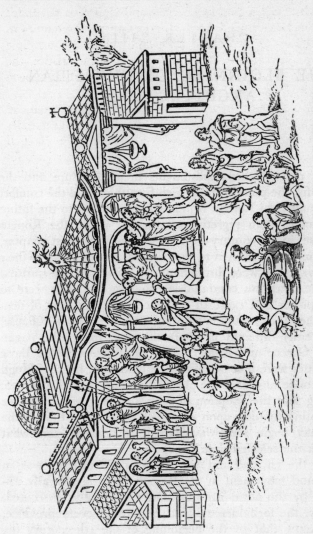

This house, drawn by a 9th-century artist, suggests a Romano-British model; though the house he copied may not have been in Anglo-Saxon England. This drawing, made from the Harleian Manuscript, No. 603, by F. W. Fairholt, is included in Thomas Wright's books, *The Homes of Other Days* and *A History of Domestic Manners and Sentiments in England*. (London: 1862)

CHAPTER XIII

THE BEGINNING OF CHRISTIAN ARCHITECTURE

THE material accomplishments in architecture and the crafts, the plumbing, the rich furnishing and the comfort of houses in Roman Britain could transmit to the future nothing more than regretful memories. While the Roman villa-houses in the country were, as we said in the last chapter, oases of luxury, dedicated to the comfort and pleasure of their proprietors, there were throughout the province little spiritual oases—the Christian communities, that in due time were to grow in power and exert an influence upon the lives of men so that when they rebuilt civilisation after the Roman collapse, it was wholly different in character from the blithe pagan world of Greece and Rome. At what time or where those communities were first established is unknown, but Dr. Hugh Williams once suggested the purely arbitrary date of A.D. 200, explaining that the adoption of such a date was a device for concentrating thought upon a particular period, " though the period may begin somewhat earlier, or, maybe, somewhat later than the selected date ".(98)

During the 1st, 2nd and 3rd centuries, Christianity was an underground movement in the Roman Empire, officially discouraged by the administration and periodically persecuted. Gradually, the forbidden religion permeated every province, and we know that by the beginning of the 4th century the Church was well established in Britain, and within two years of the martyrdom of St. Alban in A.D. 305, the persecution of Christians was stopped, and, according to Bede, those who " during the time of danger, had hidden themselves in woods and deserts, and secret caves " again appeared in public and " rebuilt the churches which had been levelled with the ground ;

founded, erected, and finished the temples of the holy martyrs, and, as it were, displayed their conquering ensigns in all places . . ."(99) Bede tells us that Alban was killed " near the city of Verulam, which is now by the English nation called Verlamacestir, or Varlingacestir, where afterwards, when peaceable Christian times were restored, a church of wonderful workmanship, and suitable to his martyrdom, was erected ". (100) Three British bishops attended the Council of Arles in A.D. 314, namely Eborius of York (known in Roman times as Eboracum), Restitutus of London, and Adelphius of either Lincoln or Caerleon, for he is described as being of Londinensium, which may have been a mis-spelling of Lindum or Legionensium, the former being Lincoln, the latter Caerleon, or Civitas Legionum.(101) The name " Eborius of Eboracum " is " rather suspicious " as Dr. William Bright observes in his *Chapters of Early English Church History*, and he suggested that the name may have been some native British name mis-read. It could conceivably have been Ivor, which was an old British name, and is mentioned by Geoffrey of Monmouth.(102) With those three bishops went Sacerdos, a presbyter, and Arminius, a deacon.

Apart from the names of a few martyrs and those who repre-sented the British church at the Council of Arles, little is known of the early history of that Church. " We know nothing of its episcopal succession, very little of its internal life, or of its efforts at self-extension," wrote Dr. Bright. But that Church began to demand and inspire architecture. Bede's reference to the church that was built to commemorate St. Alban's martyrdom has been quoted : his statement that it was erected " when peaceable Christian times were restored " is no guide to the date when the building that subsequently became the abbey church of St. Albans was first begun. (The abbey was founded in the 8th century, when Bede was living.) Dr. Bright mentions Canterbury and Caerleon as well as Verulamium where some of the buildings of the British Church were known to exist, and adds Glastonbury, where the great abbey was subsequently built in place of an older church " made of twisted wands, the earliest sanctuary on that venerable ground of which Christianity has held uninterrupted possession ".(103) Walter Johnson, in a detailed examination of the use of pagan sites for Christian churches, rejects this story of an early church of primitive construction at Glastonbury, though admitting that St. Joseph's Chapel at Glastonbury Abbey is " an interesting case of probable retention of site, though not necessarily of continuous buildings ". Although he discredits the tale " told by the imaginative William of Malmesbury, a millennium after the alleged event, that, as early as the first century of the Christian era, a chapel constructed of osiers existed at this spot," he suggests that very probably " some kind of primitive church or oratory, with walls of wattle, and a roof of reeds, was set up during the Roman occupation, and it may fairly be supposed, though it cannot be proved, that no break had occurred when the Saxon Abbey was founded ".(104)

The earliest Christian church of which indisputable evidence exists was at Silchester (Calleva Atrebatum), and it was built about the middle of the 4th century ; certainly not later. According to W. R. Lethaby, its important position in the city, close to the Forum, justifies the belief that " it was a bishop's church ". The plan, he suggests, was of an Eastern rather than a Roman type.(105) He also said that " Some day, when we reverence our antiquities more, it might be excavated once again and, having a decent roof erected over it, be made a place of pilgrimage. I should like to see a copy of it put up somewhere for use—it might cost half as much as a poor stained-glass window." Lethaby concludes, from the small size of the church at Silchester, that the Christian congregation could have numbered only a few hundreds ; in the same city a temple to Mars was in use, probably up to the end of the city's existence.

Throughout the 4th century, and for many centuries after, Christianity was competing with other religions. In the early days of its freedom from persecution and its official recognition as the religion of the Empire, the most formidable rival to Christianity was the cult of Mithras. From the worship of Mithras women were rigidly excluded. The cult was enormously popular with soldiers ; it spread throughout the Empire wherever there were garrisons, and was long established in Britain. A shrine of Mithras that was discovered in 1950 at Carrawburgh, on Hadrian's Wall, dates from the early part

of the 3rd century, and was in use until the following century.
" It was once destroyed, in A.D. 296-7, but was also enlarged
as the cult attracted more worshippers, or was for a while
abandoned and renewed with fresh zeal."(106)   In the second
half of the 4th century, a great temple to Nodens, the hunter-
god of the Forest of Dean, was erected at Lydney about A.D.
365 ; an ambitious architectural undertaking, with a hostelry
and baths—one of many examples of the vitality of the old
gods whose worship was revived under Julian, the Apostate
Emperor.(107)   Nodens was a native British god, who persisted in later times as Nuada of the Silver Hand, and, still
later, as King Lear.(108)   Many of the native forms of worship
survived in Britain throughout its period of Roman rule ; some
of the native cults were romanised, and became identified with
the deities of official Roman religion.   Collingwood and Myres
describe the history of Romano-British religion as a blend of
cultures, because the Romans " were always willing to come
to terms with the *genius loci* ".   The scale of the temple to
Nodens is evidence of this tolerant attitude, so too is the temple
of Sulis, the goddess of the hot springs at Bath.(109)   These
native and Roman cults survived, and for hundreds of years
they were rivals to Christianity, at first open rivals, and then,
as the Church grew stronger, they became what Christianity
had once been, an underground movement, whose priests and
priestesses were identified with wizards and witches, who
unlawfully practised the " old religion ", that was condemned
by the early Christians as heathenism, and by mediaeval
churchmen as witchcraft.(110)   Heathenism was still firmly
rooted in Britain in the 4th century, and throughout the 5th
and 6th centuries it was constantly reinforced by pagan
invaders and settlers, who drove the Christian Britons farther
and farther west, so that British Christianity became a partisan
religion, that encouraged enmity against the barbarians.   Its
prelates felt no call to convert the Saxons and Jutes who were
gradually taking over more and more of the Roman Province ;
and at a synod of the British Church, dated by the Cambrian
Annals in 569 and called the Synod of the Wood of the Victory,
for it was held on the site of a battle fought by the Britons,
an enactment fixed a penance of thirteen years for a Christian
who had acted as a guide to the barbarians.(111)

The churches built by British Christians have not survived, though their materials and foundations may be incorporated in the Saxon and mediaeval buildings that subsequently occupied their sites. The use of Roman materials in a Saxon church does not of course prove that they were taken from a Romano-British church : Roman ruins for centuries invited builders to use their convenient materials. Apart from the church at Silchester, nothing that now exists can with certainty be identified as a Romano-British Christian church. It seems probable that secular buildings were occasionally used as places of worship, and that some of the wealthier Christian converts allowed their houses to be consecrated. Walter Johnson examines this theory in his description of churches that occupy or are adjacent to the sites of Roman villa-houses. He assumes that " from a small reception-room, arranged like an ordinary church, there might be developed a Christian building, with chancel, nave, and aisles complete ". He supports this assumption by " a scrap of testimony, slight though it may be ", namely " the discovery, on a mosaic, among the ruins of a Roman villa at Frampton, Dorsetshire, and again on a tile from the villa at Chedworth, Gloucestershire, of examples of the Chi-Rho monogram. This sacred monogram has also been met with on such objects as bowls, seals, and rings. Seeing that the symbol was not used in Rome before A.D. 312, its presence in Britain cannot date earlier."(112)

Sacred buildings of a substantial character were undoubtedly erected in Britain during the 4th century, and Bede describes the " stately church " built by St. Ninian, which was still in existence when he wrote his history, as a stone structure " which was not usual among the Britons ".(113) This stone church, dedicated to St. Martin, was built in 397 by St. Ninian in the wild part of Britain, north of Hadrian's Wall, in what is now Galloway, and its site was on the western side of Wigtown Bay, at Whithorn. Ninian called this place Leukopibia, and his church was known as the White House (Candida Casa), and he is said to have visited St. Martin at Tours, when he was returning from his period of training at Rome, " and obtained from him masons for the purpose of building a church after the Roman manner . . ."(114) The need for bringing skilled masons from Gaul suggests that the northern part of Britain was then completely cut off from the civilised south, where building craftsmen were almost certainly still available at the end of the 4th century, for only thirty-two years before Ninian founded the White House, the splendid temple to Nodens had been built at Lydney—some two hundred and thirty miles south of Whithorn. The area between the old Antonine Wall—the chain of forts running from the Clyde to the Forth—and Hadrian's Wall, had long been abandoned ; it had never been romanised, and Leukopibia was a town of the tribe of Novantae, that occupied the south-western part of Galloway, an area which is often mistakenly called the old Roman Province of Valentia—an error that Kipling's stories in *Puck of Pook's Hill* have helped to popularise and perpetuate. The building at Whithorn was the first British monastery, which " under the name of the ' Magnum Monasterium ' or monastery of Rosnat, became known as a great seminary of secular and religious instruction ".(115)

The next phase of Christian architecture in Britain begins with the mission of St. Augustine in 597 to the English kingdom of Kent, when the eastern part of the island was wholly pagan, and the British Christians had found their final refuge in Wales. But apart from architecture, British Christians had made some notable contributions to the history of the Church.

At the end of the 4th century, a Romano-British layman named Pelagius wrote some commentaries on the Epistles of St. Paul, which form the oldest known example of British literature. Therein he expressed heretical views about the natural goodness of man, and this Pelagian heresy was refuted by Augustine, the Bishop of Hippo, and condemned in 418 at the Synod of Carthage. Pelagianism was popular in Britain, and St. Germanus, a former Roman officer, who became Bishop of Auxerre, was twice sent by Rome to the province to check the spread of the heresy. His first visit was in 429, his second in 447 ; and the need for his visits is evidence that the Christian community in Britain was full of vitality, for heresy does not flourish in an atmosphere of ignorance or indifference.

CHAPTER XIV

THE GOTHIC ACHIEVEMENT AND
THE TUDOR HOME

FROM the time of St. Augustine's mission in 597 to the beginning of the 16th century, Christian architecture in England recorded the continuous and remarkable progress of skill in building and the crafts that serve the builder. Not only in England, but throughout all parts of Christian Europe the splendour and nobility of church architecture proclaimed the victory of the spirit ; the shadows of the Dark Ages receded as the light of mediaeval civilisation brightened ; and man found that faith and training could become stronger than nature. There were occasional relapses, when savagery won a momentary victory and destroyed the evidence of progress ; but although the accomplishments of material progress usually suffered, those that reflected spiritual progress survived, until the social revolution that followed the Reformation brought the mediaeval civilisation of England to an end.

After the pillage and destruction of the great religious houses in the first half of the 16th century, a new paganism emerged ; nature for a time became stronger than training ; and when that happens, the road to the jungle is reopened. The inspiration that had carried architecture forward for nearly a thousand years withered away, and in its place came fashion.

The beginning of that long record of architectural achievement has been described ; but the measurable and visible results date from the Christian re-conquest of Britain at the end of the 6th and the beginning of the 7th centuries. St. Augustine had used what appears to have been a church built in Romano-British days as a place of Christian worship. Bede describes it as being on the east side of the city of Canterbury,

" dedicated to the honour of St. Martin, built whilst the Romans were still in the island ".(116) This church of St. Martin's still exists, and though it incorporates Roman masonry and brick and tile in its structure, its present form is mediaeval. After the Augustine mission, and the slow conversion of the pagan states of England, the history of church building really begins. The tall towers of abbeys and churches rose throughout the land ; Bede's references to the work of Benedict Biscop at Lindisfarne have been quoted ; and although this first flowering of architecture did not endure, because its fruits were destroyed by the Danes in the 9th and 10th centuries, when the Danish wars were over, church building was resumed. Great churches like St. Albans Abbey, incorporating Roman bricks and tiles taken from the ruins of the nearby city of Verulamium, were indicating the latent genius for architecture that was to find expression after the Norman Conquest, and throughout the Middle Ages.

This architectural movement began in Saxon England ; and it was in the building of churches in those pre-Norman centuries that English craftsmen disclosed their promising abilities. There was immediately after the Norman Conquest a period of foreign direction for craftsmen ; but as Norman influence had penetrated to England during the reign of Edward the Confessor (1042–66) there was no disruptive change in building and the crafts, no period when craftsmen, sullen with frustration, were unable or unwilling to understand what their new masters wanted. Such a period of misunderstanding occurred over five centuries later, when the rift between art and life began, and craftsmen worked for a new modish aristocracy. But the Normans were fellow Christians ; they were great church builders, and together Normans and Saxons began to praise God with works of unexampled majesty.

The Saxon work in the large churches was in the course of time altered and amended ; throughout the Middle Ages additions were constantly made, and big churches were always webbed with scaffolding. Only a few small Saxon churches remained much as their builders left them, and they show how powerfully the example of Roman architecture still operated in the minds of Saxon architects. The rounded arches, and their mouldings, and the sturdy square towers, like the great

Right : Saxon doorway from St. Peter's Church, Barton-on-Humber, Lincolnshire

Left : Saxon doorway from Earl's Barton Church, Northamptonshire. The tower of this church is shown on the opposite page

Right : The chancel arch of Corhampton Church, Hampshire. The character of this arch between the nave and the chancel of this church shows how strongly Saxon builders were influenced by the example of Roman architecture. (These three illustrations are reproduced from Bloxam's *Principles of Gothic Ecclesiastical Architecture*)

Tower of church at Earl's Barton, Northamptonshire. The unshaded castellated parapet is restored. The masonry of this Anglo-Saxon tower suggests a timber-built prototype; and this character-istic "long-and-short" work is sometimes called "stone car-pentry". (From Parker's *Intro-duction to Gothic Architecture.* Oxford : 1849)

central tower of St. Albans Abbey, had something Roman about them, recalling the square towers that guarded the gateways of Roman cities. Those towers and those rounded arches in churches, soberly displaying their strength, were the last architectural links with Rome.

Church building received an immense impetus from Norman civilisation; and during the 11th and 12th centuries the Norman style, that Anglo-Norman version of Romanesque architecture, was superbly expressed, not only in cathedrals like Ely, Durham and Peterborough, but in hundreds of parish churches, and in many noble abbeys, like Tewkesbury, and others, now in ruins, where the stately march of cylindrical columns along each side of the nave, linked by arches, spar-ingly embellished, still maintain their calm stability. English church architecture became a splendid adventure in building ; moving on century by century to new structural discoveries and fresh conceptions of ornamentation, drawing ideas from the returned Crusaders which imparted some of the vivid warmth of oriental taste to interior decoration; slowly evolving a national interpretation of Gothic architecture, and putting into a permanent and beautiful form the artistic genius of mediaeval civilisation.

Passing from the Norman period, through the Early English phase, with its tentative use of pointed arches, the big stone masses of churches were progressively refined in form. Clustered columns soared upwards, and from their floreated capitals, arches spurted in smooth jets, curving towards each other, and meeting to form high vaults; while tall stained-glass windows dyed the lights and shadows that fell across nave and aisles. The Decorated period of English Gothic architecture gloriously enriched the austere but supple lines that had been worked out in the Early English period; and the ultimate phase of Gothic architecture—the Perpendicular—was the final triumph of what Lethaby has described as " the architecture of adventure ", which, he explained, came from " the spirit of experiment in building ".(117)   And this spirit was pre-eminent in Gothic architecture. At last, the church became a slender skeleton of stone, a huge lantern with the voids of its windows filled with coloured glass, so that within there were light and movement, a bejewelled beauty, created, not merely for the sake of decoration, but in order to relate through window after window, and on mural after mural, the story of Christianity—to tell it visually and unforgettably to people who were illiterate, but were not insensitive to beauty, and to whom art was an integral part of life.

Those names, Early English, Decorated, and Perpendicular, are convenient descriptions for the Gothic architecture of the 13th, 14th and 15th centuries : they are not rigid periods, for they merge into each other, as every period of architecture since Saxon times has overlapped its predecessor and successor. J. H. Parker observes that the Perpendicular style really began about the middle of the 14th century in some localities, for example at Gloucester and Windsor ; and points out that " the Decorated and Perpendicular styles overlapped each other for a long period, some districts retaining the older style much longer than others ".(118)

Throughout the mediaeval civilisation, the Church was the principal patron of the architect and the craftsman, and after

Right : Norman doorway from Wyken Church, Warwickshire. (After Bloxam)

Two Early English doorways from, *above*, Kidlington, Oxfordshire, and *right*, Lutton, Huntingdonshire. (From Parker's *Glossary*)

the Church came the civic authorities ; in cities and towns traders and the guilds occasionally commissioned buildings ; while gradually the patronage of the nobility became competitive, as military architecture became less important. The

Early English doorway from Great Haseley, Oxfordshire, *circa* 1220. (After Parker)

building arts of the Middle Ages in England developed under the tutelage of the Church ; and the forms that characterised the later phases of Gothic architecture were reflected when domestic building outside the walled towns again became possible and widespread, as it did from about the end of the 13th century.

Architecture, whether domestic, religious or civic, invariably reveals the character and quality of the people responsible for creating and using it: from the Middle Ages until the present day, English houses large or small, in the town or in the country, have all attempted to embody a fundamentally English characteristic—the desire for privacy. Precautions to secure privacy for families and individuals have been taken,

(142)

Decorated doorway at Banbury, Oxfordshire, *circa* 1350.
(After Parker)

Perpendicular doorway, Merton College Chapel, Oxford.
A.D. 1424. (After Parker)

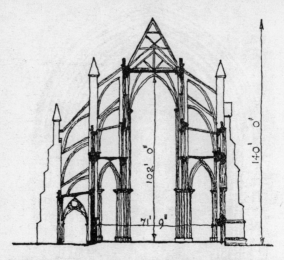

Section through the nave of Westminster Abbey showing
the thrust and counter-thrust of the vaulting and buttresses.
The nave vault is the highest Gothic vault in England, and
is strutted by flying buttresses across the aisles and north
cloister. (From a drawing by A. S. Cook)

century after century, by those responsible for building houses ;
though the coming of the Normans halted the development of
the English house for a few generations.

Military buildings, representing an architecture of fear and
intimidation, rose at strategic points throughout England after
the Norman Conquest. Outside the walls of London, that
fortress, the Tower, was erected to overawe the citizens—a
stronghold that would perpetually remind Londoners of the
King's presence and of the precariousness of the independence
they enjoyed. But the Norman kings soon realised that it paid
better to be friends with the City of London ; the Londoners
were skilled traders and merchants, they made money, and
they could confer more favours on a king than a king could
confer on them.

Within two centuries of the Norman Conquest, the two
civilisations, Norman and Saxon, became welded into something that was recognisably English ; directly the country
enjoyed a strong government, and houses were liberated from

Corner of the Chapter House at Westminster Abbey.   (From
a drawing by A. S. Cook)

A fine example of the Perpendicular period of English Gothic architecture. From a drawing by F. T. Dollman, included in *Some Account of St. Mary Magdalene, Taunton.* (Published 1845)

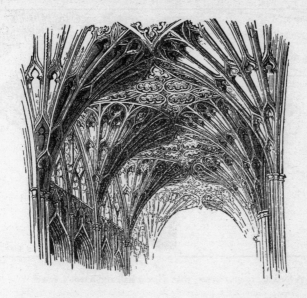

Fan vaulting in the Cloisters of Gloucester Cathedral : the ribs of the vault have the same curve and suggest the framework of a fan. It is a system of vaulting characteristic of the Perpendicular period. (After Parker)

the need for fortification, a recognisable English style of domestic architecture appeared, characteristically diversified in different parts of the country by the use of local building materials.

By the 14th century, the fortified manor house, the larger farm-houses, and the town houses of merchants and prosperous artisans began outwardly to show that their owners desired both privacy and comfort, and were actively, indeed critically appreciative, of well-equipped homes. Materials were used with confident mastery ; their limitations were a challenge to the ingenuity of the builder, who never attempted to bully them into inappropriate shapes, or to bend them to tasks beyond their capabilities. Instead he was at pains to study the character of materials and this led to a sympathetic understanding of and affection for their properties, that in the course of centuries made English craftsmanship famous not only in building but in all the arts and crafts that building

A fortified manor house, with a great hall and a watch tower

Late 13th century Stokesay Castle, Shropshire, is a complete
example of an early English castle, built between 1240–90.
The projecting half-timbered work is a late 16th- or
early 17th-century addition. (From Thomas Wright's
The Homes of Other Days)

The Hall, Great Chalfield, Wiltshire. A 15th-century
interior from a drawing in J. H. Parker's *Domestic Architecture
in England* (Oxford : 1859). At the end of such halls
there was usually a small opening, which enabled the lord
and the lady, sitting in the solar or private chamber, to keep
an eye on what was going on in the household. Parker
records that at Great Chalfield openings from chambers at
either end of the hall " were concealed in the form of stone
masks, through the eyes and mouth of which a full view of
the hall could be obtained ". One of these masks is shown
in the drawing, on the wall above the wooden screen

Norrington Manor House, Wiltshire. (See page opposite)

inspires and employs. There is a world of difference between being a master of materials and being mastered by them.

Throughout the history of the English house, the builder's mastery of materials is consistently apparent. Before the 13th century, wood, plaster and stone were the principal building materials, for brickmaking in England was not re-introduced until then, and, according to John Aubrey, was revived in London in the 16th century by Sir John Popham (1531–1607), the Lord Chief Justice.

Mediaeval country houses were stoutly built; there was often a grim defensive air about them, because, whether they were small fortified manor houses, or the living quarters of a castle, the need for protection conditioned their character. A typical example of a mediaeval house was Penshurst Place in Kent, that was built in the first half of the 14th century, and was in the form of a great hall, from which other chambers budded off, as it were. This large hall had a central hearth, and at its west end was a dais or raised platform for the high

Manor House, South Wraxhall, Wiltshire. The illustrations above and opposite are examples of 15th-century domestic building. (From Parker's *Domestic Architecture in England*. Oxford : 1859)

table, and behind and above the dais was the solar, which was the retiring room for the lord and the lady. New habits of privacy were being formed ; the existence of the solar, and the increasing tendency of the lord and lady to retire there away from the noise and bustle and smell and hearty social life of the great hall, provoked critical comments from William Langland, the English poet who was born in 1332, some nine years before Penshurst Place was built. Before the end of the 14th century, the heads of the household were deserting the hall ; a habit Langland condemned when he wrote : " There the lorde ne the lady liketh noute to sytte."(119)

At the end of the great hall at Penshurst were the pantry and the buttery, and the passage to the kitchen, and these were entered through doors in a screen, above which was a gallery. Externally Penshurst Place seemed to combine the characteristics of a castle and a church : pointed windows, embattled

Two views of Woodlands House, near Mere, Wiltshire. Although this is a 15th-century building, the windows retain the characteristic form and tracery of the previous century. (From Parker's *Domestic Architecture in England*. Oxford : 1859)

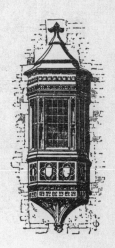

By the second half of the 15th century a rich, satisfying native domestic architecture had developed in England, which reflected the characteristics of the Perpendicular phase of Gothic. Windows expanded, and the generous amount of light admitted to rooms is shown by this stone-built house in Small Street, Bristol, which was illustrated in Parker's *Domestic Architecture in England* (Oxford: 1859). Bay windows and oriel windows, like the example on the right from Vicar's Close, Wells, Somerset (illustrated in Parker's *Glossary*), gave a new significance to glass, which corresponded with improvements in the technique of its manufacture. (See pages 154 and 155)

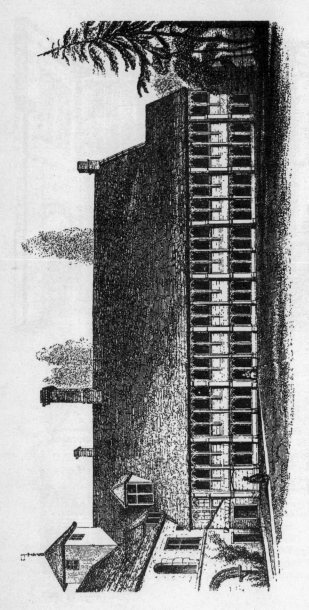

The Abbot's House at Wenlock Abbey, Shropshire. This shows the double cloister, which accommodated the passages, running along one side of a court-yard. Parker mentions that " A similar arrangement was continued very com-monly in Elizabethan houses, and long afterwards, and even to our own day in country inns." (From Parker's *Domestic Architecture in England*)

Compton Wynyates, Warwickshire, completed in A.D. 1520 by Sir William Compton, a London merchant. The house was built round an open court. This illustration, from Parker's *Domestic Architecture in England*, shows a bay window in the court

Town houses of late 15th-
and early 16th-century
character, copied by
F. W. Fairholt from an
engraving in the reprint
of Alexander Barclay's
translation of Sebastian
Brant's *Ship of Fools*, which
was published in 1570.
(Included in Thomas
Wright's *History of Domestic
Manners and Sentiments in
England*)

walls, towers, turrets and stout buttresses gave the place an
air both of strength and, oddly enough, of welcome.

An earlier building that shares some of the characteristics of
Penshurst Place and is also a typical mediaeval house is Stokesay Castle in Shropshire. Here, too, a great hall forms the
core of the building, and the solar, high above the floor level
of that hall, has small windows on either side of its fireplace,
which open on to the hall. Stokesay was built during the first
half of the 13th century, but the form is not unlike that of
Penshurst; though in common with many English country
houses, it has continued to grow, acquiring additions and outbuildings and new internal furnishings century by century.
By the end of the 15th century, when fortification was no longer
necessary, the English house began to acquire the same
structural characteristics as the church; but, instead of being
a stone lantern for coloured glass, it was a strong wooden cage,

(156)

with the spaces between the wooden framework filled with glass, brickwork, or plaster—a great articulated frame of timber, infinitely flexible in form, admitting light generously, and using windows, not merely as apertures, but as integral parts of the structure. Ockwells Manor at Bray in Berkshire, built in the second half of the 15th century, is an early example of such a half-timbered house, and the wooden cage remained a standard structural form for nearly two centuries. This same form was followed even when stone was used, as it was in the west country, and in Yorkshire ; the same generous use of windows and their incorporation into the structure of the house is apparent, particularly in such small examples as Tribunal House and the George Inn at Glastonbury in Somerset, and in large early 16th-century country houses, such as Cowdray House at Midhurst in Sussex, and Compton Wynyates in Warwickshire.

When Henry VII came to the throne and the long Tudor period began, a rich and beautiful native domestic architecture had become established. Its kinship with the Perpendicular phase of Gothic architecture was marked, and that likeness was impressed upon all the products of the ancillary building crafts, woodwork and metalwork, providing a formal unity with the interior treatment and furnishing of the churches and religious houses. During the first third of the 16th century this native style flourished : then it was interrupted by fashions introduced from the continent that ineptly imitated the modes of the Italian Renaissance. The Roman Orders of architecture, disused for centuries, returned to England. Apart from a few bleak masses of masonry—the Jewry Wall in Leicester, the fragments of the baths at Wroxeter—no Roman ruins remained above ground as late as the 16th century, nor did the subject of Roman remains arouse much interest, although the antiquary, John Leyland (1506–1552), recorded a visit to Silchester, and made some observations of the site. So to the builders and craftsmen this revival of Classical architecture was an unwelcome incursion of foreign ideas, and was resented as such. The resentment is apparent in the clumsy handling of those classical forms by English craftsmen, and their inept parodies of the orders of architecture suggest an uncomprehending dislike. The real significance of the orders as a

Window and corner post from a house at Lavenham,
Suffolk, showing the elaborate ornamentation of the wood
framework of late 15th- and early 16th-century houses.
(From Parker's *Domestic Architecture in England*)

flexible system of design was not even suspected. Their use had been imposed by masters who were harder to understand than the Normans had ever been—for the Normans, though conquerors and hard, ruthless men, were spiritually akin to the conquered. The new men who made the social revolution during the first half of the 16th century were spiritually withdrawn from the people of England. During that century a new mastery of building materials was acquired, and men built houses and furnished and decorated them with an exuberance that was generated by a new surge of national vitality. England was now standing independently ; with the loss of Calais went the proud memory of all the disastrous continental military adventures, the useless wars of conquest in France. At last the English looked, not to war-torn Europe, but to the western seas, and the new world beyond them. There they found new inspiration, adventure, wealth, power ; and all those intoxicating discoveries stimulated them to build great country houses, and palaces in the towns, and to improve their estates with new farm-houses and cottages for their tenants.

Between the accession of Queen Elizabeth and her death in 1603, the architectural character of England changed. Meanwhile, mournfully neglected, despoiled, and falling into ruin throughout the land, were churches and monasteries ; some fragment of a noble church occasionally surviving to serve the needs of a parish, like the fragment of Malmesbury Abbey, which to this day is the parish church of that small town. These ruins were the casualties of a social and spiritual revolution ; of a transition rapidly and often brutally made from a co-operative to an acquisitive society. Old securities and kindly institutions had been swept away ; new men with new codes—members of a new mercantile aristocracy—had enriched themselves, and had created many problems, unknown in the Middle Ages, of which unemployment was the darkest.

The whole story of the rise and decline of mediaeval civilisation, and the birth pangs of a new form of society, is told by the buildings, great and small, that were erected during the five centuries which lay between the Norman Conquest and Elizabeth's long reign. But England under Elizabeth inherited more than wreckage from the Middle Ages ; England inherited an astonishing body of skill in the crafts ; and it was during the

The half-timbered house was a strong, wooden cage, with the spaces between the timber framework filled with glass, brickwork or plaster. A house at Tamworth, Staffordshire : second half of the 16th century. (From Parker's *Domestic Architecture in England*)

Elizabethan period that the character of the English home was formed. It is to this period that nearly everybody in this harassed 20th century looks back, when the magic of those words " the good old times " takes us, momentarily, away from the bewildering present ; for there are two phrases that always coax English minds into the past ; one, full of pure magic, we hear first in the nursery ; it is " Over the hills and far away " ; the other, also charged with magic and incommunicable romance, is " the good old times ". Today, there is a frustrated groping after visible history ; a feeling, inarticulate, though not unexpressed, for some tangible reminder of an old and vanished England. It is, perhaps, a desire for something characteristically English, with which to stay a national appetite, ill served by a diet of mechanised buildings furnished with " export rejects ". The bleak neutralities of mid-20th-century life have sharpened this desire, which has for over a century been struggling for adequate expression in popular taste and the vernacular architecture by which that taste is partly satisfied.

The characteristic national style of domestic architecture we had perfected in the late 15th and early 16th centuries, that warm, comfortable and singularly inviting style of building which employed brickwork with such agreeable originality, was something that agreed so well with our English ways, and seemed so profoundly and satisfyingly to symbolise what we felt about life, and particularly home life, that we have thought tenderly about the early Tudor period ever since. We have constantly recalled those sturdy cages of timber with the spaces between the stout structural bones of oak filled in with plaster or small bricks laid in decorative patterns ; we have pictured streets of those half-timbered houses, the beams blackened or darkened by age, contrasting with the interstices of sparkling white plaster or rosy brickwork ; and since the second quarter of the 19th century, we have been imitating that early Tudor domestic architecture, whose development was arrested by the Italianate fashions of the Renaissance. To a vast number of people living today, home, sweet home, conjures up a vision of the thatched, half-timbered house, with carved oak panelling and low-beamed ceilings, and diamond-leaded window-panes —everything in fact that suggests an imagined Golden Age, wistfully recalled and architecturally placed in the reigns of Henry VII and " bluff King Hal ", though socially in the Elizabethan period.

It was during Elizabeth's reign that England was stimulated by the threat of Spanish aggression to become a great maritime power ; when she found herself in literature and the arts of life, and to the Queen's subjects life seemed fuller, more adventurous and satisfying than it had ever been for the men and women of mediaeval England—for the miseries of the early Tudor transitional period were by then becoming old folks' memories—a rich, full life, denied alike to their forebears and to their socially and economically circumscribed descendants. Today, the popular appeal of the half-timbered house, and the " off-Tudor " and " pseudo-Elizabethan " trimmings that are veneered over the exteriors and interiors of road-houses and the saloon bars of spaciously comfortable public houses in place of the solid mahogany, the carving and the gilding, the red velvet, and the incised glass panels of the Victorian pub, suggest how the vernacular architecture of England is nostalgic rather than creative ; drawing its inspiration from a haphazard mixture of early Tudor and Elizabethan prototypes. That vernacular architecture is as remote in sympathy and understanding from the period from which it derives its form and ornamentation, as it is from the intellectual architecture of the " modern movement in design ", whose original practitioners gave aesthetic priority to a chilly asepsis of form. The publican whose saloon bar is dark with carved stained oak, and who fills the large bricked fireplace opening with a gas fire, or an electric one designed to imitate blazing logs, and the dweller in the suburbs, who delights in a little, imitation, half-timbered bungalow or house, are closer to an understanding of what England once was, and could be again, than the modern intellectual architect who, with an arrogance akin to that which leads the atheist to declare : " There is no God ", says : " I will have none other gods but functionalism, and I will cast out humanity, and file the people in beautiful, hygienic cells, and compel them to be tidy."

Unconsciously, ordinary people sense and resent the needless separation between art and life ; and, again unconsciously, they believe—though they would be unable to clothe their beliefs in words—that once upon a time such separation did not exist. Nor did it, until what Frank Pick once called " the devils of fashion " invaded England during the 16th century, and introduced to the intellectual and artistic aristocracy of the middle and late Tudor period, all the delights of " exclusive " taste—something that was neither of nor for the people. The fact that those new fashions in architecture and in furniture,

Half-timbered house at Wingham, Kent, with the barge-boards (the wood work covering the joint between the gable end and the roofing tiles) elaborately carved. Late 15th or early 16th century. (From Parker's *Domestic Architecture in England*)

and the equipment of houses—which represented " the modern movement in design " in the mid-16th century—had nothing to do with popular art, although they were executed by native craftsmen, did not perturb the aristocratic patrons of the Italianate modes. Unlike our contemporary intellectuals, the noblemen of the Early English renaissance were not roused to fury and contempt by the passive but unremitting resistance to the modern movement in design that is now displayed by all classes, apart from that comparatively small circle of " the enlightened " that discovers pleasure and moral elevation (though scarcely spiritual sustenance) in functional forms and abstract shapes and pastel shades and rigid abstinence from ornamentation.

The new architecture, the new ornamental ideas brought from abroad by the " devils of fashion ", encountered more than the passive resistance of craftsmen in the 16th and early 17th centuries : the foreign, " Italianate " notions inspired protests from poets like Ben Jonson, who in praising the homely virtues of Penshurst Place, condemned the arrogant extravagance of many of the new edifices whose architects had struggled, often vainly, to achieve a classical elegance. His poem to Penshurst opens with these lines :

> Thou art not, Penshurst, built to envious show
> Of touch or marble ; nor canst boast a row
> Of polish'd pillars, or a roof of gold :
> Thou hast no lantern, whereof tales are told ;
> Or stair, or courts ; but stand'st an ancient pile,
> And these grudg'd at, art reverenced the while.

The last four lines of the poem repeat the condemnation of extravagance and proclaim the basic function of the house, which is to be a home.

> Now, Penshurst, they that will proportion thee
> With other edifices, when they see
> Those proud ambitious heaps, and nothing else,
> May say, their lords have built, but thy lord dwells.

About a century later, Pope made a similar and rather more sprightly protest against the sumptuous palace built for the Duke of Marlborough at Blenheim by Sir John Vanbrugh, when he wrote :

> See, sir, here's the grand approach ;
> This way is for his grace's coach :
> There lies the bridge, and here's the clock,
> Observe the lion and the cock,
> The spacious court, the colonnade,
> And mark how wide the hall is made !

The chimneys are so well design'd,
They never smoke in any wind.
The gallery's contrived for walking
The windows to retire and talk in ;
The council chamber for debate,
And all the rest are rooms of state.
   Thanks, sir, cried I, 'tis very fine,
But where d'ye sleep, or where d'ye dine ?
I find, by all you have been telling,
That 'tis a house, but not a dwelling.

Display and extravagance in architecture have always been deprecated by English critics and writers and by less gifted people, except in periods of great wealth, too rapidly acquired for education to modify its owners' innocently vulgar desire to show off. In such periods of abundant and swiftly accumulated wealth, the common art of the country is deprecated, if not actually suppressed ; so the rift between art and life is widened. But popular art—the common art of a country—is sturdy and persistent ; it survives, in changing and different forms, despite systematic and continuous efforts to discourage its manifestations ; it still raises its head, and peeps out unexpectedly, sometimes with comical effect, as if laughing at its enemies. The desire to imitate our old, arrested national style of architecture and decoration, that was submerged during the 16th century, re-emerging briefly in the middle of the 17th century during a period of freedom from the dictatorship of fashion, suggests undeveloped powers of national appreciation for art of a much higher standard than that associated with popular taste. Such powers are unlikely to be developed by the evangelical approach to design and architecture that insists upon bleak logic ; for it is quite useless to say to a man who finds pleasure in the surroundings provided by a half-timbered road-house that he ought to want something which, in his view, resembles the inside of a refrigerator.

Popular art and vernacular architecture today preserve a tenuous link with 16th-century England, a period which has left innumerable remains that provide not only material for inept imitation, but burnish the memory of a time when with robust confidence we expressed ourselves nationally in architecture and the arts and crafts. To this extent our visible history reminds people everywhere that once " the good old times " were for some few fortunate generations of Englishmen their own times, and the longing for them is appeased not only in the simulation of old forms in buildings, but in furniture that caricatures some antique shape and is stained to suggest age. Affection for such crude imitations is generated by the same desire for homeliness that was expressed both by Ben Jonson and Alexander Pope when in their vastly different ways they extolled the virtues of a comfortable dwelling.

CHAPTER XV

"COMMODITY, FIRMNESS AND DELIGHT"

THAT the Italianate Englishmen of the 16th century were strangers to the majority of their countrymen, both in morals and taste, is confirmed by that most entertaining of chroniclers, William Harrison (1534–1593), in his *Description of England* when he deplores the habit of the nobility and gentry of sending their sons to Italy to finish their education. From that country, he wrote, "they bring home nothing but meere atheisme, infidelitie, vicious conversation, & ambitious and proud behaviour, whereby it commeth to passe that they return fare worsse men than they went out".(120) Small wonder that the taste of these men in architecture and furnishing should have been resented, and their desires misinterpreted and mishandled by the English craftsmen. Renaissance Italy had become the artistic and intellectual light of Europe in the 15th and 16th centuries through the revival of classical learning and architecture; though that revival was tinctured with paganism, and there were perhaps many secret flirtations with the darker aspects of pre-Christian Rome and its cults—though no figure comparable in stature with or enjoying the power of Julian, the apostate Emperor of the 4th century, arose to command a movement for reinstating paganism. According to Harrison all the intellectual vigour was missed by the young Englishmen who visited Italy; they returned with a few sordid platitudes about self-interest, and crude criticisms of Christian principles. He furnishes the following examples:

"A gentleman at this present is newlie come out of Italie, who went thither an earnest protestant, but coming home

A late 15th-century house, with 16th- and 17th-century
additions, with the church incorporated in the general lay-out
of the house and grounds. An engraving of Coberly, by
Kip : late 17th century

Shepton Moyne, showing the transitional style of the late
16th and early 17th centuries.   From an engraving by Kip,
late 17th century

he could saie after this maner : ' Faith & truth is to be kept,
where no losse or hinderance of a further purpose is susteined
by holding of the same ; and forgivenesse onelie to be shewed
when full revenge is made.' Another no lesse forward than
he, at his returne from thence could ad thus much : ' He is a
foole that maketh accompt of any religion, but more foole that
will loose anie part of his wealth, or will come in trouble for
constant leaning to anie ; but if he yeeld to loose his life for
his possession, he is stark mad, and worthie to be taken for
most foole of all the rest.' This gaie bootie gate these gentlemen by going into Italie, and hereby a man may see what fruit
is afterward to be looked for where such blossoms doo appeere.
' I care not (saith a third) what you talke to me of God, so as
I may have the prince & the lawes of the realme on my side.'
Such men as this last, are easilie knowen ; for they have
learned in Italie, to go up and downe also in England, with
pages at their heeles finelie apparelled, whose face and coun-
tenance shall be such as sheweth the master not to be blind
in his choice. But least I should offend too much, I passe over
to saie anie more of these Italionates and their demeanor, which
alas is too open and manifest to the world, and yet not called
into question."(121)

So much for the intellectual enlightenment the Italianate
Englishmen imported : there was a corresponding paucity of
inspiration in the artistic ideas he collected ; and there was a
conservative reluctance on the part of his untravelled countrymen to abandon the established methods of building and
adorning their houses, though throughout the 16th century
everything was built and furnished on a more lavish and
magnificent scale than formerly, as Harrison has described in
instructive detail. He recorded that " The ancient manours
and houses of our gentlemen are yet, and for the most part, of
strong timber, (in framing whereof our carpenters have beene
and are worthilie preferred before those of like science among
all other nations.) Howbeit such as be latelie builded, are
comonlie either of bricke or hard stone, (or both ;) their
roomes large and comelie, and houses of office further distant
from their lodgings. Those of the nobilitie are likewise
wrought with bricke and hard stone, as provision may best be
made ; but so magnificent and statelie, as the basest house of

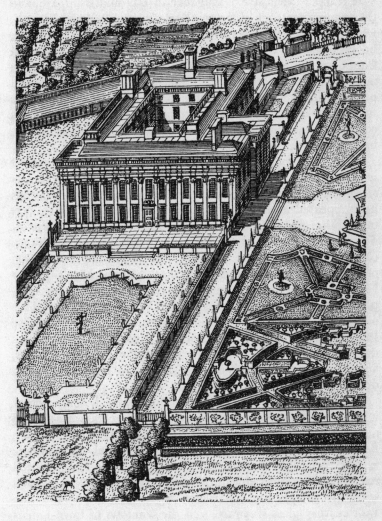

Lees Court, Faversham. Attributed to Inigo Jones. From
an engraving by Kip

a baron dooth often match (in our daies) with some honours of princes in old time."(122)

A reaction against extravagance in building is apparent in the opening sentence of Francis Bacon's essay " On Building ", when with less grace than Ben Jonson and less wit than Pope, he expressed a blunt John Bullish view of what he expected from domestic architecture. " Houses are built to live in and not to look on ", he wrote ; " therefore let use be preferred before uniformity except where both may be had." This suggests a dour, utilitarian approach ; but Bacon, like his contemporary, Sir Henry Wotton, was concerned with the basic principles of architecture.

In Wotton's paraphrase of Vitruvius, that has been quoted in Chapter XI, he begins his essay which he entitled *The Elements of Architecture*, with a statement, first set forth in 1624, that has been repeated ever since. " In architecture ", he wrote, " as in all other operative arts, the *End* must direct the *Operation*. The *End* is to build well. *Well-building* hath three Conditions, *Commodity*, *Firmness*, and *Delight*." He begins the second part of his essay with the statement that " Every Man's proper Mansion House and Home, being the Theater of his Hospitality, the Seat of Self-fruition, the Comfortablest part of his own Life, the noblest of his Sons Inheritance, a kind of private Princedome ; Nay, to the Possessors thereof, an Epitomie of the whole World ; may well deserve by these Attributes, according to the degree of the Master, to be decently and delightfully adorned."

The furnishing and adornment of the English home, whether it was large or small, in the town or in the country, were carried out with great and loving skill when William Harrison, Francis Bacon, and Sir Henry Wotton were writing about domestic architecture ; but it was not until large windows had liberated rooms from shadows that furnishing became closely associated with the design and character of rooms. Until the late 15th century glass was rare, and the windows of town houses were usually protected by panes of horn, ground very thin, or oiled linen or parchment ; in country houses, windows were high up in the wall and narrow, except when they looked upon an inner courtyard. Windows are always the first victims when military precautions become necessary. After

St PAULS COVENT GARDEN

Church of St. Paul's in Covent Garden, as rebuilt by Inigo Jones (A.D. 1631-38).
From a contemporary copy of the engraving by Wenceslaus Hollar

the Wars of the Roses were over, all the excuses for fortification disappeared, nor were the form or amenities of houses again affected by military needs until the Second World War, when windows were once more sacrificed to military necessity. When at last the moats that surrounded manor houses and castles were drained and turned into gardens, walls were pierced, and generous window spaces admitted light to rooms : in some of the early 16th-century country houses, tall bay windows would ascend through two or more storeys, so that the house front appeared to be made almost entirely of glass, framed by stone mullions.

From the early Tudor period to the beginning of Victorian times, houses in England developed an astonishing variety of forms ; but there was one basic characteristic of homes, large or small, in town or country : they were places where a man and his family could be private. That at least was the intention, though it was not always fulfilled, because sometimes cheap and ineffective building materials were used and work was skimped, for the jerry builder is by no means a modern product—he appeared at least three hundred years ago. As we have seen, by the opening of the 16th century English domestic architecture had attained a high standard of accomplishment in design. Externally houses possessed a gracious and inviting air, with their warm red-brick walls, stone-framed doorways and sturdy oak doors, and windows with leaded glazing, the pattern of little diamond-shaped panes being occasionally interrupted to accommodate heraldic roundels of coloured glass. Within, the walls were clothed by oak panelling, surmounted by friezes of coloured and gilded plasterwork. The floors were of oak boards ; the ceilings of plaster, painted and gilded ; fabrics hung here and there upon the walls ; and there were generous fireplaces that really worked and guided the smoke up the flues, to be expelled through chimneys wrought in fantastic and decorative shapes. William Harrison has described how astonishing the proliferation of chimneys seemed to the older generation of men in the mid-16th century. He said : " There are old men yet dwelling in the village where I remaine, which have noted three things to be marvellouslie altred in England within their sound remembrance. . . . One is, the multitude of chimnies

The great system of design, represented by the classic orders
of architecture, was thoroughly understood by English
architects after the middle years of the 17th century.
Williamstrip, from an engraving by Kip

latelie erected, wheras in their yoong daies there were not above two or three, if so manie, in most uplandith townes of the realme (the religious houses, & manour places of their lords alwaies excepted, and peradventure some great personages) but ech one made his fire against a reredosse in the hall, where he dined and dressed his meat."(123)

In the country, as Harrison has recorded, local materials were generally used, and the farm-houses and groups of cottages and the small manor houses crouched comfortably upon the land, giving the impression that they were growing naturally, that they were part of the countryside. But this apt and agreeable national development of domestic architecture which was arrested by " Italianate " fashions, was followed by a period of muddle and confusion in building, during which many large, vulgar and ostentatious houses were erected, and it was not until the restoration of Charles II in 1660 that classical architecture in England was again widely understood and practised with confidence. It took nearly a hundred years for that classical system of design to be thoroughly understood by English architects. Inigo Jones was the man who first established that understanding, and his own work gave expression to the precepts of his contemporary, Sir Henry Wotton. His buildings exemplified commodity, firmness and delight, and he was really the father of all the graceful architecture of the late 17th, 18th and early 19th centuries.

During the period that elapsed between the restoration of Charles II and the death of William IV, we created an astonishing volume of coherent and ordered beauty in domestic architecture and in town planning. Cities like Bath were replanned and rebuilt by architects—the Woods, father and son, were responsible for the rebuilding of Bath. Those enterprising and talented Scotsmen, the brothers Adam, working in the latter part of the 18th century, replanned and largely rebuilt Edinburgh, and after settling in London they planned and developed new parts of the West End, notably the Adelphi.

The town house in that golden age of English design, which began in 1660, became an elegant and finely equipped home. Country houses, large and small, were light and comfortable ; and all houses alike shared the incomparable benefit of well-proportioned windows. Observe any of the houses built

"See, sir, here's the grand approach;
This way is for his grace's coach. . . ."

Pope's lines on the Duke of Marlborough's palace at Woodstock were applicable
to the lay-out and orderly grandeur of many of the lesser mansions of the late 17th
and early 18th centuries, when the nobility and gentry built unashamedly for
pleasure. Sandywell, from an engraving by Kip

Temple Bar, designed by Sir Christopher Wren. From a
mid-18th-century engraving

during the late 17th and 18th centuries : the windows appear
to smile. Those windows were large, generous and well
shaped, and the sash, that was used almost universally throughout the country, not only conferred an air of distinction, but
by its division into rectangular panes gave an external bright-
ness to the houses, for those divisions—glazing bars as they are

(178)

called—were always cheerfully painted, and against mellow red or soft yellow brick, or the golden brown or warm grey of stonework, became a dominating feature of the house. Although a window tax was imposed on houses with more than six windows and worth over £5 per annum, it did not affect the size or shape of windows, though it reduced their number. It became law in 1697, and was not repealed until 1851.

Early in the 19th century houses were plastered externally and painted, and during the Regency period many elegant housing schemes were designed. That was the time when John Nash laid out Carlton House Terrace, Regent Street, and Regent's Park in London ; and places like Brighton, Hove, Worthing, Tenby and Cheltenham were enriched with bright and commodious houses. The sash window remained ; the bow window was used more extensively. Verandahs and balconies adorned the fronts of houses, and this phase of English architecture was the last expression of a true national style before the Victorian period.

During the middle years of the 19th century taste became confused, and in some ways this period resembled the age of confusion that had occurred in the 16th and early 17th centuries, when architecture was afflicted with foreign fashions which builders regarded with uncomprehending dislike. All manner of ancient, romantic and foreign ideas were imported ; taste declined ; a new rich class demanded plenty of ostentation and got it, and although a few 18th-century graces survived until well into the eighteen-fifties, the Victorian age was our dark age of design for houses and everything they contained. We are just emerging from it ; and for the last thirty years we have been reviving some of the beauties of the Georgian period, but, what is much more important, we are at last developing a contemporary way of building which imitates nothing and really represents the gifts and genius of our own century.

CHAPTER XVI

THE ENGLISHMAN'S COMFORT

As houses in the country and in the town progressively acquired refinements, when windows were enlarged, and after they were glazed, the real development of furnishing began. The furnishing of a house in the Middle Ages was not an integral part of the design of the house; the various articles of furniture did not provide a series of complementary shapes and forms to the interior of a room; no uniform principle of design or standardised types of ornamentation were employed. Furniture was then sturdy in structure; receptacles were made of joined and pegged boards; there was vigour in colour and decoration and in the patterns of fabrics; but both furniture and fabrics were put into a room without being a part of it: the mediaeval house merely provided a number of spaces, which were usually unrelated to the shapes of the things that furnished them. From Saxon times until the 15th century furniture consisted largely of receptacles and primitive seats, forms and chairs. There were movable tables, that were generally called boards, and with these few strong timber articles the rooms of a house or an inn could be furnished. Beds were generally made up on the floor, and all luxury, warmth and decorative qualities were introduced by the use of fabrics. Walls were hung with fabrics, benches were set up against a wall with a strip of fabric called a " dorcer " behind them; fabrics were draped over tables; canopies of rich materials with draperies depending from them were hung from the rafters of the ceiling above beds, chairs of state, and alcoves where people sat. The mediaeval interior, the smaller rooms that opened off the great hall, the solar and the sleeping chambers, glowed with rich fabrics. Beds themselves, although often made up on the floor, were occasionally elevated upon platforms or frames, and the draperies that turned the more luxurious type of bed into an elaborate tent, consisted of the tester (or canopy), the sellore (or celure), which was the panel of fabric that formed the head, and the curtains or vallances, which could be drawn to enclose the bed completely. An elaborately furnished bed is described by Chaucer in *The Book of the Duchesse* (lines 251–256) as follows :

> I wil yive him a fether-bed,
> Rayed with golde, and right wel cled
> In fyn blak satin doutremere,
> And many a pilow, and every bere
> Of clothe of Reynes, to slepe softe ;
> Him thar not nede to turnen ofte.

For most people, sleeping conditions were simple : everybody slept naked, but despite that, several beds were often put into one room. In *The Reves Tale*, Chaucer describes the hospitable preparations made by the miller to entertain John and Aleyn, the two clerks :

> And in his owne chambre hem made a bed
> With shetes and with chalons faire y-spred,
> Noght from his owne bed ten foot or twelve.
> His doghter hadde a bed, al by hir-selve,
> Right in the same chambre, by and by ;
> It mighte be no bet, and cause why,
> There was no roumer herberwe in the place.

William Harrison gives a depressing description of the poor lodging that before his day was the general rule. Saying that such conditions had been improved, he recalled that " our fathers (yea) and we our selves (also) have lien full oft upon straw pallets, (on rough mats) covered onelie with a sheet, under coverlets made of dagswain or hopharlots (I use their owne termes,) and a good round log under their heads in steed of a bolster (or pillow.) If it were so that our fathers or the good man of the house, had (within seven yeares after his mariage purchased) a matteres or flockebed, and thereto a sacke of chaffe to rest his head upon, he thought himselfe to be as well lodged as the lord of the towne, (that peradventure

An early 15th-century bedroom, drawn from a contemporary
manuscript of John Lydgate's metrical Life of St. Edmund
by F. W. Fairholt, and included in Thomas Wright's *Homes
of Other Days*. Furnishing is still in the fabric and framework stage of development

laie seldome in a bed of downe or whole fethers ;) so well were
they contented, (and with such base kind of furniture : which
also is not verie much amended as yet in some parts of Bed-
fordshire, and elsewhere further off from our southerne parts).
Pillowes (said they) were thought meet onelie for women in
childbed. As for servants, if they had anie sheet above them,
it was well, for seldome had they anie under their bodies, to
keepe them from the pricking straws that ran oft through the
canvas (of the pallet,) and rased their hardened hides." (124)

Up to the end of the 15th century furnishing was arrested
in what might be called the framework and fabric stage.
Thereafter it began to acquire new forms and to cater for new

needs. Once released from the demands made by fortification, country houses, towns and villages began to grow in new ways, and the house itself expressed the new freedom from the fear of internal war by enlarging its windows. Slits in the wall, high up beyond the reach of scaling ladders, and the mean dimensions generally imposed upon windows, were no longer necessary. The old chivalrous aristocracy of England had committed class suicide in the Wars of the Roses. That last mediaeval monarch, Richard III, had been killed, and with him had been killed many ways of thought and standards of conduct—though their passing was unperceived at the time and remained unmourned for some generations. But in that second half of the 15th century a new mercantile hard aristocracy arose, outwardly caparisoned like their chivalrous forerunners, inwardly as alien as the Saxon barbarians had been to the Roman provincials a thousand years earlier.

Church building still continued in those early decades of the Tudor period ; extensions to great abbeys were projected and carried out ; here a Lady chapel would be added, there a new rich porch for some fine village church ; monasteries extended their buildings, and farmed their lands and collected their tithes ; and with visible, though as yet unacknowledged and unsuspected rivalry, the homes of the new rich began to overshadow in magnificence the great buildings that had been dedicated to the service of God, and the monastic houses that were an integral part of a social system wherein charity and hospitality were identified and practised as virtues, and usury was stigmatised as sin. In the town and in the countryside the forms of buildings everywhere proclaimed an innate appreciation for beauty, respect for solid worth in construction, and a disregard for amenities other than those that affected the eye. In few civilisations have the senses of sight, smell and hearing been simultaneously respected and accommodated. In the 20th century we have a high respect for the sense of smell though we tend to minimise the importance of sight and sound, because we live amid surroundings that are often hideous and intolerably noisy. Houses and towns, villages and people, in the Middle Ages stank ; but although there was plenty of noise, it was not always unmelodious, like a mechanical by-product.

The pattern of life at the end of the Middle Ages was easily comprehended : men and women understood, not only their own work and place in society, but knew and respected the work and social position of their fellows. Only since the middle of the 19th century have so many people been ignorant of what their fellow men do, why they do it, and how they live. Today, largely as a result of the Industrial Revolution, most people are ignorant of the thousands of specialised jobs that people are doing in industry, and in commerce, and of the auxiliary activities that arise from the work of a great trading community. But in England at the end of the 15th century, at the beginning that is to say of the modern world, although there were divisions in the ranks of society, there was less separation between man and man. In the building trade there was, for example, a far greater interchange of skills than there is now ; this interchange lasted only until the end of the 16th century, thereafter craftsmen became more specialised and even one particular activity like furniture-making developed several separate branches.

At the beginning of the Tudor period there were carpenters and joiners, masons, plumbers and glaziers, smiths specialising in the different metals, smith being the term ordinarily given to those who worked in iron, but there were coppersmiths and goldsmiths ; there were also leatherworkers—" cordwainers " as they were called, the term being derived from the word " cordovan " that was the name given to the fine leather imported from Cordova in Spain in the 11th and 12th centuries. Leatherworkers were also known as " coffer-makers ", or " cofferers ", because they covered hard timber with leather, and the chief article upon which their skill was thus employed was the coffer, the mediaeval forerunner of the travelling trunk. There were also coffer-maker's chairs, with leather-covered X-shaped frames supporting leather seats or leather straps which held cushions.

The history of furniture and furnishing in England from the end of the 15th to the middle of the 19th century is a record of increasing mastery over materials, the development of new skills, following the invention of new tools and the introduction of new materials, and a consistent disposition on the part of the English craftsman to do the sensible and straightforward thing

Interior of a 15th-century hall, showing the cupboard for the display of plate by the dais, and the minstrels' gallery at the end of the hall. Reproduced from a contemporary manuscript and included in Parker's *Domestic Architecture in England*

rather than anything extravagant and eccentric. The makers of furniture had the Englishman's comfort in mind. Common sense was the thread upon which all experiments in furniture-making were strung; and although common sense was occasionally twisted by fashion, it always prevailed in the end, no matter what extravagance in decorative forms and costly materials was demanded by the patrons of the cabinet-

(185)

maker and the joiner. During the 16th, late 17th, and throughout the 18th centuries, English craftsmen and furniture makers were constantly called upon to accommodate foreign fashions ; and their skill in anglicising them grew, generation by generation.

The apparatus for furnishing rooms at the beginning of the 16th century was fairly simple. Furnishing was still in the mediaeval stage of dependence upon fabrics draped over frames ; receptacles were solid, seats and tables were stoutly supported, and there was a variety of boards—for the table was only rarely called a table, was sometimes called a table board, and when it was fixed was known as a table dormant. As late as the mid-17th century, the under frames of a table were still called " dormants ". Boards had specific functions. There was a dressing board for example, upon which food was dressed, and from which the dresser was ultimately derived ; later, this became the sideboard. There was also the cup board, upon which plate was displayed ; and types of boards devoted to special types of food, such as the meat board, and the oyster board. During the 16th century, seats, tables and receptacles were elaborated. Chairs which were by no means uncommon in mediaeval times, became a little more elaborate. Before the 16th century, they had been solid, box-like affairs, though from representations in mediaeval illustrations some were fitted with rounded backs, and at some time during the 16th century, the turned leg was used both for stools and tables, and probably for chairs. Turning may indeed be very much earlier than is supposed. Our knowledge of furniture before the 16th century is based largely upon illustrations and inventories that have survived, for few articles of furniture have endured for more than four centuries. There are some exceptions : notably the coffer-maker's chair from York Minster, with its X-shaped frame, and a good many parish chests in churches throughout the country. But these are rare exceptions : the ordinary, simple household goods, and many of the more elaborate contents of palaces, royal and episcopal, have powdered away with time. Inventories record many items of furniture ; though they are seldom described in any great detail. For the furnishing of the mid-16th-century house, Harrison again supplies a lively and detailed account. He tells us that "The furniture of our houses also exceedeth, and is growne in maner even to passing delicacie : and herein I doo not speake of the nobilitie and gentrie onelie, but likewise of the lowest sort (in most places of our south countrie,) that have anie thing at all to take to. Certes, in noble mens houses it is not rare to see abundance of Arras, rich hangings of tapistrie, silver vessell, and so much other plate, as may furnish sundrie cupbords, to the summe oftentimes of a thousand or two thousand pounds at the least : whereby the value of this and the rest of their stuffe dooth grow to be (almost) inestimable. Likewise in the houses of knights, gentlemen, merchantmen, and some other wealthie citizens, it is not geson to behold generallie their great provision of tapistrie, Turkie worke, pewter, brasse, fine linen, and thereto costlie cupbords of plate, worth five or six hundred (or a thousand) pounds, to be deemed by estimation. But as herein all these sorts doo far exceed their elders and pre-decessors, (and in neatnesse and curiositie, the merchant all other ;) so in time past, the costlie furniture staied there, whereas now it is descended yet lower, even unto the inferiour artificers and manie farmers, who (by vertue of their old and not of their new leases) have (for the most part) learned also to garnish their cupbords with plate, their (joined) beds with tapistrie and silke hangings, and their tables with (carpets &) fine naperie, whereby the wealth of our countrie (God be praised therefore, and give us grace to imploie it well) dooth infinitelie appeare."(125)

The term cupboard during the 16th century was applied both to open tiers of shelves, like the court cupboard—some-times called a buffet—and the press cupboard with doors. The enclosed cupboard was a mediaeval invention which probably began as a recess in a stone wall, protected by doors that were pierced to admit ventilation. The aumbry evolved from a recess in a wall fitted with doors, a piece of fitted furniture in fact, which was called an almery. The aumbry was a small cupboard, used in bedrooms for storing food and drink, as our ancestors in the 15th and 16th centuries had a habit of taking a snack during the night. People rose early then, and there was often a long interval before breakfast, which might be substantial or consist only of a morning draught of ale or wine. Thomas Tusser's critical couplet, included in his *Five Hundred points of good husbandry united to as many of good huswiferie* (1573), seems rather severe.

> Some slovens from sleeping, no sooner be up,
> But hand is in aumbrie, and nose in the cup.(126)

Kingsley may have had this bit of contemporary reproof in mind when he made Mrs. Leigh, that pallid Elizabethan lady with the mid-Victorian outlook, say to the hero of *Westward Ho !* : " My dear Amyas, you will really heat your blood with all that strong ale ! Remember, those who drink beer, think beer."

The reply was at least as robust as Amyas and the age he lived in, for he said : " Then they think right good thoughts, mother. And in the meanwhile, those who drink water, think water."

The aumbry was supplanted during the 16th century by what was called the livery cupboard ; though this was probably another name for a more commodious and elaborate type of aumbry. The name was derived from " liveries " : those little stores of food and drink that were given to guests and members of the household to guard them against " night starvation ". Livery cupboards remained in use throughout the following century, and an item in an inventory, dated January 2nd, 1672, is " One Livery Cupboard of juniper ".(127)

The 16th-century house was designed with each floor occupied by a series of rooms of various sizes and shapes ; a dwelling was no longer conceived as a cluster of apartments, adjacent to a large central hall, and this created the need for appropriate furnishing, and gave new shapes and functions to many articles that had appeared only in an elementary form in earlier periods. Settle and chest, court cupboard and press cupboard, tables whose tops could be extended, small, simple and convenient joined stools with turned legs, and elaborate beds with heavily carved posts, headboards and testers, all appeared during this century of prolific invention and accomplishment in the crafts. We look at all these things today often with a reverence for their age, often with so much admiration for the rich glowing colour that has been acquired by centuries of polish, that we occasionally forget the crudity

A 15th-century bed with an aumbry beside it, the small cupboard where little stores of food and drink were kept. (Drawn from a contemporary manuscript by Henry Shaw, and included in his *Specimens of Ancient Furniture*: the first English book on antique furniture, published in London in 1836)

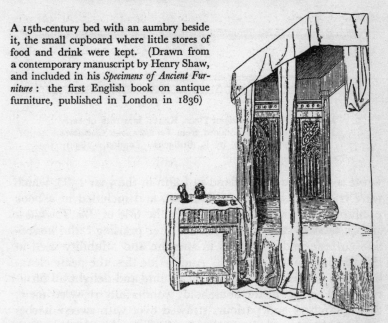

and overcrowding of the ornament, the ill proportion of the supporting columns of beds—which were often eccentric caricatures of classical columns—and forget, too, that when they were originally made, these massive pieces of furniture were of bright golden coloured oak, waxed till they shone like burnished metal, though much paler in hue than is now realised. When we think of oak today it is so often in terms of " old oak " ; and it is the age rather than the property of wood, its marking, and its strength that we admire—so much so that since the middle of the 19th century many new things made of oak have been stained to imitate the colour that age confers.

But it was not only the richness and variety of furnishing that made the 16th-century Englishman's home such an agreeable place : it was during that century, and especially in Queen Elizabeth's reign, that the art of home-making became one of our greatest national accomplishments. How English homes impressed contemporary travellers is recorded with frank admiration by the Dutch physician, Levinus Lemnius, who

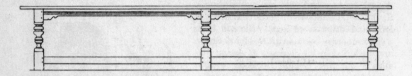

Long table from Penshurst Place, Kent : late 16th or early
17th century. (Reproduced from *Furniture with Candelabra
and Interior Decoration*, by R. Bridgens. London : 1838)

wrote some notes on England in Latin in the year 1560, which
were translated by Thomas Newton, and included in a book
published in London in 1581 under the title of *The Touchstone
of Complexions*.(128)   Dr. Lemnius after praising " the incred-
ible curtesie and frendlines in speache and affability used in
this famous realme " says : " And beside this, the neate clean-
lines, the exquisite finesse, the pleasaunte and delightfull furniture in every poynt for household, wonderfully rejoysed mee ;
their chambers and parlours strawed over with sweete herbes
refreshed mee ;   their nosegayes finely entermingled wyth
sundry sortes of fragraunte floures in their bedchambers and
privy roomes, with comfortable smell cheered mee up and
entirelye delyghted all my sences."
    Then he adds : " And this do I thinck to be the cause that
Englishmen, lyving by such holesome and exquisite meate, and
in so holesome and healthfull ayre be so freshe and cleane
coloured : their faces, eyes and countenaunce carying with it
and representing a portly grace and comelynes, geveth out
evident tokens of an honest mind ; in language very smoth
and allective, but yet seasoned and tempered within the limits
and bonds of moderation, not bumbasted with any unseemely
termes or infarced with any clawing flatteries or allurementes.
At their tables althoughe they be very sumptuous, and love to
have good fare, yet neyther use they to overcharge themselves
with excesse of drincke, neyther thereto greatly provoke and
urge others, but suffer every man to drincke in such measure
as best pleaseth hymselfe, whych drinck being eyther Ale or
Beere, most pleasaunte in tast and holesomely relised, they
fetch not from foreine places, but have it amonge themselves
brewed.   As touching theyr populous and great haunted cities,

the fruitfulnes of their ground and soile, their lively springs and mighty ryvers, their great heards and flockes of cattell, their mysteries and art of weaving and clothmaking, their skilfulnes in shooting, it is needlesse heere to discourse—seeing the multitude of marchaunts exercisinge the traffique and arte of marchaundize among them, and ambassadoures also sente thyther from forrayne Prynces, are able aboundantly to testifye that nothing needeful and expedient for mans use and commodity lacketh in that most noble Illande."

This gentle and kindly Dutch doctor certainly makes Elizabethan England sound like the good old times of our dreams, that we still try wistfully to recall by superficial and inept imitation in our vernacular architecture and machine-produced furniture.

CHAPTER XVII

FURNITURE, MANNERS AND HABITS

URNITURE, like architecture, has a revealing story to tell about the manners and social outlook of people. The aumbry and the livery cupboard recorded a habit that was common throughout the country from the 15th to the 17th century. The introduction of tea during the sixteen-fifties, when it was sold in England by the pound at prices ranging from £6 to £10, and the popularity tea-drinking rapidly acquired by the end of the 17th century, created a demand for special types of furniture that helped the new habit to become an elegant ceremony, and a delightful excuse for conversation, unclouded and uncoarsened by the fumes of wine, and largely under feminine control. The garnishing of cupboards with plate that Harrison mentions was a practice that created the plate cupboard with its high superstructure, that was called a desk, upon which cups and flagons were displayed, and from which the court cupboard with its tiers of open shelves was derived. The habit of displaying plate, not only richly decorated vessels of precious metals, but brass and pewter, also created the dresser, which was a modification of the plate cupboard, a less elaborate though commodious piece of furniture used in the spacious living-rooms of farm-houses, which usually combined the functions of kitchen and dining-room, and in a humble way kept alive the tradition of the great hall, the house place, as a centre of social life, though the parlour, unlike the mediaeval solar, was not yet a private place, an almost sacred apartment, used only for special occasions : it was often a bedroom, as contemporary inventories suggest.

Of all articles of furniture that serve the needs of the home, seats disclose more about manners and social habits and conventions than any other. The changes in the form and character of chairs from the Middle Ages to the mid-20th century relate, as clearly as written history, the social changes that have occurred during five hundred years ; and of all such unwritten records they are perhaps the easiest to read. They show how chair-making began by being a plain statement of utility—for no memory or relics of the luxurious furnishing of Romano-British homes remained to influence the ideas of the mediaeval joiners. Thereafter, the desire for elaboration brought the chair through various periods of ornamentation, eventually achieving great elegance, which was afterwards obliterated in the Victorian period when " comfort was mistaken for civilization ". The study of chair design from the 15th century to the present day, apart from its intrinsic interest, gives all kinds of hints about the personal taste, the clothes, posture and way of life of rich and poor alike.

England has always been pre-eminent in chair-making, and during that golden age of design from 1660 to 1830 or thereabouts, we had some chair-makers of genius, and their names have survived. During the 15th century chairs were straightforward pieces of furniture. The hard, wooden box-like upright chairs and the coffer-maker's chairs, covered with leather or with leather seats slung from X-shaped frames, have been mentioned in the previous chapter ; but by the beginning of the 16th century the severe lines of the former type were often enriched with carving that reproduced the prevailing Gothic forms of ornamentation. Those early Tudor chairs resembled the stalls in great churches ; they were like chairs of state, with arms and high backs ; and throughout the first half of the 16th century they retained a throne-like quality. There were also simpler types of chairs, but forms and stools provided the seating for most people. Inventories of the late 16th and 17th centuries often include references to buffet stools, and these were most probably joint, or joyned, stools—small, flat-seated, stout pieces of furniture with four turned legs, braced by stretchers.

Stretchers both on chairs and stools, raised an inch or so above the floor level, were desirable not only for the additional strength that they gave, but to allow people to keep their feet

An oak chair in St. Mary's Hall, Coventry. Mid-15th
century. This chair was probably the right-hand seat of a
triple chair, which occupied the dais of the Great Hall, built
in the early part of the 15th century for the united guilds of
St. Mary, St. John the Baptist, and St. Catherine. Like
the 14th-century oak Coronation Chair in Westminster Abbey
the design reflects contemporary Gothic architecture and
ornamentation. (See opposite page)

The back view of the chair in St. Mary's Hall, Coventry, shown on the opposite page. Both drawings are reproduced from *Furniture with Candelabra and Interior Decoration*, by R. Bridgens. (London : 1838.) Compare the decorative character of this chair with the fireplace from Sherborne Abbey on page 119, the bay window of Compton Wynyates, page 155, the carved corner post at Lavenham, page 158, and the barge-boards on the house at Wingham, page 163. Architecture always exerts a powerful influence on the design of furniture

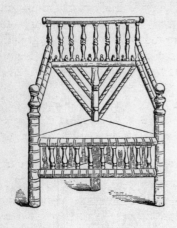 

Left : A late 16th-century chair made of turned posts and spindles. This early example of the craft of the turner finally developed into the Windsor or stick-back chair. (From Thomas Wright's *Homes of Other Days.*) *Right :* A double bow back Windsor chair, with cabriole legs in front : mid-18th century. From a drawing by Ronald Escott

off the floor, which was not always clean. Rushes were used on the floors of living-rooms long after the Middle Ages. In the public rooms of inns the floors were sanded. Despite the generous and glowing praises of Dr. Lemnius, the mid-16th-century room would hardly satisfy the standards of a family living four hundred years later in a council house. The use of sweet-smelling herbs and flowers that Dr. Lemnius mentions seems most agreeable, but those sweet scents were often struggling for the mastery with other odours. Dried lavender and woodruff and other scented herbs may have performed the same function as the nosegay that is given to the judge in Court. That little bunch of sweet-smelling flowers was originally regarded partly as a prophylactic against jail fever, partly to relieve the judge now and then from the oppressive atmosphere of the Court. The practice survives—its origin is not always remembered.

Chairs and stools in the Elizabethan period generally had hard wooden seats, with loose cushions or pieces of cloth on them. It has been mentioned how in the Middle Ages a form or bench placed against the wall had a back cloth, hung on the wall, called a dorcer (or dorsal), that allowed people to lean against the plastered stonework without being chilled. It is likely that the high-backed settle, which is really a bench with a back to it, evolved from the bench and the dorcer. The addition of side pieces, lugs or wings, to the settle back not only braced the whole structure, but kept off draughts, and from the high-backed settle with its side pieces the high-backed easy chair of the late 17th century most probably evolved.

In addition to joint stools and chairs with turned legs, there was a type of chair consisting almost entirely of turned spindles, representing a technique of chair-making that appears to have originated in East Anglia. For some reason or other a tradition has grown up that such chairs were associated with Henry VIII, and in many books of furniture issued during and since the Victorian period illustrations of chairs with turned spindles are often labelled " Henry VIII's chair ". Although turned chairs were probably in existence in the early Tudor period, few existing specimens could be dated earlier than the second half of the 16th century.

At the end of Elizabeth's long reign, chairs with upholstered seats and straight backs were being made, and a modern fancy name for them is the " farthingale chair ", because it is presumed that they were designed to accommodate that voluminous garment ; but that is not a contemporary term and such chairs were then called " back stools "—a descriptive name, because they really were stools with backs. The terms arm chair and elbow chair did not come into use until the 17th century, and they were applied to back stools that had arms, and the contemporary name was " a chair with arms ", or " armed " or " arming chairs ". Among the items in an inventory dated January 25th, 1673, is " one great arm'd chaire " (129) ; and another reference in an inventory dated November 7th, 1678, is to " a armed rush chaire, 12s. 6d."(130) Coffer-makers' chairs were still made in the early 17th century and they frequently preserved the mediaeval structure of an X-shaped under-frame, that was covered either with leather or fabric.

The small back stool type of chair was known later in the

Early 17th-century armchair, with a cushioned seat supported on an X-shaped frame. Chairs that were covered either with leather or some fabric, like velvet, were sometimes called coffer-maker's chairs. This armchair from Knole was drawn by Charles L. Eastlake and included in his *Hints on Household Taste* (Fourth edition, 1878). This chair is at an early stage in the history of upholstery : the easy chair did not arrive until the end of the 17th century. Compare this with the Hepplewhite easy chair on page 277.

17th century as an " upholsterer's chair ", or an " embroiderer's chair ". Sets of these chairs were made, and people hired them from upholsterers for dinner parties. Pepys tells us that his set of chairs and a couch cost £40, and they may well have been richly embroidered.(131)   These sets of upholsterers' chairs made the idea of a suite of furniture more generally acceptable ; and with the introduction of the suite, a new orderliness and coherence came into furnishing. Suites of upholstered chairs had been made in Elizabeth's reign, but they lacked the comprehensive character of the suites that were introduced during the latter part of the 17th century, which brought into the galleries and withdrawing rooms of the nobility and wealthy upper classes a new and elegant relationship between chairs, stools and couches ; for a suite might have as many as twenty-four chairs and stools and two or four couches.

Upholstered furniture was covered with fabrics and ornamented with embroidery and fringes until the Puritan period made such decorative extravagance inadvisable ; then the grim godliness of England's rulers during the Commonwealth

At the end of the 16th century, and throughout the 17th century, chairs with upholstered seats and straight backs were called back stools : they were made in sets, and were let out on hire by upholsterers for dinner parties. *Right :* An early 17th-century upholstered chair from Knole, Kent, drawn by Charles L. Eastlake and included in his *Hints on Household Taste* (Fourth edition, 1878). *Below :* Laying a dinner table : copied by F. W. Fairholt from an engraving made in 1633, and included in Thomas Wright's *Homes of Other Days*. This shows a set of upholstered back stools

imposed a period of utility, when austerity was inflicted on people, not for their economic salvation, but for their spiritual welfare. Tassels and fringes vanished ; the Puritan chairs were severe, upright, and structurally akin to coffer-makers' chairs, with leather-covered seats and backs garnished with nails, and with the wood under-frame exposed.

From about 1630 to 1660 furniture-makers were absolved from the obligation to satisfy modish taste. The devils of fashion were temporarily exorcised ; and during that time the form of English furniture was refined—the corpulent outlines, so expressive of Elizabethan and early Stuart lavish living and copious luxury, were reduced, and some of the suppressed native characteristics restored. National expression, both in building and woodwork, that had been checked when Englishmen became " Italianate ", was released ; and a new phase of design began. The craft of turning attained new standards of achievement at that time, bobbin-turning and twisting, including the barley-sugar twist, appeared on chair legs and table legs. Those middle years of the 17th century were marked by a great resurgence of inventiveness and increased skill in chair-making and furniture-making generally.

Upholstered furniture was found chiefly in the homes of wealthy people : chairs of sturdy and simple structure were in general use from the late 16th century. This type, known as a panel back and sometimes as a wainscot chair, had a panel framed in the back, with the upper part of the back frame decorated by lightly carved cresting, and arms jutting forward, the legs turned, and braced with stretchers. Sometimes the back panel would be decorated by carving or inlaid patterns. The term wainscot was used during the latter part of the 16th, and throughout the 17th and 18th centuries for any piece of furniture of solid wooden construction, particularly in country districts. The word, of Dutch origin, describes a material, namely quarter-cut oak, for the two planks that are cut from the centre of an oak log provide the wainscot boards. The term meant not only strongly made furniture, but pieces of loose board, table tops, and the panelling of rooms. By the beginning of the 19th century Thomas Sheraton in *The Cabinet Dictionary* (published in 1803) was defining the term as " The Wooden work which lines the walls of a room as high as the

A wainscot chair, late 16th or early 17th century; sometimes described as a panel back chair, though that term is not contemporary. From a drawing made by Charles L. Eastlake, and included in his book, *Hints on Household Taste* (Fourth edition, 1878)

surbase." Surbase is an architectural term for the moulding on the upper part of a pedestal, and the pedestal of an order in architecture corresponds to the dado in a room ; so according to Sheraton a wooden dado was a wainscot : but it was also used frequently to describe walls that were panelled from floor to ceiling.

A mid-16th-century reference to wainscot furniture occurs in an inventory of the goods of Sir Henry Parkers (dated 1551–1560), where an item " in the Wardroppe " is : " A louse beddstedd of waynscott, iijs, iiijd."(132) There are many references to various types of wainscot furniture in 17th-century inventories, and wainscot chairs are often mentioned. The frequency of the term is an indication of the extensive use of oak as a material for furniture making, and although other native woods were used—ash, beech, elm, yew and the fruit woods, such as apple and cherry—oak predominated. Walnut was used as early as the 16th century, but did not become fashionable until the second half of the 17th century. While it is convenient to classify the various ages of furniture-making under the woods that were chiefly employed, this method of studying the history of design can be misleading, for it suggests rigidly marked periods and an exclusive use of certain materials. The late Percy Macquoid first adopted this form of classification in his monumental work, *A History of English Furniture*, published in four volumes (1904–1908), which covered : I. The Age of Oak. II. The Age of Walnut. III. The Age of Mahogany. IV. The Age of Satinwood.(133)

Although oak was the principal material used for furniture from the Middle Ages until the late 17th century, the divisions suggested by those four labelled " Ages " are artificial, for oak, walnut and mahogany were used concurrently during the third, fourth and fifth decades of the 18th century ; and satinwood was used only for a comparatively few costly examples of furniture, at a time when mahogany was still the most popular material, and rosewood was coming into use. In the countryside, all the native woods were used from mediaeval times until the late 19th century.

All through the 17th century skill was increasing, and several inventions in furniture were made—not only fanciful jokes like the piece of furniture at Sir William Batten's house which Pepys described after a visit there : " Among other things he showed me my Lady's closet, wherein was great store of rarities ; as also a chair, which he calls King Harry's chaire, where he that sits down is catched with two irons, that come round about him, which makes good sport."(134)

An equally ingenious, but far more useful invention was a piece of dual-purpose furniture, named in contemporary inventories as a " table-chair " or a " table chairewise ", and consisting of a chair with arms and a hinged, circular back, that could swing over and rest upon the arms, thus forming a small round-topped table. These table chairs were in common use during the second half of the 17th century, and the modern name of " monk's bench " is a romantic invention. Tables were made in new and convenient forms such as the draw or extending table, with the top divided into three leaves, those at each end sliding under the centre leaf when the table was closed ; and the gate-leg table, for which the earliest term was a falling table. Those sliding receptacles that were originally called " boxes to shoot in and out " or " drawing boxes ", were fitted in cupboards and chests, and had been used in aumbries and below table-tops during the 16th century and probably much earlier. It was not until the 17th century that their use was widened and they were known generally as drawers. The mule chest, which was a large chest mounted upon a base with two drawers in it, was the ancestor of the chest of drawers. Before the end of the 17th century chests of drawers were in many homes. At first they were mounted either on a solid plinth or upon a stand with legs ; but during the late 17th and early 18th centuries they took the form that has remained basically unchanged ever since.

The increasing complexity and convenience of receptacles of all kinds that occurred between the reigns of Elizabeth and Anne indicated rising standards of comfort, but the enjoyment of comfort was tempered by an increasing regard for elegance in the form and proportions of furniture. In every class of home labour was lightened. The replacement of the large chest with a hinged lid for storing clothes and linen by the far more get-at-able chest of drawers was an example of labour-saving. The history of furniture in the 17th century was distinguished by inventiveness and, during the second half, by the establishment of cabinet-making, for the cabinet-maker's craft was created and developed by the technique of veneering, which was introduced after the restoration of Charles II, among many other decorative and luxurious accomplishments. The inventions and fresh skills made and introduced during the 17th century were refined and elaborated during the 18th, and the Georgian age was one of supreme ability in cabinet-making and chair-making.

Only people whose manners were polished and ornate and whose appreciation of beauty demanded elegant surroundings could have lived appropriately against the exquisite background provided by the architects and furnishers of that period, when nothing ugly was made, and every article in a room was harmoniously adjusted because of the universal respect paid by designers to the great system of design represented by the classic orders of architecture. There was an urbane family likeness between the form of the house, the porch, the front door, the knocker, the iron lamps on the gate-posts, the coach that drew up before the gates, and within, the chairs, tables, cabinets, silver candlesticks and tea things, again reflected that likeness. This bland relationship in terms of design was untainted by the standardisation that had often disfigured the architecture of that earlier period, when houses in the Roman

A seat designed by William Kent (1685–1748), the architect who began life as a coach-painter's apprentice, and whose patron was Richard Boyle, the third Earl of Burlington. The ornamentation is a little heavy, but characteristic of the early Georgian period. (From *Some Designs by Mr. Inigo Jones and Mr. Wm. Kent*, published in 1744 by John Vardy)

province of Britain were built and furnished in accordance with a universal system of design and ornamentation. Unlike Roman architects and craftsmen, English architects and cabinet-makers and silversmiths of the Georgian period were liberated from a rigid respect for the precedents and rules that had curbed their Roman forerunners. Designers mastered the rules and used them with imagination, as craftsmen mastered their materials, and used them with sympathy. The master designer was the architect, who was respected alike by his patrons and those who built and carved and decorated under his direction.

Throughout this orderly pattern of design ran a pleasing and highly individual thread of eccentricity ; taste might be guided by impeccable rules ; great noblemen like Richard Boyle, the third earl of Burlington, might take up architecture, both as a practitioner and a patron ; nothing might disturb the serene rhythms of interior decoration and furnishing, but there was no accounting for the queer turns and fancies of the English character, manifest in every class, and finding expression in odd and sometimes outrageous ways. Occasionally the form of furniture would indicate a transient craze for some fashion, and there was during the mid-18th century an affectionate weakness for Gothic forms of ornament—yet another example of nostalgic longing for times past. It was regarded as a passing fashion, and described by William Whitehead, writing in March 1753 in that sprightly periodical, *The World*, as something already outmoded. "A few years ago every thing was Gothic," he said ; "our houses, our beds, our book-cases, and our couches, were all copied from some parts or other of our old cathedrals."(135)

This was not another revival of the interrupted national style, which had been resumed a hundred years earlier during the Puritan period ; it was merely a fashion, based on superficial copying, when, as Whitehead observed : "Tricks and conceits got possession everywhere." There was supposed to be something in this form of taste that was "congenial to our old Gothic constitution . . ." Whitehead considered that it was really congenial "to our modern idea of liberty, which allows everyone the privilege of playing the fool, and of making himself ridiculous in whatever way he pleases ".(136) He proceeded to describe the rise and spread of another fashion, which had visited England before. "According to the present prevailing whim," he wrote, "everything is Chinese, or in the Chinese taste ; or as it is sometimes more modestly expressed, *partly after the Chinese manner*. Chairs, tables, chimney-pieces, frames for looking-glasses, and even our most vulgar utensils, are all reduced to this new-fangled standard ; and withoutdoors so universally has it spread, that every gate to a cow-yard is in T's and Z's, and every hovel for the cows has bells hanging at the corners."

In a later number of *The World*, in the same year, the Chinese manner of furniture is criticised in greater detail. After a

fashionable upholsterer had been given a free hand in the
refurnishing of a country house, it became, the owner complained, " so disguised and altered, that I hardly knew it
again ". He added : " There is not a bed, a table, a chair,
or even a grate, that is not twisted into so many ridiculous and
grotesque figures, and so decorated with the heads, beaks,
wings, and claws of birds and beasts, that Milton's ' Gorgons,
and hydras, and chimaeras dire ' are not to be compared with
them."(137)

The contents are then enumerated : " Every room is completely covered with a Wilton carpet ; I suppose to save
the floors, which are all new-laid, and in the most expensive
manner. In each of these rooms is a pair or two of stands,
supported by different figures of men or beasts, on which are
placed branches of Chelsea china, representing lions, bears, and
other animals, holding in their mouths or paws sprigs of bays,
orange, or myrtle ; among the leaves of which are fixed sockets
for the reception of wax candles, which by dispersing the light
among the foliage, I own, make a very agreeable appearance.
But I can see no use for the lions and bears : to say the truth,
I cannot help thinking it a little unnatural ; for it is well known
that all kinds of savages are afraid of fire. But this I submit to
you ; having observed of late several wild beasts exhibited on
the stage, without their shewing the least surprise at the lamps,
or even at the loud shouts of applause which have been
bestowed upon them from the galleries. The upper apartments of my house, which were before handsomely wainscoted,
are now hung with the richest Chinese and India paper, where
all the powers of fancy are exhausted in a thousand fantastic
figures of birds, beasts, and fishes, which never had existence."

Following this general account of the furnishing and interior
decoration is a description of the state bedroom and the dress-
ing-room ; and the illustrations that appeared in the trade
catalogues of the fashionable furniture-makers and upholsterers, like *The Gentleman and Cabinet-Maker's Director* issued
by Thomas Chippendale in 1754, and the interiors shown in
some of Hogarth's satires on fashionable life, prove that the
description was by no means a burlesque exaggeration.

" The best, or, as my wife calls it, the state bedchamber, is
furnished in a manner that has half undone me. The hang-

A china case or china cabinet in the Chinese taste. From
the third edition of *The Gentleman and Cabinet-Maker's Director*,
by Thomas Chippendale (1762)

ings are white sattin, with French flowers and artificial moss stuck upon it with gum, and interspersed with ten thousand spangles, beads, and shells. The bed stands in an alcove, at the top of which are painted Cupids strewing flowers and sprinkling perfumes. This is divided from the room by two twisted pillars, adorned with wreaths of flowers, and inter-mixed with shell-work. In this apartment there is a cabinet of most curious workmanship, highly finished with stones, gems, and shells, disposed in such a manner as to represent several sorts of flowers. The top of this cabinet is adorned with a prodigious pyramid of china of all colours, shapes and sizes. At every corner of the room are great jars filled with dried leaves of roses and jessamine. The chimney-piece also (and indeed every one in the house) is covered with immense quantities of china of various figures; among which are Talapoins and Bonzes, and all the religious orders of the east." (138)

The ornate artificiality of high life is disclosed by the suc-ceeding paragraph.

"The next room that represents itself is my wife's dressing room; but I will not attempt to describe it to you minutely, it is so full of trinkets. The walls are covered round with looking-glass, interspersed with pictures made of moss, butter-flies, and sea-weeds. Under a very magnificent Chinese canopy stands the toilette, furnished with a set of boxes of gilt plate, for combs, brushes, paints, pastes, patches, pomatums, powders white grey and blue, bottles of hungary, lavender and orange flower water, and, in short, all the apparatus for dis-guising beauty. Here she constantly pays her devotions two hours every morning; but what kind of divinity she adores, may be safer for you to guess than for me to tell. By this time I imagine you will conceive my house to be much fuller of furniture than my head. Alas! sir, I am but a husband, and my wife is a woman of quality."

The furnishing of the English home in the mid-18th century might exhibit such extravagances, but they were confined to the luxuriously equipped town houses and country seats of the nobility and gentry: the small manor houses of the country-side, the larger farm-houses, also the cottages, and the town dwellings of the professional classes and artisans, were sensibly

A ribband back chair : one of the most elaborate examples
of mid-18th-century furniture by a master chair-maker.
From the first edition of Thomas Chippendale's *Director*
(1754). Ribband was the contemporary form of ribbon

and adequately furnished with simpler versions of the fashions that had been in vogue in high society perhaps a generation earlier. Solid, sensible and well formed, such simple furniture, made chiefly by country craftsmen, had nothing crude about it, representing as it did the needs of people who were well endowed with common sense, and had neither the time nor the money to indulge in the fastidious pursuit of pleasure. Indeed, only a small, though most influential section of the community lived openly for pleasure, without being either apologetic or ashamed of a life of self-indulgence. Because the aristocracy preserved their sense of social obligation to the community, they were respected, and their taste was emulated ; they seldom avoided their obligations, and the bad landlord was never so common as the bad employer was to become after the industrial revolution had altered the social structure of the country. And through all this variegated life ran that eccentric streak, which made people do the most unexpected things, and choose the most unexpected and queer ways of calling attention to their prejudices and predilections, and which incidentally led to all manner of experiments being tried, for, as William Whitehead had said, the contemporary idea of liberty allowed " every one the privilege of playing the fool, and of making himself ridiculous in whatever way he pleases ".

Here is an example of the rich vein of eccentricity that has in the past made the English character and English life so curiously incomprehensible to people whose actions and pastimes are steadied by a greater respect for logic and personal dignity. In *The London Daily Post and General Advertiser*, on March 5th, 7th and 10th, 1739–40, the following advertisement appeared, issued, apparently, by one Henry Marsh :

Fuller on Exercise

(A Book worth reading)

Nothing ought to be thought ridiculous, that can afford the least Ease, or procure Health. A very worthy Gentleman, not long ago, had such an odd sort of Cholick, that he found nothing would relieve so much as lying with his Head downwards ; which Posture prov'd always so advantageous, that he had a Frame

Furniture of mid-18th-century design, displayed for sale by a cabinet maker. (From *The Gentleman's Magazine*, October, 1814)

made, to which he himself was fastened with Bolts, and then was turn'd Head downwards, after which manner he hung till his Pain went off. I hope none will say, that this was unbecoming a grave and wise Man to make use of such odd Means to get rid of an unsupportable Pain. If People would but abstract the Benefit got by Exercise from the Means by which it is got, they would set a great Value upon it, if some of the Advantages accruing from Exercise were to be procured by any one Medicine, nothing in the World would be in more Esteem than that Medicine.

This is to answer some Objections to the Look of the Chamber-Horse (for Exercise) invented by HENRY MARSH, in Clement's-Inn Passage, Clare-Market; who, it is well known, has had the honour to serve some Persons of the greatest Distinction in the Kingdom; and he humbly begs the Favour of Ladies and Gentlemen to try both the Chamber-Horses, which is the only sure Way of having the best. This Machine may be of great service to Children.

The first three sentences of this advertisement are quoted from pages 275–277 of a book on the use of exercise in the treatment of disease by Francis Fuller (1670–1706) entitled : *Medicina Gymnastica, or a Treatise concerning the Power of Exercise with respect to the Animal Œconomy, and the great necessity of it in the Cure of Several Distempers*, which was published in 1705, and had reached its sixth edition in 1728.

There is no trace of Henry Marsh at the Patent Office, either among the accepted official patentees, or among those who were merely granted a degree of protection for their inventions ; but although he claims to be the inventor of the chamber horse, he may have been only the first maker to advertise the device. It was certainly in use during the second half of the 18th century, when its novelty had probably worn off, and in the records of the firm of Gillow, which are preserved at Lancaster, there is an entry ordering such a machine, dated January 1st, 1790 ; one is also illustrated on plate 3 of Thomas Sheraton's book, *The Cabinet Maker's and Upholsterer's Drawing Book*, which was originally published between 1791 and 1794. The device consisted of springs encased in a leathern envelope resembling a large concertina, the whole being framed in mahogany ; and as the motions of horse exercise could be

An article of furniture that recalled the painful side of life in 18th-century England. It was known as a gouty or gout stool ; it had an adjustable seat, " the construction of which, by being so easily raised or lowered at either hand, is particularly useful to the addicted." The stool is commended in those words in Hepplewhite's *Guide* (1788), from which this illustration is reproduced

performed upon it, the name " horse exercising machine " was sometimes used.

Even the horse exercising machine, and the defence of the remarkable cure adopted by the worthy gentleman who suffered from " an odd sort of Cholick " which occupied the first part of Henry Marsh's advertisement, reveal a basic love of natural pursuits, of which exercise in rural surroundings is characteristically English. Before his strictures on Gothic and Chinese mannerisms in design and ornamentation, William Whitehead had written : " People may have whims, freaks, caprices, persuasions, and even second-sights if they please ; but they can have no Taste which has not its foundations in nature, and which, consequently, may be accounted for." This love of nature and natural simplicity was not an intellectual affectation, like Rousseau's Naturalism—it was an inherited love, which came into the life of most Englishmen,

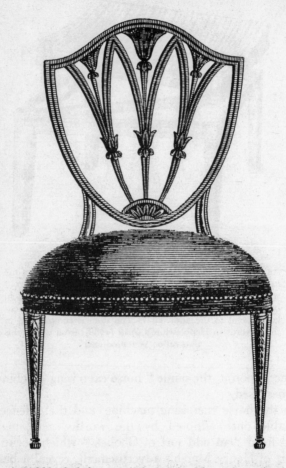

A shield back chair : a typical example of the work associated with the name of Hepplewhite, and indicative of the increasing refinement of form that characterised furniture in the second half of the 18th century. It is far less exuberant than the Chippendale design shown on page 209, and about twenty to twenty-five years later

A shield back chair with a vase splat: compare this with
the design on the opposite page. Both examples are from
Hepplewhite's *Cabinet-Maker and Upholsterer's Guide*, which
was published in 1788, two years after his death. Hepplewhite had served as an apprentice to the Lancaster firm of
Gillow, and when he came to London he opened a shop in
Red Cross Street, Cripplegate

and was occasionally acknowledged, and with it went that distrust for over-much magnificence that Ben Jonson had expressed in his praise of Penshurst.

In one of his early poems, Pope had set down the dream of many an Englishman, who longed for an independent home and place of his own, and the first two verses of his " Ode to Solitude " would when written have appealed alike to the contented countryman or to the man wearied of the pleasures and fatigues of the town (also to a good many people who have lived since).

> Happy the man, whose wish and care
>   A few paternal acres bound,
> Content to breathe his native air
>   In his own ground.
>
> Whose herds with milk, whose fields with bread,
>   Whose flocks supply him with attire,
> Whose trees in summer yield him shade,
>   In winter fire.

John Pomfret, in his poem *The Choice or Wish*, written in 1700, had described the modest home and the surroundings a cultivated man desired.

> Near some fair town I'd have a private seat,
> Built uniform ; not little, nor too great ;
> Better if on a rising ground it stood,
> On this side fields, on that a neighb'ring wood :
> It should within no other things contain
> But what are useful, necessary, plain :
> Methinks 'tis nauseous, and I'd ne'er endure
> The needless pomp of gaudy furniture.
> A little garden, grateful to the eye,
> And a cool rivulet run murm'ring by,
> On whose delicious banks a stately row
> Of shady limes or sycamores should grow ;
> At th' end of which a silent study plac'd,
> Should be with all the noblest authors grac'd.

Such temperate desires were throughout the 18th century reflected in the form and furnishing of the smaller houses of the town and countryside. The professional furnishers, the cabinet-makers and upholsterers who, either independently or under the direction of architects, catered for the wealthy classes, had a sense of what was fitting ; they had standards of judgment and workmanship, and their patrons had the same standards, and could appraise the design and workmanship of any article with knowledge. In concluding their preface to *The Universal System of Household Furniture,* which was published in 1760, the authors William Ince and Thomas Mayhew, said :

" In Furnishing all should be with Propriety—Elegance should always be joined with a peculiar Neatness through the whole House, or otherwise an immense Expense may be thrown away to no Purpose, either in Use or Appearance ; and with the same Regard any Gentleman may furnish as neat at a small Expense, as he can elegant and superb at a great one."

Nearly everything made in the Golden Age of design showed a universal appreciation of good proportion, common sense, elegant embellishment and both propriety and neatness. It was then that our national reputation as master designers and makers of furniture was established, and was attached chiefly to the names of a few men whose trade catalogues happened to be signed : Thomas Chippendale, George Hepplewhite and Thomas Sheraton. But there were others, like the Gillows of Lancaster, and Ince, Mayhew and Robert Manwaring, and architects like Robert and James Adam who designed furniture and employed cabinet-makers like Chippendale to carry out their designs. All these master craftsmen and master designers flourished, because the arts of life were respected and fully and freely enjoyed.

CHAPTER XVIII

THE ENGLISHMAN'S INN

NEXT to the home itself, the inn for centuries has claimed the affectionate regard of Englishmen, and its furnishing and general character have to this day preserved something of its air of ancient welcome. No artificial, paper-planned " community centre " can provide a substitute for an institution that gives such agreeable expression to the English tradition as the inn. Towns on the highways that carried a lot of traffic, had according to Harrison " great and sumptuous inns builded in them for the receiving of such travellers and strangers as pass to and fro ". The inn as an institution changed, like many other things in England, at the end of the Middle Ages ; it was less companionable and democratic than the Tabard, that " gentil hostelrye " at Southwark where the Canterbury pilgrims put up for the night ; but it was a briskly efficient and comfortable place when Harrison described it in the late 16th century, and certainly justified his use of the word sumptuous. Still more revealing was his statement that " every man may use his inne as his owne house in England, and have for his money how great or little variety of vittels, and what other service himself shall think expedient to call for ".(139) That tradition of welcome remained for a long time, and many writers have made much of it, and, where welcome was lacking, were as savagely critical as Thomas Hughes, who wrote these lines :

> If ever you go to Dolgelly,
> Don't stay at the —— Hotel ;
> There's nothing to put in your belly,
> And no-one to answer the bell.

A mediaeval hostelry at night. Copied from a 15th-century
MS. by F. W. Fairholt and included in Thomas Wright's
Homes of Other Days. This was before the days of the " great
and sumptuous inns " described by William Harrison in the
16th century

Dickens rejoiced in praises of the inn—though he had some
unkind things to say about the Great White Horse at Ipswich,
particularly the manners of the waiters and the quality of the
food. But elsewhere in *Pickwick* his approval is warmed to a
fine glow, as, for example, when Mr. Pickwick, accompanied
by Bob Sawyer, Benjamin Allen and Sam Weller, travelling
from Birmingham to London in the pouring rain, was persuaded by Sam Weller to put up at the Saracen's Head at
Towcester. " There's beds here," said Sam to Mr. Pickwick,
and added, " everything clean and comfortable. Wery good
little dinner, sir, they can get ready in half an hour—pair of
fowls, sir, and a weal cutlet ; French beans, 'taturs, tart, and
tidiness." When the decision had been taken to stay for the
night, and the travellers entered the inn, " the candles were
brought, the fire was stirred up, and a fresh log of wood thrown
on. In ten minutes' time, a waiter was laying the cloth for
dinner, the curtains were drawn, the fire was blazing brightly,

The parlour of an Elizabethan inn, as it appeared in the
early 19th century. (Published by R. Ackermann, 1819)

and everything looked (as everything always does, in all decent
English inns) as if the travellers had been expected, and their
comforts prepared, for days beforehand."

From the 16th century to the end of the coaching days, such
conscientious attention to the comfort of travellers was the
rule ; providing, of course, that the travellers arrived in a
vehicle or on horseback. The pedestrian was not so welcome,
and, unless the innkeeper was satisfied that a traveller had
either money or social standing, he could expect to be directed
to the nearest ale-house. Tow-wouse, the innkeeper in
Fielding's *Joseph Andrews*, gave the most candid support to this
policy when he said to his wife : " ' If the traveller be a
gentleman, though he hath no money about him now, we shall
most likely be paid hereafter ; so you may begin to score
whenever you will.' "(140)

The names of the inns often indicated the quality of their
customers, and Thomas Heywood, the dramatist who was born
about 1575, introduced into *The Rape of Lucrece* (1608) a song
about them.

The Gintry to the King's Head,
  The Nobles to the Crown,
The Knights unto the Golden Fleece,
  And to the Plough the Clowne.

The Churchmen to the Mitre,
  The Shepheard to the Star,
The Gardener hies him to the Rose,
  To the Drum the Man of War.

The Huntsmen to the White Hart,
  To the Ship the Merchants goe,
But you that doe the Muses love,
  The sign called River Po.

The Banquer out to the World's End,
  The Fool to the Fortune hie,
Unto the Mouth the Oyster-wife,
  The Fiddler to the Pie.

The Punk unto the Cockatrice,
  The Drunkard to the Vine,
The Beggar to the Bush, there meet,
  And with Duke Humphrey dine.

The names of English inns for a long time kept alive memories of hunting and heraldry and old trades; but the original names became blurred and distorted, and the incongruous results, as well as the habit of anglicising foreign names, were critically examined by Addison in an early number of the *Spectator* (April 2nd, 1711). "Our streets," he wrote, "are filled with blue boars, black swans, and red lions, not to mention flying pigs, and hogs in armour, with many other creatures more extraordinary than any in the deserts of Africa. Strange! that one who has all the birds and beasts in Nature to choose out of should live at the sign of an *ens rationis*!

"My first task therefore should be, like that of Hercules, to clear the city from monsters. In the second place, I would forbid that creatures of jarring and incongruous natures should be joined together in the same sign, such as the Bell and the Neat's Tongue, the Dog and Gridiron. The Fox and Goose may be supposed to have met, but what has the Fox and the Seven Stars to do together? And when did the Lamb and Dolphin ever meet except upon a sign-post? As for the Cat and Fiddle, there is a conceit in it, and therefore I do not intend that anything I have here said should affect it. I must, however, observe to you upon this subject, that it is usual for a young tradesman, at his first setting up, to add to his own sign that of the master whom he served; as the husband, after marriage, gives a place to his mistress's arms in his own coat. This I take to have given rise to many of those absurdities which are committed over our heads, and, as I am informed, first occasioned the Three Nuns and a Hare, which we see so frequently joined together. I would therefore establish certain rules for the determining how far one tradesman may give the sign of another, and in what cases he may be allowed to quarter it with his own.

" In the third place, I would enjoin every shop to make use of a sign which bears some affinity to the wares in which it deals. What can be more inconsistent than to see a bawd at the sign of the Angel, or a tailor at the Lion? A cook should not live at the Boot, nor a shoemaker at the Roasted Pig; and yet, for want of this regulation, I have seen a goat set up before the door of a perfumer, and the French king's head at a sword cutler's.

" An ingenious foreigner observes that several of those gentlemen who value themselves upon their families, and over-look such as are bred to trade, bear the tools of their fore-fathers in their coats of arms. I will not examine how true this is in fact; but though it may not be necessary for posterity thus to set up the sign of their forefathers, I think it highly proper for those who actually profess the trade, to show some such marks of it before their doors."

A most appropriate tradesman's sign was that of Hugh Granger, a London cabinet-maker, who conducted his business during the late 17th and early 18th centuries, at " The Carved Angell " in Aldermanbury.(141) Thomas Chippendale's business was carried on at 60, St. Martin's Lane, London, at the sign of " The Chair ".

Addison's complaint about the odd inconsistency of some signs and the strange associations of objects they included had

A Country Inn Yard by William Hogarth

been anticipated a year earlier by an anonymous writer in
The British Apollo, in the following doggerel :

> I'm amazed at the Signs
> As I pass through the Town,
> To see the odd mixture :
> A Magpie and Crown,
> The Whale and the Crow,
> The Razor and Hen,
> The Leg and Seven Stars,
> The Axe and the Bottle,
> The Tun and the Lute,
> The Eagle and Child,
> The Shovel and Boot.

That observant English traveller and writer, Fynes Moryson
(1566–1630), published in 1617 a large work on his journeyings
about Europe, entitled *An Itinerary*, that included a passage
about English inns, which accords with William Harrison's
views about the welcome and comfort they provided. He
wrote : "I have heard some Germans complaine of the
English Innes by the high way, as well for dearenesse as for
that they had onely roasted meates : but these Germans,
landing at Gravesend, perhaps were injured by those knaves
that flocke thither onely to deceive strangers, and use Englishmen no better, and after went from thence to London, and
were there entertained by some ordinary Hosts of strangers,
returning home little acquainted with English customes. But
if these strangers had knowne the English tongue, or had had
an honest guide in their journies, and had knowne to live at
Rome after the Roman fashion (which they seldome doe, using
rather Dutch Innes and companions), surely they should have
found that the World affoords not such Innes as England hath,
either for good and cheape entertainement after the Guests owne
pleasure, or for humble attendance on passengers ; yea, even
in very poore villages. . . . For assoone as a passenger comes
to an Inne, the servants run to him, and one takes his horse
and walkes him till he be cold, then rubs him and gives him
meate, yet I must say that they are not much to be trusted in
this last point, without the eye of the Master or his servant to
oversee them. Another servant gives the passenger his private
chamber, and kindles his fier, the third puls of his bootes and

The Talbot Inn, Borough High Street, Southwark, as it appeared in the early 19th century. (From *The Gentleman's Magazine*, September, 1812)

makes them cleane. Then the Host or Hostesse visits him, and if he will eate with the Host, or at a common table with others, his meale will cost him sixe pence, or in some places but foure pence (yet this course is lesse honourable, and not used by Gentlemen) ; but if he will eate in his chamber, he commands what meate he will according to his appetite, and as much as he thinkes fit for him and his company, yea, the kitchin is open to him, to command the meat to be dressed as he best likes ; and when he sits at Table, the Host or Hostesse will accompany him, or if they have many Guests, will at least visit him, taking it for curtesie to be bid sit downe : while he eates, if he have company especially, he shall be offred musicke, which he may freely take or refuse, and if he be solitary, the musitians will give him the good day with musicke in the morning. It is the custome and no way disgracefull to set up part of supper for his breakfast. In the evening or in the morning after breakfast (for the common sort use not to dine, but ride from breakefast to supper time, yet comming early to the Inne for better resting of their Horses) he shall have a reckoning in writing, and if it seeme unreasonable, the Host will satisfie him either for the due price, or by abating part, especially if the servant deceive him any way, which one of experience will soone find. . . . I will now onely adde, that a Gentleman and his Man shall spend as much as if he were accompanied with another Gentleman and his Man, and if Gentlemen will in such sort joyne together to eate at one Table, the expences will be much diminished. Lastly, a Man cannot more freely command at home in his owne House, then hee may doe in his Inne, and at parting if he give some few pence to the Chamberlin and Ostler, they wish him a happy journey."(142)

Harrison has in two sentences described the well-appointed inn, when he said : " Our Innes are also very well furnished with naperie, bedding and tapestrie, especially naperie : for beside the linen used at the tables, which is commonly washed daily, is such and so much as belongeth unto the estate and calling of the guest. Each commer is sure to lie in clean sheets, wherein no man hath been lodged since they came from the laundry, or out of the water wherein they were last washed." (143)

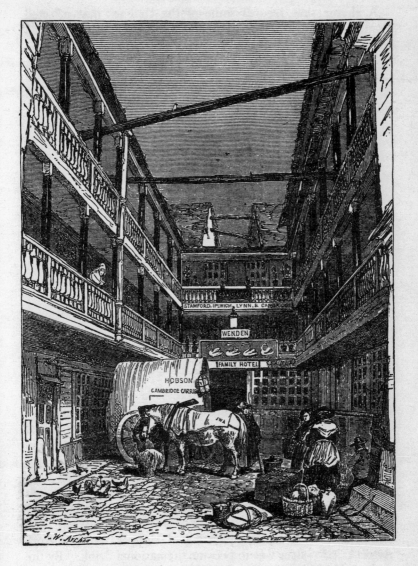

The Four Swans inn-yard, Bishopsgate Street Within, in the mid-19th century. A double row of bedroom galleries overlooks the yard, and the general character of the building resembles the country inn by Hogarth on page 223, and the Talbot, on page 225. The form goes back to the 16th century

A rhyme that records some of the changes that affected English life in the 16th century, and which particularly affected the life of the inn, is quoted in Stowe's *Annales*, and runs thus :

> Turkeys, Carpes, Hops : Piccarels, and beere,
> Came into England : all in one yeere.

Another version runs thus :

> Hops, reformation, bays, and beer,
> Came into England all in one year.

Yet another variation of the first line is :

> Hops, heresy, turkeys and beer . . .

All these versions suggest that the use of hops introduced the name of beer, to distinguish it from ale, the old and softer malt liquor. Thomas Tusser, whose *Five Hundred points of good husbandry* has been quoted in Chapter XVI, said in praise of the hop :

> The hop for his profit I thus do exalt,
> It strengtheneth drink and it flavoureth malt ;
> And being well brewed, long kept it will last,
> And drawing abide, if ye draw not too fast.

Shakespeare's reference to turkeys in the first part of Henry IV anticipates their introduction, which occurred over a century after the death of that monarch. In Scene I of Act II, one of the carriers says : " God's body ! the turkeys in my pannier are quite starved."

Turkeys, Stow tells us, were called " Guyney cockes " by all other nations, and were " generally said to bee brought into England between the tenth, and fifteenth year of Henry the eight " ; and about the same time, that is between 1518 and 1524, " came in the planting of Hoppes, brought from Artois . . ." Beer was to become the national drink. By the end of the 16th century, the last vestiges of the old English wine-growing industry had disappeared. Harrison reminds us that the Isle of Ely in Cambridgeshire was in Norman times called *Le Ile des vignes*, and that the bishop there " had yearlie three or four tunne at the least given him, *Nomine*

The George Inn, Southwark, drawn by A. S. Cook. In
many inns, two or three centuries of building were melted
into an harmonious structure, which might incorporate
Tudor half-timbered work, brick, weather-boarding or
plaster, open galleries and the orderly sash windows of the
Georgian period

decimoe, beside whatsoever over-summe of the liquor did accrue to him by leases and other excheats . . ." He pointed out that " our soil is not to be blamed " for the neglect and disappearance of the English vineyards.(144) He had referred to " the old notes of tithes for wine that yet remain in the accounts of some parsons and vicars in Kent " and to the records of " sundrie suits commenced in divers ecclesiastical courts, both in Kent [and] Surrey, also the enclosed parcels almost in every abbey, yet called the vineyards . . ."

The vineyards had been characteristic of the great monastic establishments of the Middle Ages : and wine was produced in great quantity, chiefly white : but the art of tending vines was lost, most probably after the dissolution of the monasteries and the dispersal of the monks who had mastered the art.(145) Some localities like Norfolk may have continued wine-growing during the 16th century.(146) That Norfolk at one time produced a great deal of wine, is attested by the survival of the names Vineyard and Vineyard Street, which occur in many towns and villages in that county, recalling the existence of a big but now utterly forgotten home industry.

Many other sites have thus been marked by name, even in London. At the beginning of the 19th century, John Lockie recorded in his *Topography of London* (1810) a Vineyard near Drury Lane, which was losing its identity and becoming part of Wooburn Street ; another Vineyard at Tooley Street " at 110, about ⅓ of a mile on the left from London Bridge " ; also Vineyard Gardens and Vineyard Walk in Clerkenwell. The home-grown wines could not compete with imports ; and at this distance of time it is impossible even to conjecture what those English white wines were like. No attempt was made to encourage or preserve the home industry, although from the early years of Elizabeth's reign until the end of it one of the chief objects of official policy was to reduce imports of luxuries, like wines and rich cloths.(147)

The importation of foreign wines began over two thousand years ago, before Britain was a Roman province. Those tall, two-handled jars called amphorae, in which wine was brought over from Europe, have been found in such large quantities that the wine-trade with the Roman Empire must have been considerable.(148) In the 3rd century, the Emperor Probus gave permission for vines to be planted in Gaul, Spain and Britain; the first vineyards in this country date from that time, " and a quantity of vine-stems have actually been found near a villa in Hertfordshire, on a sheltered south-western slope ".(149) Bede writing in the 8th century stated that the country " produces vines in some places ", and home-grown wines were abundant before and at the time of the Norman Conquest, though shortly after that event foreign wines were again introduced, and imports increased throughout the Middle Ages. Although wine-growing as an industry ended after the 16th century, vineyards continued to flourish in some localities ; directions for tending them and for wine-making were included in such popular works as *A Dictionary of Husbandry, Gardening, Trade, Commerce and all sorts of Country Affairs*, which went into its second, enlarged edition in 1717 ; and at the beginning of the 18th century, English wine was still being made, though it was not the white wine that had come from the vineyards of mediaeval monasteries. J. C. Loudon records that a vineyard at Hammersmith " produced annually a considerable quantity of Burgundy wine " in the early years of the 18th century,(150) and during that century sporadic attempts were made to revive the culture. " Thus, one of the dukes of Norfolk made from a vineyard at Arundel Castle, a considerable quantity of wine, which is said to have much excelled Burgundy ; of which there are stated to have been in the cellars of the castle, sixty pipes in the year 1763. At Chart Park, near Dorking, in Surrey, was a similar vineyard ; and upon the house being taken down about twenty years since, we saw there a circular stone resembling that used in a mill, by which the grapes were pressed. In the Isle of Wight an experimental vineyard was planted about fifty years since, but with little success ; and another vineyard at Painshill, is said to have been equally unproductive."(151) This particular reference was made in 1835.

These experiments in wine culture were sponsored by the enthusiasms of a few landlords ; but in the countryside all kinds of wines were made from flowers and herbs, roots and berries. Recipes for cowslip and elderberry wine have been in use for a very long time, and are included in the *Dictionary of Husbandry* ; and among other home-made wines are currant, damson, dandelion, gooseberry, parsnip, raspberry and rhubarb. Many of these wines can be made dry or sweet, and their character and potency determined by the amount of sugar used : for example, some parsnip wine may have the quality of a mild hock, and despite its deceptive gentleness, can be about three times as potent.

Although foreign wines were supplied in inns, beer was the basic drink, and the humbler inns that served the rustic population were called ale-houses. Beer was also brewed at home, and up to the end of the 18th century, as Cobbett said, " to have a house and not to brew was a rare thing indeed ".(152) In his *Cottage Economy*, which was issued in six parts between August 1st, 1821 and January 1st, 1822, Cobbett gave detailed directions for brewing beer. They were preceded by a ferocious attack on tea, and some uncomplimentary remarks about brewers and the public houses they owned. He asserted that " tea drinking fills the public house, makes the frequenting of it habitual, corrupts boys as soon as they are able to move from home, and does little less for the girls to whom the gossip of the tea table is no bad preparatory school for the brothel ".

He advocated the use of a brewing machine, and in Part 2 of *Cottage Economy* he included a plate of the appliance, being careful to explain that he had " no *private interest*, direct, or indirect, in the success of the proprietor of this Machine. I bought mine at the recommendation of a gentleman, who has long had a *six-bushel* one, and who gave me some beer, of different strengths and age, that he had made with it. In pointing out the many and great advantages of the Machine, I have solely the public good in view ; and, if I were to-morrow, to discover, or to hear of, any thing preferable to this Machine for accomplishing the same ends, I should undoubtedly hasten to communicate the discovery to my readers. The Patentee has, of course, furnished the *Plate* and paid for the *advertizing* of his prices, on which advertizing I myself *pay a tax*. He has reduced the prices, I believe, in consequence of representations made to me by several persons, and with the substance of which representations I made him acquainted."(153)

At the very end of Part 6, he abruptly announces that the brewing machine is no good. " Having, in the former Numbers, spoken of *brewing-machines*, I cannot conclude my

Work without stating, that further experience has induced me to resolve to *discontinue* the use of all sorts of brewing machines, and to use *the old sort of utensils*." Whether the patentee of the machine got his money back for the advertisement which Cobbett had published, is not disclosed.(154)

From mediaeval times down to the present day, ale and beer are mentioned with affection, and the word *ale* is associated with various feasts. For example, " *bridal*, or *bride-ale*, is the feast in honour of the bride, or marriage ; *leet-ale* denoted the dinner at a court leet of a manor, for the jury and customary tenants. *Lamb-ale* was the annual feast at lamb-shearing ; *Whitsun-ales* were the sports and feast of Whitsuntide. The *Church-ale* was a festival for the repairs of the church, and in honour of the church saint, when the people went from after-noon service on Sundays to their lawful sports and pastimes in the churchyard, or in the neighbourhood, or in some public-house, where they drank, and made merry : and by the benevolence of the people at these pastimes, many poor parishes cast their bells, beautified their churches, and raised stock for their poor. *Clerk-ales* were for the better maintenance of the parish-clerk, who, in poor parishes, being but ill paid, the people sent him in provisions, and then came on Sundays, and feasted with him : by which means, the clerk sold more ale, and tasted more of the liberality of the parishioners than their payments would have amounted to in many years.

" A *Bid-ale* was when a poor decayed housekeeper was set up again by the generosity of his friends at a Sunday feast. The people delighted in all these recreations, and the bishop recom-mended them, as bringing the people more willingly to church, as tending to civilize them, to compose differences among them, and to increase love and unity. But the justices of the peace complained that evil-minded persons perverted these merry meetings into profanation of the Lord's day, riotous tippling, quarrels, murders, &c. : they prayed that they might be discontinued. . . ."(155)

These festivals progressively degenerated, until they were little better than orgies, and the churchyard was obviously no place for them, so they were held on the village green or the main street of the town. Far better order was kept at inns : landlords as a class were against orgies, and seldom had to cope with them so long as their guests stuck to ale, "Good ale, the true and proper drink of Englishmen", as George Borrow declared, adding : "He is not deserving of the name of Englishman who speaketh against ale."

An old proverb in praise of ale runs thus :

He that buys land buys many stones,
He that buys flesh buys many bones,
He that buys eggs buys many shells,
But he that buys good ale buys nothing else.

Enormous quantities of ale were consumed, and it was estimated in 1688 that 12,400,000 barrels were brewed in England in a single year, when the population of the country hardly exceeded five millions. Cobbett, writing 134 years later, assumed that a cottager's family would drink ten gallons of beer weekly.(156)   Until about 1730, the chief malt liquors were ale, beer, and twopenny, which was ale sold at twopence a quart, and they were usually mixed—like old and mild or mild and bitter today. A tankard of "half and half" was a mixture of ale and beer, or beer and twopenny. According to *Domestic Life in England*, "It next became customary to call for *three threads*, meaning a third of ale, of beer, and of twopenny, and thus, the publican had to go to three casks, and often to turn three cocks for a pint of liquor. To avoid this inconvenience and waste, a brewer named Harwood invented a liquor which should partake of the united flavour of ale, beer, and twopenny ; this he called entire, or entire butt ; and, as it was a strengthening drink, it was much drunk for porters and other working people ; whence its name *Porter*."(157)

It was also appreciated by those whose work was neither strenuous nor exacting. In *Martin Chuzzlewit*, Mrs. Gamp remarks that "my half a pint of porter fully satisfies ; perwisin', Mrs. Harris, that it is brought reg'lar, and draw'd mild". There is a story, possibly apocryphal, that Mrs. Siddons after sending for some refreshment during a rehearsal, reproved the messenger by exclaiming : "I asked for porter, boy : thou hast brought me beer ! "

Published in 1835, *Domestic Life in England* records that in 1830 some 8,000,000 barrels of beer were brewed yearly, of which four-fifths were strong beer. This was less than in 1688,

Gin Lane by William Hogarth. The lettering on the arch
to the cellar reads : "Drunk for a Penny. Dead drunk for
two pence. Clean straw for nothing."

although the population had risen to about 9,000,000 in the
interval. During that time ale and beer had a serious rival ;
for in the early part of the 18th century a taste for gin drinking
grew so rapidly that the English nearly became a nation of
drunkards. The most shameful advertisement ever displayed
in England was "Drunk for a penny. Dead drunk for two-

(235)

pence. Clean straw for nothing." The gin shop was a travesty of the inn—a vile place, with dismal and filthy cellars, strewn with straw, into which the customers who had spent twopence were dragged to sleep off the effects. This vice enormously increased poverty, crime and disease, and thousands of men and women were bloated with dropsy. "The average of British spirits distilled, which is said to have been only 527,000 gallons in 1684, and 2,000,000 in 1714, had risen in 1727 to 3,601,000, and in 1735 to 5,394,000 gallons. Physicians declared that in excessive gin-drinking a new and terrible source of mortality had been opened for the poor. The grand jury of Middlesex, in a powerful presentment declared that much the greater part of the poverty, the murders, the robberies of London, might be traced to this single cause."(158)

In "Beer Street" and "Gin Lane", Hogarth depicted the contrast between the sound, nourishing, traditional drink, and the debilitating spirit that was called in the slang of the time "Strip-me-naked", for in order to buy gin, men and women parted with all they possessed and reduced themselves to the bitterest poverty. London and other cities had not then acquired the appalling slums that could give such sad conviction to the drunkard's remark that "Gin was the nearest way out of Whitechapel". Hogarth's two prints were issued in 1751, and in that year Fielding published a pamphlet, entitled *An Inquiry into the causes of the late increase of robbers, &c., with some proposals for remedying the growing evil*, in which he blamed "a new kind of drunkenness, unknown to our ancestors", and stated his belief that gin was "the principal sustenance (if it may so be called) of more than 100,000 people in the metropolis . . ." Stringent legislation was introduced to restrict the distilling and sale of gin ; and after the middle of the 18th century, the evil diminished, but although unlicensed dealers still kept a black market alive, the penalties were severe, and it was a hazardous rather than a flourishing business. But the "barrow boys" have always been with us, and their boldness in peddling gin was the subject of a news paragraph in *The General Evening Post*, London (No. 478), dated October 21st, 1736. "Notwithstanding the Diligence of the Magistracy in putting the late Act against retailing of Spirituous Liquors in force, the People are so madly fond of it, that it

Beer Street by William Hogarth

was sold publickly on the Road at Horn-Fair, by People with Wheelbarrows, Baskets, &c." The report added : "The Benefit of the aforesaid Act begins to be felt already in the Suburbs and Out-parts of the Town, where some Bakers vend (at least) one third more of Bread than they did before the Commencement thereof. The People will have it, according to the Adage, in Meal or in Malt."

Beer was reinstated, and the "British Burgundy", as it

was sometimes called, remained unchallenged as the national drink.

Love of good, simple food and drink has characterised English taste from the Middle Ages until the end of the 19th century : in the oldest English book on hunting, *The Master of Game*, written between 1406 and 1413 by Edward, the second Duke of York, the hunter is advised to " order well his supper, with wortes [roots] and of the neck of the hart and of other good meats, and good wine or ale ". Old Brooke in *Tom Brown's Schooldays* deplores " fuddling about in the public-house, and drinking bad spirits, and punch, and such rot-gut stuff ", and reminds his audience of hero-worshippers that " you get plenty of good beer here, and that's enough for you . . ."

During the 16th and 17th centuries, ale and beer were drunk by all classes ; though Fynes Moryson's *Itinerary* records that " Cownes and vulgar men onely use large drinking of Beere or Ale, how much soever it is esteemed excellent drinke even among strangers ; but gentlemen garrawse onely in Wine . . ." (159) A mid-16th-century French observer, Estienne Perlin, in his *Description d'Angleterre* (1558), noted that the English " consume great quantities of beer, double and single [strong and small], and do not drink it out of glasses, but from earthen pots with silver handles and covers, and this even in houses of persons of middling fortune ; for as to the poor, the covers of their pots are merely pewter, and in some places, such as villages, their beer pots are made only of wood. With their beer they have a custom of eating very soft saffron cakes, in which there are likewise raisins, which give an excellent relish to the beer . . ."(160)

Harrison mentions " pots of earth of sundrie colours and moulds, whereof many are garnished with silver, or at the leastwise in pewter ".(161) Pewter, which is an alloy of tin and lead, with tin forming about four-fifths of the composition, was known as early as the 11th century, and the pewterer's craft was an important one in mediaeval times. By the 16th century, the material was used for plates and tankards and spoons. Inns would have a big range of pewter pots, from the pottle—which held four pints—to the gill. Many drinking vessels were made of wood—elm, boxwood or holly ; leather was used too, and black leather pitchers, tipped with silver or pewter, were called jacks—the use of large black jacks or bombards not only in inns but in the great houses of noblemen and even at court, caused some foreigners to say that the English drank out of their boots.(162) The smallest type of wooden vessel, that contained a dram for one person, was called a noggin. During the 17th and 18th centuries glass came into general use, but pewter and wood were still commonly used in inns and cottages and farm-houses. "Anything," wrote Cobbett, "is better than crockery ware." He believed that a cottager's " plates, dishes, mugs, and things of that kind, should be of *pewter*, or even of wood ". He added : " As to *glass* of any sort, I do not know what business it has in any man's house, unless he be rich enough to live on his means."(163)

There was much to recommend the pewter tankard and mug, for at the inn and particularly the ale-house they often got rough usage. Travellers on coaches would order a pint or so of beer, which was handed up to them as the stage coach halted at an inn for the horses to be changed, and the mugs would be thrown down as the coach drove off, if the waiter was not spry enough to collect the empties. The dented mugs were restored to their proper shape by means of a wooden stretcher, that was inserted in the battered vessel, and expanded by means of a pair of handles, so that the mug was pressed back into its proper shape from within. Manners were rough, coaches were as punctual as clocks could make them and waited for nobody, and the scene Marryat described in the second chapter of *Peter Simple* of the drunken sailor returning to Portsmouth as an outside passenger was probably not overdrawn. " Whenever the coach stopped, the sailor called for more ale, and always threw the remainder which he could not drink into the face of the man who brought it out for him, just as the coach was starting off, and then tossed the pewter pot on the ground for him to pick up." In their journey to Rochester, Mr. Pickwick and his companions listened to the anecdotes of Jingle, " with an occasional glass of ale, by way of parenthesis, when the coach changed horses . . ."

The punctuality of the mail coaches during the century before the coming of the railways was proverbial ; Englishmen could rely on their timing, in hard weather or fine. The inns that served the coaches usually ran large stables and let out chaises and other vehicles for hire, and they displayed a characteristic time-piece, that is often wrongly called an act of parliament clock. This name for the typical coaching-inn clock, or tavern clock, is based on the belief that such clocks were introduced and used generally by innkeepers after Pitt's Act of 1797 (which taxed watches and clocks), presumably for the convenience of customers. But these large, plain, weight-driven mural clocks, with a big wooden dial usually japanned black with gilt numerals on it, and a short trunk or case below, were in use at the coaching inns from the middle of the 18th century, when the mail coaches began to run on fixed time-tables. Every stop was timed.

" ' Twenty minutes here, gentlemen,' said the coachman, as they pull up at half-past seven at the inn door." Twenty minutes for breakfast during Tom Brown's journey on the outside of the Tally-ho coach from the Peacock at Islington to Rugby. And what a breakfast, served in a "low, dark wainscoted room hung with sporting prints ; the hat-stand (with a whip or two standing up in it belonging to bagmen who are still snug in bed) by the door ; the blazing fire, with the quaint old glass over the mantelpiece, in which is stuck a large card with the list of the meets for the week of the county hounds ; the table covered with the whitest of cloths and of china, and bearing a pigeon-pie, ham, round of cold boiled beef cut from a mammoth ox, and the great loaf of household bread on a wooden trencher. And here comes in the stout head waiter, puffing under a tray of hot viands—kidneys and a steak, transparent rashers and poached eggs, buttered toast and muffins, coffee and tea, all smoking hot. The table can never hold it all. The cold meats are removed to the side-board—they were only put on for show and to give us an appetite. And now fall on, gentleman all. It is a well-known sporting-house, and the breakfasts are famous. Two or three men in pink, on their way to the meet, drop in, and are very jovial and sharp-set, as indeed we all are."(164)

Thomas Hughes wrote *Tom Brown's Schooldays* during the eighteen-fifties, and it was published in 1857, when the stage coach was already becoming a memory, the roadside inns and

The stage coach arrives at a country town : the scene might be from *Tom Brown's Schooldays* or *Pickwick Papers*

post houses had lost the customers the through traffic had brought, and the highway, save for a little local traffic, was deserted.

Food, drink and accommodation were to be had not only at the great coaching inns, but at the better class of village ale-house. Mr. Tupman, when he retired to the Leather Bottle at Cobham, to recover from being jilted by Rachael Wardle, did very well at that " clean and commodious village ale house ", as his three friends found when they " entered a long, low-roofed room, furnished with a large number of high-backed leather-cushioned chairs, of fantastic shapes, and embellished with a great variety of old portraits and roughly-coloured prints of some antiquity. At the upper end of the room was a table, with a white cloth upon it, well covered with a roast fowl, bacon, ale, and et ceteras. . . ."

Something quite as important as food and drink was pro-vided by inns during and after the 17th century, for tobacco was introduced into Europe about 1560, and was being culti-vated in England ten years later. It was sold at first by druggists, who also sold pipes—Winchester pipes, they were called—and maple blocks upon which tobacco could be cut or shredded. Face, the housekeeper in Ben Jonson's play *The Alchemist*, describes the stock-in-trade of Abel Drugger, in these lines :

> He shall do any thing.—Doctor, do you hear !
> This is my friend, Abel, an honest fellow ;
> He lets me have good tobacco, and he does not
> Sophisticate it with sack-lees or oil,
> Nor washes it in muscadel and grains,
> Nor buries it in gravel, under ground,
> Wrapp'd up in greasy leather, or piss'd clouts ;
> But keeps it in fine lily pots, that, open'd,
> Smell like conserve of roses, or French beans.
> He has his maple block, his silver tongs,
> Winchester pipes, and fire of Juniper. . . .

Juniper wood was used for making charcoal fires, and pieces of glowing charcoal were lifted with silver tongs to light a customer's pipe. Ursula, the pig-woman, in Ben Jonson's *Bartholomew Fair*, mentions both the price and the adulteration of tobacco, when she says : " Three-pence a pipe-full, I will have made, of all my whole half-pound of tobacco, and a quarter of a pound of colt's-foot mixt with it too, to eke it out " (Act II, Scene I). In the same play, Humphrey Waspe says : " I thought he would have run mad o' the black boy in Bucklersbury, that takes the scurvy, roguy tobacco there " (Act I, Scene I). The Black Boy was the tobacconists' trade sign, and remained so for generations. An inventory of the goods of Daniell Bridges of Drury Lane, a grocer, dated February 26th, 1724/5, includes the item : " 2 black boys, 3s.", as well as various quantities of tobacco and snuff.(165)

The figure of a kilted Highlander used to be a popular snuff-shop sign ; and other figures used by tobacco dealers included the Sailor and the Moor or Oriental.(166) In the United States, the figure of a Red Indian, with a handful of cigars, was usually displayed outside a tobacco store, and this may have been suggested by the much older figure of a Moor.

Three centuries ago we grew our own tobacco, but the English tobacco industry was deliberately suppressed during the 17th century, because it competed with the Virginian plantation monopoly. Despite official discouragement the home industry persisted for a hundred years. From the first record of the cultivation of tobacco in England, in Lobel's *Stirpium Adversaria Nova*, published in London in 1570, to the experiments in planting that were begun in 1910 by Colonel Brandon of Church Crookham in Hampshire, English growers have proved their ability to produce good tobacco crops. Both James I and Charles I made tobacco a royal monopoly, and instructed their troops to trample down any secretly-grown crops they might find. But planting was impossible to suppress, for it paid handsomely, and no government, royalist or puritan, could curb the lawless enterprise of the English growers. For example, " in Gloucestershire the whole region prospered : sheriffs, magistrates, and squires, as well as the common farmers, were involved in cultivation—which, of course, added to the difficulties of putting it down. Crime decreased as the people prospered, and, as an anonymous pamphleteer complains, there was no work for the hangman, since sheep-stealing declined as the plantations flourished."(167) But the law extinguished planting after the end of the 17th century ; and, apart from some illicit crops raised in Yorkshire during the reign of George III, for two hundred years there is no record of any tobacco having been grown in the British Isles.

Occasionally some protest was made, and the fact that good tobacco crops could be raised in England was not easily forgotten. Thomas Mun, a London merchant, wrote an economic treatise called *England's Treasure by Foreign Trade*, which was published in 1664, in which he advocated the raising of tobacco, for, as he said, " although this Realm be already exceeding rich by nature, yet might it be much encreased by laying the waste grounds (which are infinite) into such employments as should no way hinder the present revenues of other manured lands, but hereby to supply our selves and prevent the importations of Hemp, Flax, Cordage, Tobacco, and divers other things which we now fetch from strangers to our great impoverishing ". Two hundred and eighty-seven years later, Mr. Ronald Duncan, in his book, *Tobacco Cultivation in England*, pointed out that " there are over 2,000,000 acres in England still derelict, still growing nothing, and of these at least 70% could grow tobacco ".(168) Restrictions on planting tobacco in England and Scotland were removed in 1909, subject to planters being licensed and paying excise duty. In 1913 the British Tobacco Growers' Society was formed, and cultivation was carried on until 1920, when its prosperity was ended by imperial preference and the importation of Dominion tobaccos. Since then tobacco-planting has continued on a small scale, and with modest success. In the spring of 1948 the Government made a concession which allowed individual growers to raise a few plants, free of duty, for their own consumption. The man who smokes 1 ounce of tobacco, or 20 cigarettes, a day, needs only 220 plants to cover this consumption at a cost of approximately twopence, exclusive of the cost of his labour. (Such figures are apt to fire productive and perhaps revolutionary trains of thought.)

The suppression of the home industry made no difference to the spread of the tobacco habit, and smoking was one of the few pleasures in life that was not denounced and prohibited by the Puritan government in the mid-17th century. Evelyn, describing the funeral of Oliver Cromwell, said " it was the joyfullest funerall I ever saw, for there were none that cried but dogs, which the soldiers hooted away with a barbarous noise, drinking and taking tobacco in the streets as they went ".(169)

Smoking became increasingly popular with all classes during the 17th century save that small, exclusive, vivacious clique that adorned the court after the Restoration. Full wigs and the ornate clothes that marked the joyful reaction from Puritan austerity imposed a certain foppish neatness, a stately carriage that made pipe-smoking seem incongruous ; also those flowing wigs would have held the smell of tobacco. But men of fashion used tobacco in the form of snuff, which allowed an infinity of elegant and decorative gestures to be cultivated, and gave jewellers and goldsmiths opportunities for designing exquisite receptacles.

Pipes had no such ornamental pretensions ; they became foul in use, and from the first gave offence to ladies : John Aubrey mentions that when Sir Walter Raleigh took a pipe of tobacco when he was in a stand at the park of Sir Robert Poyntz at Acton (which, as Aubrey said in his frank way, had been built by Sir Robert's grandfather " to keep his whores in ") all the ladies present left, until he had finished smoking. Aubrey also records, on the authority of his grandfather, Lyte, that the first pipes were made of silver, and the commoner sort of a walnut shell and a straw, and that they were smoked in a communal way, being handed round from man to man. Clay was a far more satisfactory material for pipes than metal or straw ; and towards the end of the 17th century a long-stemmed clay pipe, with a glazed mouthpiece, was introduced, and was known as an " alderman ". The " churchwarden " or " yard of clay " had a much longer stem, and according to G. L. Apperson, the author of *The Social History of Smoking*, did not come into general use until the early 19th century ; though contemporary engravings occasionally show the long " churchwarden " type of clay in use during the previous century.(170)

The social importance of tobacco has been emphasised by J. B. S. Haldane, who believes that its use " has slight but definite effects upon the character " and that the London coffee-houses of the 17th and 18th centuries " and cafés in modern Europe were and are civilising influences of incalculable value ".(171)   Addison's description of the cheerful friendliness of smokers is familiar.   In the *Spectator*, for July 16th, 1714, he writes : "I was yesterday in a coffee-house not far from the Royal Exchange, where I observed three persons in close conference over a pipe of tobacco ; upon which, having filled one for my own use, I lighted it at the little wax candle that stood before them ; and after having thrown in two or three whiffs amongst them, sat down and made one of the company.   I need not tell my reader, that lighting a man's pipe at the same candle is looked upon among brother-smokers as an overture to conversation and friendship."

Early in the 19th century, Thomas de Quincey, reflecting upon the soothing and civilising influence of tobacco, wrote that " Many a wild fellow in Rome, your Gracchi, Syllas, Catilines, would not have played ' h—— and Tommy ' in the way they did, if they could have soothed their angry stomachs with a cigar : a pipe has intercepted many an evil scheme." But for the first three centuries after its establishment as a social habit, tobacco smoking in any form aroused the almost universal hostility of ladies.   In Vanbrugh's play, *The Provoked Wife*, which was first acted and published in 1697, Lady Brute and her niece, Belinda, agree to tease Sir John Brute, who is sitting with them and smoking.   When Belinda says that she should especially dislike a husband who smoked tobacco, Lady Brute replies : " Why, that, many times, takes off worse smells."

Belinda.   Then he must smell very ill indeed.
Lady B.   So some men will, to keep their wives from coming near them.
Belinda.   Then those wives should cuckold them at a distance.

(*Sir John runs in a fury, throws his pipe at them, and drives them out, crying :*) Oons ! get you gone up stairs, you confederating strumpets you, or I'll cuckold you with a vengeance !
(Act III, Scene I.)

An engraving of this scene, made in 1776, portrays Garrick in the part of Sir John Brute, and the pipe he is just about to throw at his tormentors is a clay with a long, straight stem. Although smoking was unpopular in the home until the end

Act III.   The PROVOK'D WIFE.   Scene I.

MR GARRICK in the Character of SR JOHN BRUTE.

'Oons, get you up Stairs, you confederating Strumpets you, or I'll cuckold you with a Vengeance.

From an engraving made in 1776

(247)

of the Victorian period, and men had their special smoking rooms, their smoking jackets and their smoking caps, so that the smell of tobacco should not cling to their clothes or their hair, the coffee-house and particularly the inn were places where the pipe-smoker was always able to indulge his taste. Celia Fiennes travelling from Newcastle to Cornwall in 1698 spent a night at an inn in St. Austell, where she was " much pleased with " her supper, " tho' not with the custome of the country, which is a universal smoaking both men women and children have all their pipes of tobacco in their mouths and soe sit round the fire smoaking, which was not delightful to me when I went down to talke with my Landlady . . ."(172) This was the typical reaction of the gentlewoman, whose menfolk, unlike Sir John Brute, would not have smoked in the presence of ladies. Smoking was periodically unfashionable with the nobility and gentry, though it always remained in favour with the majority of the population. The Hon. John Byng, who became the fifth Viscount Torrington, when he stayed at an inn in the Cotswolds in 1785, mentions that he smoked a pipe after dinner, but added that " this sport has been decaying . . ."(173)

The habit of smoking was always being revived, and early in the 19th century cigars restored it to favour ; this particular revival was due probably to the experiences of British officers during the Peninsula War, for cigar smoking was common in Spain and Portugal.(174) During the eighteen-twenties a special type of accommodation for cigar smokers was introduced, and became fashionable and popular under the name of a cigar divan. The origin of such divans is described in a satirical book, published anonymously in 1827 under the title of *Every Night Book, or Life After Dark*—an obvious jibe at William Hone's *Every-day Book*, which had appeared a year earlier. After giving twelve golden rules for smokers, the author describes the original cigar divan as follows : " In the month of February, 1825, Mr. Gliddon, a man well known as a choice collector and retailer of rare snuffs, and noticed by Blackwood as generally having the best cigars in the market, opened a very elegant Cigarium at the back of his shop in King Street, Covent Garden. The Divan, for so he called it, by the beauty and taste of its fittings up, the comfort it afforded, the excellence of the cigars purveyed, its central situation, ' the fine drinks, and warmth, and quiet, and literature '—for its tables were covered with papers, periodicals, and standard works of piquancy—fully merited, and soon obtained popularity. Two others were afterward set up, one in Catherine Street, and the other near the Temple Gate ; but they were by no means equal to the original, which was, in fact, a little paradise to the smoking lounger. The walls were handsomely draperied ; but in this particular an alteration has taken place, it being found that the cloth, or whatever material was used for the purpose, held the smoke. In other respects, as well as we remember, the Divan looks nearly as it did when it was first opened. Filthy gas, the fumes of which would pollute the pure Havannah atmosphere of the place, has been wisely excluded, and handsome ground-glass lamps, in which oil of fine quality only is burnt, are used ; they shed a rich, mellow, subdued light, which is far more pleasant than candles could afford ; and, what is more material, they are void of offence to the choicest nostril. Here a man may smoke in luxury, obtain a cup of capital coffee, and feed his curiosity with the tattle of the day from the best publications. The company may be described as a pleasant, gentlemanly miscellany— ' theatre-goers, officers who have learnt to love a cigar on service, men of letters, and men of fortune, who have a taste for letters, and can whirl themselves from their own fire-sides to these.' We are often to be found at the Divan ; we profess a fondness for it, and that there are few places of evening resort, to us, so pleasant and unexceptionable.

" At the other Divans there are more characters of humour, more eccentrics, and persons who make themselves conspicuous than at the quiet, decorous Cigarium of Mr. Gliddon. Several droll folks start up to our mind's eye, whom we have met with on our occasional visits to the Rural, in Catherine Street, and its twin parody in Fleet Street on the original Divan ; but all of them are so well known in print or person—with one exception—that to describe them here would be a matter of little gratification either to ourself or our readers."(175)

The divans catered for the wealthy and leisured classes ; but during the 19th century, cigars were within the reach of everybody, as they are today in the United States. (The duty on them was reduced in 1829 from 18 shillings to 9 shillings a pound.) When Mr. Pickwick visited the Magpie and Stump to see Mr. Perker's clerk, Lowten, he was introduced to the company over which Lowten presided as chairman, and after he had ordered a drink and seated himself, the silence that followed was presently broken. " ' You don't find this sort of thing disagreeable, I hope, sir ? ' said his right-hand neighbour, a gentleman in a checked shirt, and Mosaic studs, with a cigar in his mouth.

" ' Not in the least,' replied Mr. Pickwick, ' I like it very much, although I am no smoker myself.'

" ' I should be very sorry to say I wasn't,' interposed another gentleman on the opposite side of the table. ' It's board and lodging to me, is smoke.'

" Mr. Pickwick glanced at the speaker, and thought that if it were washing too, it would be all the better."

Those habitually impecunious medical students, Bob Sawyer and Benjamin Allen, were, as Sam Weller reported to Mr. Pickwick, during the Christmas visit to Dingley Dell, " a-smoking cigars by the kitchen fire ", while they ate oysters, and when Mr. Pickwick met them at breakfast, he observed that Mr. Allen presented, altogether, " rather a mildewy appearance, and emitted a fragrant odour of full-flavoured Cubas ".

The cigar divan was never a competitor of the inn ; it was a specialised type of coffee-house, and its name accorded with the fashion for Turkish things that came in during the eighteen-twenties, when the long, low, upholstered seat without back or arms was introduced and was called an ottoman, and sometimes, if it was very long and broad, a divan. (A form of corner ottoman was developed that became at the end of the 19th century the famous " cosy corner ", and was also known as a " Turkish corner ".)

There were a few taverns that were famous for some particular drink, and one of the sketches in the *Every Night Book* describes the Cider Cellar, that was beginning to lose its popularity. " On the left-hand side of Maiden Lane, if you enter it from Southampton Street, close to the stage-entrance of the Adelphi Theatre, and a short distance only from the house kept by Preist, who lately performed Shylock two or three times on the boards of Drury Lane Theatre, at a considerable nightly expense, as it was said, to himself, is the once famous house of public resort, called the Cider Cellar. It is entirely underground, the entrance to it is by a broad flight of stairs, the place is low, but sufficiently spacious for comfort, and, when tolerably well-filled, is admired by many for its snugness of appearance. Eggs, Welch rabbits, oysters, porter, cider, ale, cigars, spirituous liquors, etc. are to be obtained here, of excellent quality, and at a moderate price. We are told by a lively writer that, a few years ago, the frequenters of the Cider Cellar consisted of gentlemen of the sword, templars, some *petit-maîtres* from the adjacent theatres, a few respectable tradesmen, two or three parsons, an idle old bachelor or so, two or three members of parliament, and occasionally a lord."

Tea-drinking has affected the character and the prosperity of the English inn probably more than any other social habit. Tea had become a national beverage, notwithstanding the denunciations of Cobbett, who after admitting that " the drink, which has come to supply the place of beer has, in general, been *tea* ", said : " It is notorious, that tea has no *useful strength* in it ; that it contains nothing *nutricious* ; that it, besides being *good* for nothing, has *badness* in it, because it is well known to produce want of sleep in many cases, and, in all cases, to shake and weaken the nerves. It is, in fact, a weaker kind of laudanum, which enlivens for the moment and deadens afterwards. At any rate, it communicates no strength to the body ; it does not, in any degree, assist in affording what labour demands. It is then, of no *use*."

The popularity of tea was unassailable, and a verse from *An Ode to my Tea-Pot*, some doggerel published in 1825, indicates the growing rivalry between tea and stronger drinks.

> I scorn the hop, disdain the malt,
> I hate solutions sweet and salt—
> Injurious I vote 'em ;
> For tea my faithful palate yearns,
> Thus,—though my fancy never *turns*,
> It always is *tea-totum* !(176)

Directions for making tea-gardens in country inns were included by John Claudius Loudon, in his huge *Encyclopaedia of Cottage, Farm and Villa Architecture and Furniture*, which was first published in 1833. "The Tea-Garden", he wrote, "should be planted with deciduous and evergreen shrubs; taking care that the nurseryman who supplies them does not plant more than two of a sort, and that the sorts have showy and odoriferous flowers. The alcoves may be formed of trellis-work, and covered with honeysuckle, virgin's-bower, and other creeping shrubs; and, in general, where nothing else will grow, and it is desirable to have a covering of vegetation, Virginian creeper and ivy may be planted. The fountain may be of artificial stone, if real stone is found too expensive; or it may be of cast iron."(177)

Already the process had begun that was to end in Chesterton's lament that

> . . . the wicked old women who feel well-bred
> Have turned to a tea-shop "The Saracen's Head".

But the inn survived, like many other English institutions, and it changed to accommodate new needs. Over a century ago, Loudon could say confidently that "inns in a wealthy and highly civilised country like England contain all the luxuries of a private mansion; and the traveller who stops in them with plenty of money, may enjoy many of the comforts of the home, without its cares". He added that in other countries, "such as the south of Germany and many parts of North America, the inn is frequently a place where greater luxuries are to be obtained than in the private houses of most of its citizens". And then, cautious Scot though he was, Loudon made a prophetic reference to the sort of state that, in the mid-20th century, we are trying to establish, and for want of a more stirring name have called the Welfare State. "With the progress of things in all countries," he wrote, "this is likely to be more and more the case; for, as equality of education and rights become general, it will be followed by a comparative equality in the distribution of property; and great entertainments, such as are now given by wealthy merchants and princes, will only be obtainable by public assemblies or associations at inns. This will, in time, give rise, in every country, as it has already done in Britain, to inns of recreation and enjoyment, as well as inns of accommodation and convenience for travellers."(178)

Loudon then described what he called " Inns of Recreation ", which would not merely afford accommodation and indoor comforts, but would " embrace also all that can be afforded by gardens, pleasure-grounds, parks, forests, and farms ; all the sports of the field, and all the games and exercises that have been known to contribute to human gratification. In one word, all that now can only be obtained by sovereign princes or the most wealthy nobles, will, by the modern system of inns of recreation, be within the reach of every one who has a little spare money and time. In ages and countries of ignorance, and of a privileged and consequently wealthy and all-grasping aristocracy, there will necessarily be many enjoyments, the very nature of which cannot be even imagined by the mass of society, much less can the spectacles displayed by them be seen ; but, in an age such as we contemplate, there will not be a single enjoyment which is not within the reach of all to see and understand ; and in which most of the inhabitants may not be able to participate."

As Loudon lived in an age when people had begun to approve of imitating the styles and fashions of the past, and mediaeval ideas of building were encouraged with a romantic and sometimes religious fervour, he proceeded to " the business of laying down principles for arranging the architectural characteristics of inns ", and illustrated them with " a few miscellaneous designs ". Those designs included a country inn in the Italian style, a small village inn or ale-house in the Italian Gothic manner, a suburban public house in the Old English Style, and a small inn or public house in the Swiss style. His directions for furnishing inns favoured Gothic ornamental shapes in cast iron, such as brackets and frames for supporting tables and sideboards, also chairs. Loudon's copiously illustrated *Encyclopaedia* was a best-seller ; it was one of the key copy books for every type of building and furnishing, and gave practical support to the taste for reproducing old English styles that led ultimately to the nostalgic character of present-day design in architecture and furniture. But despite all such external insincerities, the character of the English inn, like that of the English home, was preserved by the power of tradition, which has always proved stronger than fashion.

CHAPTER XIX

LEGEND AND TRADITION

SINCE the beginning of the 19th century millions of people, countrymen excepted, have come to respect and rely upon what used to be called "book learning", and have allowed their powers of personal observation to become atrophied. One result of such increasing dependence upon the printed word has been the loss of a considerable body of learning that was formerly acquired by word of mouth, and put into practice in everyday life. Knowledge of the proper use of herbs and simple remedies, methods of dressing food and brewing drinks, was traditional ; a great deal of such knowledge was first discredited and then lost ; and although a few discerning Englishmen, like William Cobbett, saw what was happening, and protested, a process had begun that could not be halted, though it could have been intelligently directed. A way of life was being undermined, not by conscious revolutionary action, but by an unacknowledged revolution, that everywhere belittled beliefs which had been handed down from father to son, and consigned the lore of the countryside to the oblivion that was supposed to await the ideas of the unlettered. Soon all rustic beliefs and ideas were to be dismissed as superstitions and " old wives' tales ", and the fabric of unwritten history, in which the bright threads of legend and tradition were interwoven to form a brave pattern, was torn across—almost beyond repair.

Occasionally a belief long held by country folk, and scorned by the learned, would be awkwardly justified by some discovery that disclosed the strength and the length of local memory. Occasionally such memories reach back to the days of the Roman province, and two examples from the west country suggest that the prestige and customs of Roman

Britain probably survived there for generations after they had
been obliterated in the eastern and central parts of the old
province that eventually became England. Up to the early
19th century, a cairn named Bryn-yr-Ellyllon (goblin or fairy
hill), near Mold in North Wales was, according to the country
folk, haunted by the ghost of a warrior in golden armour.
William Boyd Dawkins, the famous Victorian archaeologist,
opined that " This superstition is merely a survival of the idea
so universal among cairn-builders, in all ages and countries,
that the tomb was the home of the spirit, whence it issued
into the upper world."(179)

But was it a superstition ? It may have been a legend that
had lived on in the minds of generations of countrymen for
fifteen hundred years or for more ; because in 1832 a Mr. John
Longford excavated that burial mound, and after removing
three hundred cart-loads of stones, discovered a skeleton, " laid
at full length, wearing a corselet of beautifully-wrought gold
. . . which had been placed on a lining of bronze ".(180)
Boyd Dawkins described the corselet as being formed " of a
thin plate of gold, three feet seven inches long, eight inches
wide in the centre, and weighing seventeen ounces ", and it
was " ornamented in *repoussé* with nail-head and dotted-line
pattern ". He stated that it was an Etruscan work of art,
though it may well have belonged to some Roman officer of
high rank. Mold is in Flintshire, some twelve miles from
Chester, where the XXth Legion, Valeria Victrix, had its
permanent headquarters.

Another memory of Roman Britain, preserved in a locality
where the IInd Augustan Legion had once been quartered,
endured until the middle years of the 19th century. It has
been recorded by Arthur Machen, who was born at Caerleon,
in Monmouthshire ; and in his essay, " Why New Year ? ",
he relates that when he was a boy, New Year's Day was
celebrated in Caerleon in a rather strange fashion. The town
children would take a large brightly coloured apple, make it
still brighter with patches of gold leaf, then stick raisins into
it, also little sprigs of box, with hazel nuts affixed to them, so
" that the nuts appeared to grow from the ends of the box
leaves, to be the disproportionate fruit of these small trees ".
Into the base of the apple three pieces of stick were inserted,

and upon this tripod it was carried round from house to house, and the householders gave sweets and cakes to the children. Arthur Machen identified this as the ancient custom of the *strena*. " Nobody ", he wrote, " knew what it was all about. And here is the strangeness of it. Caerleon means the fort of the legions, and for about three hundred years the Second Augustan Legion was quartered there, and made a tiny Rome of the place, with ampitheatre, baths, temples, and everything necessary for the comfort of a Roman-Briton. And the Legion brought over the custom of the *strena* (French, *etrennes*), the New Year's gift of good omen. The apple, with its gold leaf, raisins and nuts meant : ' good crops and wealth in the New Year ' . . . And I suppose that Caerleon was the only place south of the Tweed where people took any festal notice at all of the first day in the year. For it is not an old English festival at all. It is distinctly Latin in origin."(181)

Gerald de Barri had described the Roman ruins at Caerleon in the 12th century, when he wrote about " immense palaces, formerly ornamented with gilded roofs . . . a tower of prodigious size, remarkable hot baths, relics of temples, and theatres, all inclosed within fine walls, parts of which remain standing ".(182) In Caerleon, the memory of Roman customs lasted longer than Roman masonry.

The book-fed scepticism of the 19th century was not the only influence that eroded long-established habits of thought : an unacknowledged revolution and a disruptive form of taste known as the Gothic Revival had a profound effect upon the Englishman's environment, and gradually debilitated his critical powers to the point when ugliness was accepted as an inevitable accompaniment of what was called " progress ", and very soon ugly surroundings were unperceived. The grimy foulness of the industrial towns in the Midlands and North was even excused by the saying : " Where there's mook, there's mooney ! "

The American and French revolutions of the late 18th century made no visible break with tradition. In the newly independent United States there was a transitory and superficial attempt to create a national fashion, that took the form of using the American eagle on furniture as a decorative motif occasionally ; but the English tradition of architectural design, which had been adapted to the pre-fabricated wooden frame house, still gave a Georgian elegance to the American home, with its sash windows and white-painted weather-boarded walls —a tradition of house design that still persists in the United States. In the design of furniture, the American makers interpreted contemporary English and French fashions : there was no sudden break with accepted forms, no desire to wipe the slate clean and start afresh with all things new. Regional crafts were practised and encouraged, as they were in England ; but one characteristic article was developed in America—the rocking chair. Its invention is sometimes attributed to Benjamin Franklin, though it may have originated in Lancashire in the middle years of the 18th century. Franklin is supposed to have invented it at some time between 1760 and 1770, but it was probably in use earlier, and the first types were either Windsor or ladder-backed chairs, fitted with the curved rockers that were known as bends. Rockers had been used on cradles for centuries, though the idea of applying them to chairs never apparently occurred to anybody, until Franklin, or some unknown chair-maker, thought of it two hundred years ago. The rocking chair has since become an American domestic institution, though its popularity in England died out at the beginning of the present century.

The rocking chair was invented and produced in an age when industry was still based upon organised handicrafts ; but the unacknowledged revolution that changed the shape of so many things during the 19th century was the industrial revolution, for it provided new materials and mechanical methods for the making of all manner of objects, from bridges of cast iron to bedsteads of tubular brass. The industrial revolution began early in the 18th century ; it supplanted an age of machinery that is now forgotten, but had reached a high standard of development during the 17th century, when innumerable weight-driven and spring-driven devices were perfected, and the great period of English clock-making began. The mechanical ingenuity of English craftsmen was considerable ; and John Evelyn gives several descriptions of their abilities and achievements. For example, in the gate-house of Broad-Hinton, the seat of Sir John Glanvill, Evelyn saw " such a lock for a doore, that for its filing and rare contrivances was a master-piece, yet made by a country black-smith. But we have seene watches made by another with as much curiositie as the best of that profession can brag of; and not many yeares after, there was nothing more frequent than all sorts of Iron-work more exquisitely wrought and polish'd than in any part of Europ, so as a dore-lock of a tolerable price was esteem'd a curiositie even among forraine princes."(183)

The capabilities of craftsmen as designers of great works as well as small are emphasised in Evelyn's description of the launching of " that goodly vessell the Charles " at Deptford.

" She is longer than the Soveraine, and carries 110 brasse canon ; she was built by old Shish, a plaine honest carpenter, master builder of this dock, but one who can give very little account of his art by discourse, and is hardly capable of reading, yet of greate abilitie in his calling. The family have been ship carpenters in this yard above 100 yeares."(184)

All over England there were hundreds of men like old Shish, who had profited not by book-learning, but by skill and knowledge passed on from father to son, thus maintaining continuity of tradition, in skill and the way materials were understood and sympathetically handled. Tradition was broken, as we have seen earlier, by the " Italianate " fashions of the 16th century, that affected the shape and character of so many things ; and the memory of the old forms faded before the new, lively understanding of the classical orders of architecture which enlightened the work of designers in the 17th century, and later allowed the diverse fashions of the Georgian period to be so graciously accommodated. But skill remained, though it was diverted into new channels, and some of it was drawn off by the new industrial enterprises, like the great ironfounding business established in 1707 by Abraham Darby in Coalbrookdale, that was started, like so many other enterprises, with an expanding market for its objective. Darby wanted to make life simpler and more comfortable for people in England by supplying them with cheap iron pots, and in 1707 he took out a patent on a " new Invention of Casting Iron-bellied Pots and other Iron-bellied Ware in Sand only without Loam or Clay ".(185) Skill was increasingly encouraged and employed in the devising of new methods and processes in ironfounding and other branches of industry. The industrial revolution offered innumerable opportunities to old Shish and his kind, and many talented men who would formerly have become master-craftsmen, became instead engineers, while skilled workmen instead of practising some handicraft became mechanics. This transference of skill was gradual ; its effect did not become strikingly apparent until the early part of the 19th century, and by then the life and work of the country depended more upon machinery and the new forms of industrial production than upon the traditional arts and crafts. Those arts and crafts survived, but they became even more hopelessly subservient to fashion than they had been in the " Italianate " phase of fashionable taste in the 16th century.

There had been a classical revival in the last decade of the 18th century, and architects and designers of furniture and interior decoration were prolifically ingenious in their use of Greek decorative motifs ; as a result, this phase of taste is sometimes called the Grecian or neo-Grecian revival, and it was variously expressed in the homes of the modish until the eighteen-thirties. The writings and designs of a gifted amateur of architecture, Thomas Hope (1770–1831), stimulated interest in this classical revival, and in 1807 he published a book, illustrated with his own drawings, entitled *Household Furniture and Interior Decoration*. He had travelled in Europe, Asia and Africa to study ancient buildings, and his travels also provided him with materials for a novel, called *Anastasius*, which was published anonymously in 1819, and caused a great sensation. (After the authorship was revealed, he was nicknamed " Anastasius " Hope.) The influence of Hope's writings and designs was considerable, and helped to mould the character of the style, popular during the Regency, that very properly bears its name. A modern and misleading term, English Empire, arises from the belief that Regency furniture and interior decoration were adapted from the Empire style which flourished in France under Napoleon ; but French styles had no effect upon English taste during the first fifteen years of the 19th century, when, save for the brief peace of Amiens, the two countries were at war.

This classical revival injected fresh inspiration into the practice of the great system of design that had been expounded by the writings of Sir Henry Wotton and clarified by the work of Inigo Jones in the first half of the 17th century, and had been followed by architects and designers and craftsmen ever since. It continued an established tradition of taste ; it was under the control of master designers ; it was not a disruptive or misunderstood mode ; and it was the last time that the elegant forms and ornamental conventions of classical antiquity were freshly interpreted in terms of a popular fashion.

The Gothic revival became a potent force in the first half of the 19th century, and its power during that time was moral as well as artistic, for what began as a tenderly romantic fashion in the mid-18th century was transmuted in the course of a hundred years into a form of spiritual regeneration. William Whitehead's references to Gothic fashions have been quoted earlier ; like any other urbane Georgian gentleman, he could dismiss them as ephemeral conceits ; and even Horace Walpole, who tricked out his " little plaything house " at Strawberry Hill with battlements, pinnacles, arched or quatrefoil windows, and chimney-pieces that ingeniously combined features borrowed from mediaeval tombs in Westminster Abbey and Canterbury Cathedral, could admit that the contemplation of good classical architecture restored his sense of proportion, for in writing to Richard Bentley he said about Mereworth that it was " so perfect in a Palladian taste, that I must own it has recovered me a little from Gothic . . ."(186) Horace Walpole might experience the " satisfaction of imprinting the gloom of abbeys and cathedrals on one's house ", but he had no illusions about the architectural significance of his liking for Gothic forms : he was doing, with more taste and judgment and with the discriminating eye of a collector, what many other members of the nobility and gentry were doing at the same time—indulging a romantic and nostalgic mood : nothing more. For the craftsmen and tradesmen who had to execute all these mediaeval fancies, books like Batty Langley's *Builder's Director or Bench-Mate* gave practical guidance about Gothic columns, capitals, cornices, and other details of mouldings and their enrichment, and illustrated designs for Gothic chimney-pieces, of which some suggested a pre-view of the Victorian interior.(187) Fonthill Abbey, in Wiltshire, designed by James Wyatt for William Beckford and built between 1796 and 1799, was a large-scale example of

Horace Walpole's Gothic villa at Strawberry Hill

the orderly Gothic style that was intermittently fashionable during and after the middle years of the 18th century. It was dominated by a great tower, 276 feet high, and contained a hall, " built in the ancient baronial style, seventy-eight feet high, sixty-eight feet long, and twenty-eight feet wide ".(188) Such extravagances were amusing and decorative, and nobody pretended that they elevated the mind or enlarged the spiritual perception of those who commissioned them. Not until men like Augustus Welby Northmore Pugin (1812–1852) began to proclaim the Christian significance of Gothic architecture and repudiate its use as a romantic fashion, did the Gothic revival become a serious, missionary enterprise, dedicated to the rescue of contemporary taste from the amoral acceptance and enjoyment of classical architecture, which in its final manifestation

(261)

as the Greek revival was denounced as the " revived pagan style ".

The Gothic revival drew some of its strength from the Evangelical movement, which gave moral sanction to an interest in sacred architecture ; but a popular appetite for mediaeval romance, roused by the novels of Sir Walter Scott, made large sections of the public receptive to the idea of reviving " good old English " ways of building, though to be sure the date of " the good old times " was, as usual, rather vague. In the first half of the 19th century the great mediaeval legend was invented, and it was coloured and gilded by Pugin, who was an architect of great ability, a pungent writer and a superb draughtsman. Those who believed in the Gothic revival regarded it as an instrument for reforming innumerable abuses and ills, and the growth of the town was considered a grievous ill, and one that had caused increasing anxiety since the end of the 16th century. There had been spirited protests ; and some of the critics of town life in the 18th century had been especially savage.

Reproof of vice and folly may be conveyed either with winged words, or, even more memorably, by the graphic arts. So Fielding's criticisms of the shortcomings of Georgian society in his pamphlets and novels come less readily to mind than Hogarth's pictures of them. Hogarth was as critical of slums and mean cities as any modern social reformer ; but his criticism was incidental—it was introduced as part of the squalid background of " Gin Lane " and " Beer Street " ; it was a component of his general criticisms of society, and he was content merely to show deplorable examples of housing. No remedy is suggested ; no comparisons are made with any previous phase of English civilisation ; possibly because in the 18th century good town planning and the pleasant lay-out of new squares and crescents and gardens and streets, were constantly before authors and artists. Although a few cultivated gentlemen had started to examine the past with the eager eyes of collectors, there was no desire to restore conditions which had long passed away. As we have seen, the Gothic revival was then in its sedate and gentlemanly phase—a charming fashion, not a crusade.

Not until the first half of the 19th century did it become

unpleasantly obvious that towns were losing their gracious and serene character, that they were growing anyhow, and becoming hideously congested ; and that industrial development was seldom inspired by any motive nobler than greed. The gains and losses that had occurred during four centuries of towns growing by fits and starts, were abruptly and even brutally disclosed in a most extraordinary book, written and illustrated by Pugin, which he called *Contrasts : or a Parallel between the noble edifices of the Middle Ages and corresponding buildings of the present day, showing the present decay of taste*. This bombshell burst in England at a time when complacency was being cemented firmly into the social structure by industrial prosperity. Pugin applied to architecture and town planning the same graphic criticism that Hogarth, a hundred years earlier, had used to illustrate social abuses.

The first plate in the book of *Contrasts* showed a town of 1840 compared with an idealised view of it in 1440. Those contrasting views were inspired less by a desire for objective criticism than by a passionate sense of loss—loss of beauty and serenity and spiritual significance. To restore such properties to life was, Pugin obviously felt, the mission of the Gothic revival—which was only part of the greater mission of reuniting Christendom. Who could deny, after examining his drawing of an industrialised town in 1840, that the buildings themselves reflected the inhumanity of an age that created, and found good, such harsh, fantastic chaos ?

Today, in many industrialised parts of England, mediaeval church towers and spires stand in mute reproof of our unlovely materialism, emphasising the comparison between an age of faith and an age of greed, which Pugin found intolerable—the more so because many of his contemporaries were incapable of appreciating what was missing from life. In plate after plate of his book of *Contrasts*, he attacked the shams and stupidities that had invaded civic life, and had produced an architecture which reflected only a bleak utilitarianism. The book vigorously attacked classic architecture, and was a fine bit of graphic pamphleteering for the Gothic revival.

Pugin also attacked public monuments and institutions. The plate that showed contrasted crosses was a harsh comment upon new forces that were beginning to affect everyday life.

Catholic town in 1440.

THE SAME TOWN IN 1840.

The illustration above and on the page opposite are from the 1841 edition of
A. W. Pugin's book of *Contrasts*. See the next four pages

Chichester Cross. From Pugin's book of *Contrasts*, 1841 edition.
The 19th-century version of a cross is shown opposite

He showed Chichester Cross, and displayed his great ability as
a draughtsman in doing so, for he could draw Gothic buildings with insight and sympathy. As a contrast, he selected
Kings Cross, Battlebridge, a preposterous monument to
George IV, with a police station in the base.

Pugin's *Contrasts* was published in 1836, by the author (at a

Kings Cross, Battlebridge. Pugin's dislike for his own times
and their beastly ugliness extended to the newly-formed
police force, as indicated above and on page 269

heavy loss), and the year before, borough constabulary forces
had been established by the Municipal Corporation Act (1835),
and Sir Robert Peel's metropolitan police—whose members
were known at first as " peelers "—was already in existence.
The new police force was regarded with suspicion by many
people ; and policemen and other municipal officials are

(267)

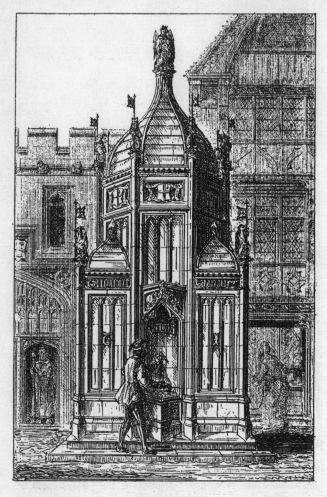

West Cheap Conduit. The illustrations on these two pages
are from the 1841 edition of Pugin's book of *Contrasts*

St. Anne's, Soho. The chained pump and the minatory policeman had in the 19th century replaced the noble fountain depicted on the opposite page

introduced in several of Pugin's drawings, always unflatteringly. To many Englishmen at that time, policemen and municipal officers were visible symbols of a new bureaucratic tyranny. Dickens lost no opportunity of deflating their dignity, and gave that supreme embodiment of parochial power, the beadle, a label that made it difficult ever to take beadles seriously thereafter, for who could respect a " Mr. Bumble " ? Pugin put both police and municipal officers in the pillory in the plates in which he contrasted conduits, and residences for the poor.

The book of *Contrasts*, which was re-issued in 1841, five years after its first appearance, has often been dismissed as an attack on the Protestant religion, mere Popish propaganda, and the religious significance attached to it somewhat diminished its potency as an exposure of civic thoughtlessness. Pugin's case was that the religion of mediaeval England instilled and maintained a sense of civic responsibility—a virtue to which he attached much importance. He was a champion of the old religion, and regarded himself as such. Michael Trappes-Lomax, in his admirable biography of Pugin, admits that he was "not entirely fair in his satire". He qualifies that admission with a sentence that should be written in letters of fire, for the instruction of every reformer : " It is hard for a man to be quite fair when he is wholly in earnest."(189)

Pugin's satirical gifts were considerable ; and in his drawings he used them with the same ferocity as Hogarth. The impact of his method upon the consciousness of his contemporaries was remarkable. He developed a method of architectural criticism that was never forgotten, and Pugin's technique has been the remote though indisputable source of inspiration for many of the illustrated commentaries which have been published during the last twenty-five years, on bad town planning and the destruction of civic and rural amenities. Of these, Osbert Lancaster's *Progress at Pelvis Bay* and *Drayneflete Revealed* are the most outstanding. Osbert Lancaster is an urbane satirist, and *Drayneflete Revealed* not only shows what we owned and enjoyed in the past, and what we have almost or completely ruined, but what we may have lost for ever. It is as resourcefully stimulating as Pugin's *Contrasts*, but written and illustrated on a better plan ; also Osbert Lancaster is bland where

Pugin is bitter, and consequently far more effective in castigating folly.(190)

There were many other contributors to the legend that mediaeval civilisation was nobler and more beautiful than anything that had preceded or followed it ; and the deliberate denigration of the achievements of the Elizabethans, and the contemptuous dislike of the period of classical elegance that began during the 17th century and endured until the reign of William IV were the conventional accompaniments of this glorification of English life in the Middle Ages. Cobbett, writing at the top of his indignant voice, published in 1824 *A History of the Protestant " Reformation ", in England and Ireland*. Early in the book he appeared to realise that his emotions were getting the better of his sense, for he said : " We must keep ourselves cool ; we must reason ourselves out of our ordinary impulses ; we must beseech nature to be quiet within us for a while ; for, from first to last, we have to contemplate nothing that is not of a kind to fill us with horror and disgust."(191) Injustice of any kind, past or present, always brought Cobbett into action ; so he unmasked his batteries of invective on Henry VIII and the noblemen and churchmen who had served him, and contrasted, as Pugin did pictorially a few years later, the country before the dissolution of the monasteries with its state in his own times. " The monastics built as well as wrote for posterity," he said. " The neverdying nature of their institutions set aside, in all their undertakings, every calculation as to *time* and *age*. Whether they built or planted, they set the generous example of providing for the pleasure, the honour, the wealth and greatness of generations upon generations yet unborn. They executed everything in the very best manner : their gardens, fish-ponds, farms ; in all, in the whole of their economy, they set an example tending to make the country beautiful, to make it an object of pride with the people, and to make the nation truly and permanently great. Go into any county, and survey, even at this day, the ruins of its, perhaps, twenty Abbeys and Priories ; and, then, ask yourself, ' what have we *in exchange for these* ' ? Go to the site of some once-opulent Convent. Look at the cloister, now become, in the hands of a rack-renter, the receptacle for dung, fodder and faggot-wood : see the hall, where for ages, the widow, the orphan, the aged and the stranger, found a table ready spread ; see a bit of its walls now helping to make a cattle-shed, the rest having been hauled away to build a *workhouse* : recognize, in the side of a barn, a part of the once-magnificent Chapel : and, if, chained to the spot by your melancholy musings, you be admonished of the approach of night by the voice of the screech-owl, issuing from those arches, which once, at the same hour, resounded with the vespers of the monk, and which have, for seven hundred years, been assailed by storms and tempests in vain ; if thus admonished of the necessity of seeking food, shelter, and a bed, lift your eyes and look at the white-washed and dry-rotten shell on the hill, called the 'gentleman's house' ; and, apprized of the 'board-wages' and the spring-guns, suddenly turn your head ; jog away from the scene of devastation ; with 'old English Hospitality' in your mind, reach the nearest inn, and there, in room half-warmed and half-lighted, and with reception precisely proportioned to the presumed length of your purse, sit down and listen to an account of the hypocritical pretences, the base motives, the tyrannical and bloody means, under which, from which, and by which, that devastation was effected, and that hospitality banished for ever from the land."(192)

After describing the monastic establishments that had formerly flourished in the county of Surrey, he said : " To these belonged *cells* and *chapels* at a distance from the convents themselves : so that it would have been a work of some difficulty for a man so to place himself, even in this poor, heathy county, at six miles distance from a place where the door of hospitality was always open to the poor, to the aged, the orphan, the widow, and the stranger. Can any man *now* place himself, in that whole county, within any number of miles of any such door ? No ; nor in any other county. All is wholly changed, and all is changed for the worse. There is now no *hospitality* in England. Words have changed their meaning. We now give entertainment to those who entertain us in return. We entertain people because we *like them personally* ; and, very seldom, because they stand in need of entertainment. An *hospital*, in those days, meant a place of free entertainment ; and not a place merely for the lame, the sick and the blind ;

and the very sound of the words, ' Old English Hospitality ', ought to raise a blush on every Protestant cheek. But, besides this hospitality exercised invariably in the monasteries, the weight of their *example* was great with all the opulent classes of the community ; and thus, to be generous and kind was the character of the nation at large : a niggardly, a base, a money-loving disposition could not be in fashion, when those institutions to which all men looked with reverence, set an example which condemned such a disposition."(193)

Such adulation of mediaeval life and conditions supplied part of the literary accompaniment to the Gothic revival in architecture ; and during the course of the 19th century the disruptive power of that revival was increasingly marked by the form and embellishment of buildings and furniture, and innumerable objects in everyday use. A great writer and teacher, John Ruskin (1819–1900), became a popular leader of taste, and in the preface to the second edition of *The Seven Lamps of Architecture* (which had first appeared in 1849) he expressed his conviction " that the only style proper for modern northern work ", was 13th-century Northern Gothic, " as exemplified, in England, pre-eminently by the cathedrals of Lincoln and Wells . . ."

It is instructive to compare the effect of Ruskin's writings with those of Sir Henry Wotton. Those two men, separated by two centuries, exerted educational powers that profoundly influenced their contemporaries. One dispelled confusion, the other encouraged it ; one wrote with a sweet reasonableness, the other with the dark fire of faith. Wotton illuminated his age with Vitruvian precepts, intelligibly presented, thus helping to reinstate the basic principles of design. Wotton, who was born in 1568 and died in 1639, was both a realist and a humanist. His reputation for realism is indicated by one of his sayings : " An ambassador is an honest man, sent to *lie* abroad for the good of his country." That sentence was translated from one which he wrote in Latin in the *albo* of Christopher Flecamore, one of his German acquaintances, and in Latin its cynical imputation is diminished. Isaak Walton gives the original sentence in his *Reliquae Wottonianae* : " Legatus est vir bonus peregre missus ad mentiendum Republicae causa." Walton said of the translation : " But the word for *lye* (being the hinge upon which the Conceit was to turn) was not so exprest in Latine, as would admit (in the hands of an Enemy especially) so fair a construction as Sir Henry thought in English."

Wotton's realism and his humanism are both copiously demonstrated by that paraphrase of Vitruvius, *The Elements of Architecture*, which has been quoted in Chapters XI and XV. He wrote at a time when the principles of architectural composition were being confused with the application of ornament. As we have seen, the classical orders of architecture, unrecognised as a system of design, were then regarded as an antique treasury of decorative ideas, that could be pillaged for the adornment of exterior and interior surfaces. Only the work of Inigo Jones showed how the classical orders could be used creatively and imaginatively, and the example of his work, supplemented by Wotton's writings, helped the English Renaissance to grow and to put forth such wonderful fruit from the mid-17th century to the beginning of the Victorian period. During that age of supreme achievement in English architecture, Vitruvian principles were respected and practised. Wotton began the educational process, that was amplified during the 18th century by great architects and great amateurs of architecture, like the third Earl of Burlington.

The urbanities of that age were destroyed by another age of confusion, and John Ruskin hailed the new darkness with rapturous and regrettably infectious enthusiasm, for he thought that the Gothic revival represented new light instead of old night. In *The Stones of Venice*, he denounced everything that Wotton and his contemporaries had admired and taught. He proclaimed the new anarchy in these words : " Whatever has any connection with the five orders ; whatever is Doric or Ionic or Corinthian or Composite, or in any way Grecised or Romanised ; whatever betrays the smallest respect for Vitruvian laws or conformity with Palladian work—that we are to endure no more."

" Ornamentation is the principal part of architecture," he said, adding : " that is to say, the highest nobility of a building does not consist in its being well built, but in its being nobly sculptured or painted."(194)

He believed that " a great architect must be a great sculptor or painter ". He called that personal opinion " a universal law ", and insisted that " No person who is not a great sculptor or painter *can* be an architect. If he is not a sculptor or painter, he can only be a *builder*."

" A Gothic cathedral," he said, " is properly to be defined as a piece of the most magnificent associative sculpture, arranged on the noblest principles of building, for the service and delight of multitudes ; and the proper definition of architecture, as distinguished from sculpture, is merely ' the art of designing sculpture for a particular place, and placing it there on the best principles of building.' " From this he concluded that in his own day there were no architects.

Wotton wrote for the instruction both of architects and laymen ; Ruskin preached rebellion against architects. He encouraged people to fall in love with words that had a romantic as well as an architectural significance. He described the " strange and thrilling interest " conveyed by words that were " in any wise connected with Gothic architecture—as for instance, Vault, Arch, Spire, Pinnacle, Battlement, Barbican, Porch, and myriads of such others, words everlastingly poetical and powerful whenever they occur. . . ." What happened, he asked, if you removed from Scott's romances " the word and the idea *turret* . . .? " He gave an example : " Suppose, for instance, when young Osbaldistone is leaving Osbaldistone Hall, instead of saying ' The old clock struck two from a *turret* adjoining my bedchamber ', he had said, ' The old clock struck two from the landing at the top of the stairs ', what would become of the passage ? And can you really suppose that what has no power over you in words has no power over you in reality ? Do you think there is any group of words which would thus interest you, when the things expressed by them are uninteresting ? "

These romantic enthusiasms for Gothic architecture and for words associated with mediaeval building all helped to establish the legend of " Merry England ". There were many recruits to the ranks of the " Merry Englanders ", and during the eighteen-thirties and -forties the legend accumulated rich decorative trimmings. The history of the Gothic revival in architecture, and all the ancillary activities it stimulated, records the growth of an artificial legend ; not one handed down from father to son, that fitted into the traditional folklore of a country ; but an amalgam of spurious beliefs, arising originally from the trivialities of fashion, and in the course of a century acquiring an emotional appeal that was partly religious and partly nostalgic.

The forms of nearly everything used for the furnishing of houses was affected by the Gothic revival ; and an interest in old furniture was encouraged by the publication, in 1836, of the first book on the subject, Henry Shaw's *Specimens of Ancient Furniture*, with descriptions by Sir Samuel Rush Meyrick. The term *antique* was not at that time applied to old furniture ; the word was used to describe the buildings and works of art of Graeco-Roman civilisation ; while *ancient* was usually reserved for artifacts of great antiquity, such as the temples of Egypt.

Antique furniture did not become a general term for old furniture until the last quarter of the 19th century ; Henry Shaw's book enlarged the meaning of the word ancient, for his beautifully engraved plates showed mediaeval, Elizabethan and late 17th-century furniture, including some elaborately carved chairs of the William and Mary period. John Claudius Loudon, in his *Encyclopaedia of Cottage, Farm, and Villa Architecture and Furniture*, that was published three years before the book by Shaw and Meyrick, included illustrated sections on Gothic and Elizabethan furniture for villas. Loudon wisely remarked that "What passes for Gothic furniture among cabinet-makers and upholsterers is, generally, a very different thing from correct Gothic designs supplied by Architects who have imbued their minds with this style of art." Pugin a few years later said " Upholsterers seem to think that nothing can be Gothic unless it is found in some church."(195)

The growing interest in old furniture, and the strength of the mediaeval legend, encouraged the use of many incorrect though romantic descriptions, such as " monk's bench " for a table-chair (mentioned in Chapter XVII) and "refectory table " for the long tables in use during the late 16th and 17th centuries. Names for articles of furniture were often adopted because they had a comfortable, old-fashioned sound : for example, the term " Grandfather Clock " for a long-case or tall-case clock, seems to have become popular shortly after

Saddle check or easy chair, from Hepplewhite's *Cabinet-Maker and Upholsterer's Guide* (1788). Such chairs were sometimes called lug chairs, and are now often known as wing chairs : but easy chair was the contemporary name. Grandfather chair is a late Victorian term, unknown before the eighteen-eighties

the year 1878, when a song composed by Henry C. Work called " My Grandfather's Clock " was published. The first verse began with the lines :

My grandfather's clock was too large for the shelf,
So it stood ninety years on the floor :
It was taller by half than the old man himself,
Though it weighed not a pennyweight more.

(277)

The " grandfather " clock may have suggested the term " grandfather chair " for a high-backed winged easy chair, as that sentimental name does not appear to have been current earlier than 1880, though such chairs had been in use since the second half of the 17th century, when some examples with adjustable backs were called " sleeping chairs ", though the name generally used was " easy chair ". In Hepplewhite's *Cabinet-Maker and Upholsterer's Guide* (1788) an upholstered high-backed chair with wings is illustrated and described as " a Saddle Check, or easy chair . . ." Another term, adopted for its comfortable sound, was the Darby and Joan chair, that was given to a seat wide enough for four people : such excessive width would certainly have been needed to accommodate the old couple after whom it was named, as Darby suffered from dropsy, and although during the 18th and 19th centuries, Darby and Joan symbolised long-standing affection, the repulsive nature of the original couple was conveniently forgotten. Like the grandfather clock, this term arose from a song, that was published in the " Poetical Essays " section of *The Gentleman's Magazine* for March, 1735, entitled " The Joys of Love Never Forgot ", and it includes these lines :

> Old Darby with Joan by his side,
> You've often regarded with wonder,
> He's dropsical, she is sore-eyed,
> Yet they're ever uneasy asunder. . . .

After the middle of the 19th century, renewed vigour was given to the mediaeval legend by the handicraft revival that was started by William Morris, a brilliantly versatile artist-craftsman, an indifferent poet (who wrote majestic prose), a social reformer, and a teacher who passionately desired to restore the standards of honest craftsmanship that had existed in the Middle Ages and to bring back into life something that had been driven out by the industrial revolution—joy and pride in work.

The proliferation of spurious legends and the interruption of tradition that occurred in the 19th century are illustrated in every city, town and village of England by the buildings and the streets. Architecture, most revealing of all unwritten records, has many unflattering things to say about the Victorian period ; for the scope and character of the Mistress Art have always been largely determined by the nature of the architect's patron.

Thus, the highly civilised Greek city states were served by an architecture that reflected the intellectual and artistic integrity of their rulers, and the perceptive public they governed. (Clive Bell in his essay, " Civilisation ", has said that " The Athenians wished to live richly rather than to be rich ; which is why we reckon them the most highly civilised people in history.") The intellectual and artistic limitations of the military, commercial and bureaucratic slave state of Rome were revealed in buildings whose splendour was often marred by the vulgar amplitude of their decoration. The rising power, both spiritual and temporal, of Christianity after the 4th century re-focused Graeco-Roman architectural genius, and inspired the Byzantine achievement ; and, thereafter, throughout mediaeval Europe, the Church became the supreme patron, collecting the wealth and keeping bright the faith that created the grave nobility and attained the structural triumphs of Gothic architecture. The mercantile aristocracy of the Renaissance, reviving the glories of classical architecture, encouraged their architects to build in the grand manner, allowing the magnificence of their designs to be disciplined by a respect for rules, but never allowing them to be intimidated— as Roman architects were intimidated—by too great a respect for standardisation. Our own great age of building in England was sustained by the most enlightened patronage that English architects have ever enjoyed ; for the Stuart and Georgian nobility and gentry, who called the tune, were visually educated, and a universal respect for common sense supplied the architectural profession with the services of appreciative craftsmen, who could interpret designs, and were masters of their materials—wood, stone, brick, plaster and metal.

Although there was a break with tradition in the 19th century, and an emotional, semi-religious revival of mediaeval ideas, certain traditional ideas persisted. The Victorian house was nearly always designed, whether it was large or small, upon the assumption that it would contain a staff of trained servants. A maid-of-all-work was always assumed to be in residence, however small the house. Such houses represented variations in scale upon the theme of the well-equipped town or country mansion ; and, even today, both in the town and countryside we find traces of these outmoded conventions. Country cottages in a hamlet often have front doors facing the road, no matter what inconvenience such siting imposes upon the interior, and even temporary, pre-fabricated houses are, generally speaking, sited in dull rows with the front doors all facing one way, a relic of the times when the front door had some significance, when it was opened by a servant, to receive the message or the cards proffered by the footman of some lady or gentleman who was paying a call.

Those architectural relics of social distinctions are likely to disappear, for a new form of patronage is emerging. It is collective patronage, operating through the bureaucracy, that is—in theory, at least—appointed and employed by the community. Architects now have the responsibility of creating an architecture for democracy, that may in future centuries be regarded as the outstanding achievement of the Welfare State. They are the only men who could give the breath of life to the architecture that the new patrons require. Only through a co-operative and understanding relationship between architect and patron, can living architecture be produced.

Many obstacles confront the architect who wants to build for democracy ; they are more troublesome to overcome or circumvent than the personal eccentricities of any individual patron ; to create an architecture for democracy, the architect must believe in its future, and look beyond the pre-fabricated creeds that at present house the ideas and aspirations of masses of innocent and credulous people. When men believe strongly in things of the mind and the spirit, they build greatly. They build greatly even if they believe only in the splendour and majesty of their patrons and the society that they adorn, for even such material beliefs are powerful tonics for creative imagination. But what does belief in democracy beget in terms of architecture ? Is it expressed only by applying efficiently—as the Roman builders did—the technical accomplishments of the age : by providing good plumbing, constant hot water, a wash-basin adjacent to every water-closet, and by making a house or an apartment block " a machine for living in " ?

William Morris had said that the " study of history and the love and practice of art " had forced him into " a hatred of the civilisation which, if things were to stop as they are, would turn history into inconsequent nonsense, and make art a collection of the curiosities of the past, which would have no serious relation to the life of the present ".(196) He had described the condition of England, always with reference to the past. " Think of the spreading sore of London," he wrote, " swallowing up with its loathsomeness field and wood and heath without mercy and without hope, mocking our feeble efforts to deal even with its minor evils of smoke-laden sky and befouled river : the black horror and reckless squalor of our manufacturing districts, so dreadful to the senses which are unused to them that it is ominous for the future of the race that any man can live among it in tolerable cheerfulness : nay in the open country itself the thrusting aside by miserable jerry-built brick and slate of the solid grey dwellings that are still scattered about, fit emblems in their cheery but beautiful simplicity of the yeomen of the English field, whose destruction at the hands of yet young Commercial war was lamented so touchingly by the highminded More and the valiant Latimer. Everywhere in short the change from old to new involving one certainty, whatever else may be doubtful, a worsening of the aspect of the country."(197)

He looked forward to a time when both luxury and poverty would be extinguished, " when the upper, middle and lower classes shall have melted into one class, living contentedly a simple and happy life ". In his *News from Nowhere* he described the architecture that was to serve this classless society, and his visions of the future fitted into the mediaeval legend that his writings and practice of handicrafts had reanimated in the second half of the 19th century. In Chapter 4 of that serene utopian romance, he wrote about Hammersmith as it would appear some centuries hence. " There were houses about, some on the road, some amongst the fields with pleasant lanes leading down to them and each surrounded by a teeming garden. They were all pretty in design, and as solid as might be, but countrified in appearance, like yeomen's dwellings ; some of them of red brick like those by the river, but more of timber and plaster, which were by the necessity of their construction so like mediaeval houses of the same materials that I fairly felt as if I were alive in the fourteenth century. . . ."

Such was the architecture of democracy, envisaged by a mediaevalist with a creative mind, and a great love for the English tradition. An alternative, that would have startled and disgusted Morris, is described in John Betjeman's poem, " The Planster's Vision ".

> I have a Vision of The Future, chum,
>> The workers' flats in fields of soya beans
>>> Tower up like silver pencils, score on score :
> And Surging Millions hear the Challenge come
>> From microphones in communal canteens
>>> " No Right ! No Wrong ! All's perfect, evermore."(198)

Centuries of achievement in the arts, crafts and sciences have given us, as we said in the first chapter, an urbanised civilisation, whether we like it or not ; and it has imposed upon the surface of England an irregular and vastly untidy pattern of cities and suburbs with thousands of miles of streets, interspersed with agricultural and industrial areas, dotted with great airfields, many of them guarding our east coast like the old Roman forts of the Saxon Shore, while innumerable streams have been dammed up and villages drowned to form the artificial lakes that supply water to far-distant towns. The vigilant guardians of public health arrange for water to be chlorinated to such an extent that a drink of fresh, crystal clear water, pleasant to the taste, may be had only from some country well. Many homes enjoy central heating that is, perhaps, slightly inferior to the hypocaust system used in the houses of the Romano-British squires and officials ; but the belief that a visible fire on a hearth does, as Wotton said, add to a room " a kind of *Reputation* " is old and strong and honoured as a part of the tradition of home-making.

The English tradition has survived the industrial revolution and the Gothic revival, and has broken through the crust of false legends that were invented and cultivated in the 19th century ; but because we acquired the habit of imitating mediaeval and Tudor and Stuart buildings and furniture during the Victorian period, many people now contentedly accept and find pleasure in counterfeit forms that suggest " the good old times ". The acceptance of such substitutes diminishes the significance of the English tradition : it is like looking at a distant view through the wrong end of a telescope, and ignoring what may be seen about us if we use our eyes.

CHAPTER XX

THE KING'S STANDINGE

L EGENDS have a stubborn grip on many localities ; and
long after they have lost their original substance, they
may bequeath a name to mark the site of a forgotten
battle, a murder, the escapades of some gallant, outrageous or
eccentric man or woman, or the existence of some extinct
industry. Old details about famous events are sometimes
handed down from generation to generation, and Arthur
Machen recorded that he once met an Oxfordshire farm
labourer, unschooled and illiterate, who had casually remarked : " Ay, Chalgrove Field, that's where they killed
Muster Hampden. *They do say it was down in oats at the
time.*"(199)

In Suffolk there is a legend that Cardinal Wolsey built
the causeways west of Southwold which carry the roadway to
Blithburgh, because when he was a lad he assisted his father
who was a butcher to drive cattle from that part of the county
to Ipswich. He is supposed to have said that " if ever his
Purse should be adequate to his Mind, he would accommodate
Travellers with the Shortest Passage ". Thomas Gardener,
who wrote a history of Dunwich, Blithburgh, and Southwold
in 1754, records this, and adds : " Accordingly, in process
of time, he was as good as his word, making Causeways to and
from the Channel, over which he laid a Bridge, that afterwards
bore the Name —— of the Founder thereof."(200)

All over southern and eastern England small eminences mark
the sites of windmills that have been demolished, sometimes a
century ago or even more, but the name Mill Hill clings to
them. (In London Great Windmill Street off Shaftesbury
Avenue still marks the eastern side of Windmill Field, where

up to the end of the 17th century a windmill stood to the north
of the Haymarket.) We have seen how the names Vineyard
and Vineyard Street are the only surviving traces of the old
English home-grown wine industry ; and a field on the outskirts of Winchcombe in Gloucestershire is still called " Tobacco
Close " to remind us that what is now a drowsy and secluded
little town was once the centre of organised resistance when
Charles I, Cromwell, and Charles II all tried unsuccessfully
during a period of over sixty years to prevent the planting of
tobacco in that part of the west country.   The men of Winchcombe intimidated the local constable, defied and seriously
injured the County Sheriff, and fought the picked troops of
the Guards sent by Charles II to subdue them.(201)

Innumerable legends have grown up about mounds and
barrows, some, like the warrior in golden armour at Mold,
have endured for fifty generations ; for mounds were usually
burial places, venerated and often feared by country folk.   In
Walter Johnson's *Byways in British Archaeology* the vitality of
such legends is acknowledged.   Writing in 1912 he said :
" Realising how potent, even to-day, are the traditions of
ghosts, and fairies, and hidden treasure, wherever the dead
are known to lie, and remembering that folk-memory has
frequently proved to be sound in the identification of graves
previously overlooked by the antiquary, we are bound to conclude that nothing short of the extermination of the whole of
the inhabitants of a country-side could completely wipe away
such recollections.   Even to-day after several centuries of the
printed book, and several decades of the day school, the most
definite legends, and those with the greatest living force, are
those which the peasant connects with graves and ghosts.
How much stronger was this kind of tradition when delivered
orally from father to son, and when all folk alike were under
the spell of superstition ! "(202)

Sometimes comparatively modern legends become attached
to ancient mounds, and an example of the growth of a popular
legend is provided by two mounds in Richmond Park, in
Surrey, of which one still exists in the grounds of Pembroke
Lodge on the western side of the park.   It was described in a
guide-book published in 1761 as " a little hill cast up, called
King Henry's Mount, from which there is a prospect of six

counties, with a distant view of London and of Windsor Castle ".(203)   On the earliest known map of the park, which is dated 1637, this mound is called " The King's Standinge ", and as it is on the highest ground in the vicinity, it has been suggested that this name was used in the ancient sense of a stand for a hunter, towards which game could be driven.(204) It is called King Henry's Mount in a conveyance dated 1686 ; in another conveyance of 1698 it is called King Henry VII's Mount ;(205) and during the 18th century it began to appear on maps and plans as Henry VIII's Mount.   On John Roque's map of London, that covers the district of Richmond in 1741–5, the mound is shown but not named, and from it an avenue runs north-east to another mound, which is marked as Oliver's Mount.   Both mounds were probably neolithic, and this is confirmed by Walter Johnson and William Wright in *Neolithic Man in North-East Surrey* when they said : " Oliver's Mound, in Richmond Park, was traditionally said to have been occupied as a camp by Cromwell, but as, in 1834, three skeletons were found at a depth of a yard from the surface, it is a fair surmise that a barrow existed there, especially as many old earthworks and mounds are foolishly connected with the name of Cromwell.   The mound, which stood in the Sidmouth plantation, exists no longer, its site being occupied by a gravel-pit."(206)

The neolithic origin of Henry VIII's Mount is strongly suggested by the considerable deposit of ashes discovered when it was opened.(207)   The avenue shown on John Roque's map still exists, though it is now almost wholly absorbed in Sidmouth Wood, through which a vista has been cut to preserve the line of the old avenue, so that looking along it towards London from Henry VIII's Mount it is possible, in clear weather, to see St. Paul's Cathedral exactly in the centre. This vista was cut when Sidmouth Wood was first planted in 1823, but it became overgrown, and was only re-opened in 1951 after being lost for a century or more.   The Tower of London could be seen from the Mount before Sidmouth Wood was planted, and this helps to sustain a legend that on May 19th, 1536, Henry VIII stood at this point in the park, to watch for the ascent of a rocket from the Tower at noon which was to be the signal that Anne Boleyn had been executed on Tower Green.   Dr. Evans prints the story in *Richmond and*

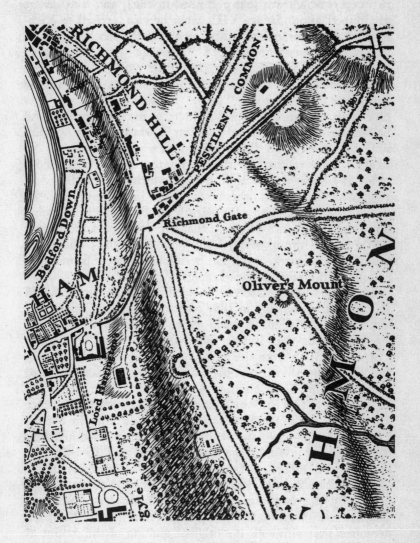

An enlarged section of John Rocque's Map of London in
1741-5, showing the North West part of Richmond Park.
Henry VIII's Mount is due South of Richmond Gate,
and the avenue leading to Oliver's Mount is clearly
marked

its Vicinity, which was first published in 1824, and is as savage as Cobbett about Henry VIII, who, he said, retired to Richmond Palace immediately after receiving the signal " to revel in his accustomed sensuality ! " Edward Jesse, writing in 1832, also mentions the story, and states that the Mount " is in a direct line with the Tower, which is readily seen with the naked eye on a clear day ".(208) Sidmouth Wood was only nine years old when that was written, so the Tower could still be seen through the young trees, for it was certainly not possible to see it down the avenue that framed a view of St. Paul's. Jesse referred to the story later, in the third of his series of *Gleanings in Natural History*, which was published in 1835, when he said that the mound had " long been celebrated as the spot where Henry the Eighth stood to watch the going up of the rocket to assure him that the death of Anne Boleyn would enable him to marry Lady Jane Seymour. This is the tradition of the park, and it has been handed down from father to son by the several park-keepers."(209)

The legend has been serenely copied by different writers, and J. T. Beighton, writing in 1887 on Richmond Park, examined some of the variations in detail about the nature of the signal. " Some tell us that it was the sound of a gun," he said ; " others the flash from the gun : one that it was a black flag, and Dr. Evans that it was the rising of a rocket, and Edward Jesse after him." In another version a signal gun and a flag on the spire of Old St. Paul's figured. Estimating the distance from the mount to the Tower at about eleven miles, he asked : " Would the sound of the artillery of those times be heard at that distance ? Would the flash from a gun, or even the bursting of a rocket, so far off, be visible at noonday in the month of May ? The visionary character of the story is confirmed by the fact that the same tradition has been long attached to high grounds near Epping Forest."(210) Beighton suggested that although the original naming of the mount as The King's Standinge might have referred to Henry VIII, it was more likely to be connected with Charles I, who completed the enclosure of the park in 1637 which is the date of the first map. Mr. C. L. Collenette, in his admirable history of Richmond Park, has pointed out that on the day Anne Boleyn was beheaded, Henry VIII spent the evening at Wolfe Hall in

Wiltshire, sixty miles from Richmond.(211) But it has been argued that he could have covered the distance by riding at seven or eight miles an hour, procuring fresh mounts in the towns through which he passed, and if he had left Richmond shortly after noon he would have reached Wolfe Hall by eight in the evening.(212) Nobody knows when the legend started : obviously it was popular long before it was printed ; it has an appealing plausibility ; it reasserts itself periodically ; and its most dramatic reappearance has been in the form of a short story by Clemence Dane, published in 1929 under the title of " The King Waits ". Inevitably it cropped up again in newspaper correspondence when the re-opening of the vista through Sidmouth Wood was suggested in 1950, and since the eighteen-twenties it has lived on by means of the printed word : its oral life before that may have been far longer, may indeed have begun on that May morning in 1536 when Anne Boleyn's head was struck off by the sword of the executioner who had been brought over specially from Calais.

The other mound, marked on John Roque's map as Oliver's Mount, has long been demolished ; but there is a tradition, unsupported by any evidence, that Oliver Cromwell viewed one of the battles of the Civil Wars from its summit, or, alternatively, that there was an assembly or review of Parliamentary troops in its vicinity. Beighton, in the article previously quoted, suggests that the name may be connected with the family that held the manor of West Sheen, whose surname was Oliver. (West Sheen, a hamlet consisting of eighteen houses, was pulled down in 1769, and the site made into a lawn and added to George III's enclosures, which are now incorporated in Kew Gardens.) This suggestion indicates a possibility, nothing more ; but to dismiss all association with the name of the Protector, as Johnson and Wright did when they said " many old earthworks and mounds are foolishly connected with the name of Cromwell ", is a bit too sweeping.

Apart from recent traditions, which associate Henry VIII and Oliver Cromwell with those two neolithic mounds, there is some significance about their alignment. From Oliver's Mount, Oliver Cromwell would have seen Old St. Paul's crowning Ludgate Hill : from the mound some 700 yards westwards, Henry VIII would have seen the same view, only in his time St. Paul's had a magnificent spire, nearly five hundred feet high. Both mounds are aligned on St. Paul's, and they may well be mark points for one of those " leys " or sighted tracks, running from the high ground of Richmond Hill, across the Thames valley to Ludgate Hill, on which for thirteen hundred years, perhaps far longer, a sacred edifice has stood. From the reign of Henry III, a tradition has been current that on or near the site of St. Paul's Cathedral a temple of Diana existed when London was Londinium Augusta. There is some archaeological evidence to support this belief: in the vicinity a small stone altar to Diana has been found, also a bronze statuette of the goddess. So the King's Standinge in Richmond Park where game was once driven up for the sport of some royal Tudor or Stuart hunter is linked with a temple dedicated to the divine huntress ; though Tudor and Stuart monarchs are people of yesterday and the Roman temple is almost modern compared with the age of that neolithic mound.

England is still a guide-book to over twenty centuries of civilisation, and these pages have attempted to show how, here and there, it may be read ; and in how many unsuspected ways the past is projected into the present.

An altar of Diana, found in 1830, when making excavations
for Goldsmith's Hall, in which building it is now preserved.
From Charles Roach Smith's *Illustrations of Roman London,*
privately printed, 1859

BOOKS REFERRED TO IN THE TEXT

CHAPTER I

(1) *The Environs of London,* by the Rev. Daniel Lysons. (London : Cadell & Davies. Second edition, 1811.) Vol. II, Part II. Note on p. 540.

(2) *London's Natural History,* by R. S. R. Fitter. (Collins, 1945.) Chapter V, p. 96.

CHAPTER II

(3) Included in *The Runagates' Club,* by John Buchan. (Nelson, 1928.)

(4) *Roman Britain and the English Settlements,* by R. G. Collingwood and J. N. L. Myres. (Oxford University Press, 1936.) Section XIX, pp. 317–18.

(5) The earliest date is given in a Calendar of Conveyances as December 21st, 1349. *Records of the Borough of Leicester,* edited by Mary Bateson. (Cambridge University Press, 1901.) Vol. II, p. 394. See Appendix I.

(6) *Diary,* August 9th, 1654.

(7) *Britannia.* (Edition of 1806.) Vol. II, p. 313.

(8) *Folk Memory, or the Continuity of British Archæology,* by Walter Johnson. (Oxford University Press, 1908.) Chapter XVI, p. 338.

(9) *A Study of History,* by Arnold J. Toynbee. (Oxford University Press, 1939.) Vol. IV, Section C.II (*a*), p. 41.

(10) *Glass in Architecture and Decoration,* by Raymond McGrath and A. C. Frost. (The Architectural Press, 1937.) Section I, p. 8.

(11) *Trade Routes and Commerce of the Roman Empire,* by M. P. Charlesworth. (Cambridge University Press, 1924.) Chapter XII, pp. 216–17.

(12) " The Development of the Glass Industry in Lancashire ", by L. M. Angus Butterworth, F.S.A.Scot. Paper prepared for Manchester University, and quoted in *Building for Daylight,* by Sheppard and Wright. (George Allen & Unwin Ltd., 1948.) p. 12.

(13) *Roman Britain and the English Settlements,* by R. G. Collingwood and J. N. L. Myres. Section XIV, p. 236.

(14) *St. Joan,* Scene IV.

(15) *The Jungle Tide,* by John Still. (William Blackwood.) Quoted from the 1947 reprint, Section V, p. 118.

CHAPTER III

(16) *Royal Commission on Historical Monuments,* Vol. III, Roman London. (H.M. Stationery Office, 1928.) p. 42 : also Appendix VI, p. 195 and map.

(17) *Some Sources of Human History*, by W. M. Flinders Petrie. (Society for Promoting Christian Knowledge, 1919.) Chapter I, p. 39.

(18) *A History of Egypt*, by J. A. Breasted. (Hodder & Stoughton Ltd., reprint of 1909 edition, 1946.) Chapter V, p. 86.

(19) *Ancient Town-Planning*, by F. Haverfield. (Oxford University Press, 1913.) Chapters II and III, pp. 27–30.

(20) *The Arab Conquest of Egypt*, by Alfred J. Butler. (Oxford University Press, 1902.) Chapter XXIV, pp. 369–70 and 390–1.

(21) Suyûtî (*Husn al Muhâdarah*), quoted by Dr. Butler.

(22) *The Arab Conquest of Egypt*, Chapter XXIV, p. 369.

(23) *The City of Tomorrow*, by Le Corbusier. (Translated from the eighth French edition of *Urbanisme* by Frederick Etchells. London : John Rodker, 1929.) Part II, p. 177.

(24) *The Architecture of Marcus Vitruvius Pollio*. Translated by Joseph Gwilt. (London : Priestley & Weale, 1826.) Book I, Chapter VI.

(25) *Ancient Town-Planning*, by F. Haverfield. Chapter IV, p. 49.

(26) *Vitruvius*, Book I, Chapter VII.

(27) *How the Greeks Built Cities*, by R. E. Wycherley. (Macmillan & Co. Ldt., 1949.)

(28) *Ibid.*, p. 39.

(29) *Ibid.*, p. 39.

CHAPTER IV

(30) *The Past in the Present*, by Arthur Mitchell, M.D., LL.D. (Edinburgh : David Douglas, 1880.) Lecture III, pp. 57–72.

(31) Quoted by R. W. Moore in his selection of Latin texts, *The Romans in Britain*. (Methuen & Co. Ltd., 1938.) XVIII, 87, p. 139.

(32) *Stonehenge and its Date*, by R. H. Cunnington. (Methuen & Co. Ltd., 1935.) Chapter VIII.

(33) *The Old Straight Track*, by Alfred Watkins. (Methuen & Co. Ltd., 1925.)

(34) *The Green Roads of England*, by R. Hippisley Cox. (Methuen & Co. Ltd., 1914.)

(35) Ordnance Survey Office, Southampton, 1933.

(36) *Landscape in History*, by Sir Archibald Geikie, D.C.L., F.R.S. (Macmillan & Co. Ltd., 1905.) p. 23.

(37) *The Roman Invasions*, by Laurence O. Pitblado. (Allen & Unwin Ltd., 1935.) Addenda, Note I, pp. 133–9.

(38) *Mediaeval Geography : an Essay in illustration of the Hereford Mappa Mundi*, by the Rev. W. L. Bevan, and the Rev. H. W. Phillott. (E. Stanford, London, 1873 : also published in Hereford by Jakeman and Jones.) Chapter I, p. 5.

(39) *The Atlas of Ancient and Classical Geography*. (Everyman Library edition.) pp. 4 and 5.

(40) *Journal of Roman Studies*, Vol. XXIV (1934), II. Inscriptions, p. 220. Described by V. E. Nash-Williams, F.S.A.

(41) *The Personality of Britain*, by Sir Cyril Fox, Ph.D., F.S.A. (Cardiff, National Museum of Wales, 1933.) pp. 44, 45.

(42) *Submerged Forests*, by Clement Reid, F.R.S. (Cambridge University Press, 1913.) Chapter VIII, p. 117.

(43) *The Personality of Britain*, by Sir Cyril Fox, Ph.D., F.S.A., p. 43.

(44) *Landscape in History*, by Sir Archibald Geikie, p. 18.

(45) *Ibid.*, pp. 18, 19.

CHAPTER V

(46) *Roman Britain and the English Settlements*, by Collingwood and Myres. Section XII, pp. 201–2.

(47) *A History of Cast Iron in Architecture*, by John Gloag and D. L. Bridgwater, F.R.I.B.A. (Allen & Unwin, 1948.) Introduction, p. 9.

(48) Quoted from the 3rd edition of *Sylva, or a Discourse of Forest-Trees*, published in 1679.

(49) *The Sword in the Stone*, by T. H. White. (Collins, 1939.) Chapter X, pp. 153–4.

(50) *The Woodlands*, by William Cobbett. (Printed and published by William Cobbett, 1825.)

CHAPTER VI

(51) *The Stranger in Liverpool*. (Printed and published by T. Kaye.) Quoted from the fifth edition, 1816. pp. 209, 210.

(52) *Outline Plan for the County Borough of Birkenhead.* Prepared for the Council by Professor Sir Charles Reilly, O.B.E., M.A., Hon. LL.D., F.R.I.B.A., Hon. M.T.P.I., and N. J. Aslan, Dip.Arch. (Liverpool), A.R.I.B.A., Dip.T.P. (London), A.M.T.P.I. Printed by Willmer Bros. & Co. Ltd., Birkenhead, 1947. (Published by the County Borough of Birkenhead.)

(53) *Rides on Railways*, by Samuel Sidney. (London : William S. Orr & Co., 1851.)

(54) *Ibid.*, p. 155.

(55) *Ibid.*, p. 151.

(56) *A Perambulation of the Hundred of Wirral*, by Harold Edgar Young. (Liverpool : Henry Young & Sons, 1909.) Chapter II, p. 18. Also Lysons' *Magna Britannia*. (London : T. Cadell & W. Davies, 1810.) Vol. II, Cheshire, p. 506.

(57) *Ibid.*, Chapter II, p. 21.

CHAPTER VII

(58) *The Ecclesiastical History of the English Nation*, by the Venerable Bede. (Everyman Library edition.) Chapter I.

(59) *Roman Britain and the English Settlements*, by R. G. Collingwood and J. N. L. Myres. (Oxford University Press, 1936.) Section XII, p. 202.

(60) *Ibid.*, p. 202.

(61) *Verulamium : a Belgic and two Roman Cities*, by R. E. M. Wheeler, D.Lit., V.P.S.A., and T. V. Wheeler, F.S.A. (Oxford University Press, for the Society of Antiquaries, 1936.)

(62) *Ibid.*, p. 2.

(63) *Roman Britain and the English Settlements*, by R. G. Collingwood and J. N. L. Myres. Section XII, p. 197.

(64) " What *matters* in Archaeology ? " An address to the Council for British Archaeology, delivered by R. E. M. Wheeler at Burlington House, London, on July 10, 1950. Printed in *Antiquity*, Vol. XXIV, No. 96. September, 1950.

CHAPTER VIII

(65) *Roman Britain and the English Settlements*, by R. G. Collingwood and J. N. L. Myres. (Oxford University Press, 1936.) Section VI, p. 101.

(66) *Royal Commission on Historical Monuments*. Vol. III, *Roman London*. (H.M. Stationery Office, 1928.) p. 103. These fragments of sculpture were preserved in the Guildhall Museum.

(67) *Ibid.*, p. 92.

(68) *Ancient Town-Planning*, by F. Haverfield. (Oxford, 1913.) Chapter XI, p. 142.

(69) *London Before the Conquest*, by W. R. Lethaby. (Macmillan & Co., 1902.) Chapter VII, p. 157.

(70) *Ibid.*, p. 156. *Londinium*, by W. R. Lethaby. (Duckworth, 1923.) Chapter II, p. 54.

(71) *Ancient Town-Planning*, by F. Haverfield. Chapter XI, pp. 140–1.

CHAPTER IX

(72) *The World Set Free*, by H. G. Wells. (Macmillan & Co., 1914.) Chapter IV, p. 199.

(73) (London. Harvey & Darton, 1814.)

(74) (London. Henry G. Bohn, 1849.)

(75) *Man and Boy*, by Sir Stephen Tallents. (Faber & Faber Ltd., 1943.)

(76) *Ibid.*, pp. 12–13.

(77) *Richmond on the Thames*, by Richard Garnett. (London : Seeley & Co., 1896.) Chapter III, p. 20.

(78) *Ibid.*, p. 206.

CHAPTER X

(79) *From Sea to Sea*, by Rudyard Kipling. (Macmillan & Co., first edition, 1900.)

(80) *Ibid.*, Vol. II, Section XXV, p. 25.

(81) *Building for the People*, by Richard Sheppard, F.R.I.B.A. (George Allen & Unwin Ltd., 1948.) Chapter 8, p. 114.

CHAPTER XI

(82) *A History of Egypt*, by J. H. Breasted. (London : Hodder & Stoughton Ltd. Reprint of 1909 edition, January 1939.) Chapter V, p. 101.

(83) *The Architecture of Marcus Vitruvius Pollio*. Translated by Joseph Gwilt. (London : Priestley & Weale, 1826.) Book VI, Chapter VIII, p. 179.

(84) *Ibid.*, p. 180.

(85) *Ibid.*, Chapter IX, pp. 181-2.

(86) *Itinerary Through Wales*, by Giraldus Cambrensis. (Everyman Library edition.) Book I, Chapter V.

(87) *The Elements of Architecture*, by Sir Henry Wotton. The First Part. (Included in *Reliquiae Wottonianae*. London : third edition, 1672.)

CHAPTER XII

(88) *The Ecclesiastical History of the English Nation*, by the Venerable Bede. (Everyman Library edition.) Book III, Chapter X.

(89) " *The Illiterate Anglo-Saxon* ", and other Essays on Education, Medieval and Modern, by John William Adamson. (Cambridge University Press, 1946.) Chapter I, p. 15.

(90) *Anglo-Saxon Art*, by T. D. Kendrick. (Methuen, 1938.) Chapter VI, p. 119.

(91) *The Lives of the Holy Abbots of Wearmouth and Jarrow*, by the Venerable Bede. (Everyman Library edition.)

(92) *Ibid.*

(93) *Building for Daylight*, by Richard Sheppard and Hilton Wright. (George Allen & Unwin Ltd., 1948.) Introduction on " English Window Design ", by John Gloag. pp. 13, 14.

(94) *The Ecclesiastical History of the English Nation*, by the Venerable Bede. Book II, Chapter VI.

(95) *The Transition from Roman Britain to Christian England*, by Gilbert Sheldon. (Macmillan & Co., 1932.) Chapter V, p. 86.

(96) *Ibid.*, pp. 86, 87.

(97) *Roman Britain and the English Settlements*, by R. G. Collingwood and J. N. L. Myres. (Oxford University Press, 1936.) Section XIX, pp. 317-18.

CHAPTER XIII

(98) *Christianity in Early Britain*, by Hugh Williams, M.A., D.D. (Oxford : Clarendon Press, 1912.) Chapter IV, p. 78.

(99) *The Ecclesiastical History of the English Nation*, by the Venerable Bede. (Everyman Library edition.) Book I, Chapter VIII.

(100) *Ibid.*, Book I, Chapter VII.

(101) *Christianity in Early Britain*, by Hugh Williams, M.A., D.D. Chapter IX, p. 142. *Chapters of Early English Church History*, by William Bright, D.D. (Oxford : Clarendon Press, 3rd edition, 1897.) Chapter I, p. 10.

(102) *The British History*, by Geoffrey of Monmouth. (Aaron Thompson's translation, London, 1718.) Book III, Chapter XVIII.

(103) *Chapters of Early English Church History*, by William Bright, D.D. Chapter I, p. 11.

(104) *Byways in British Archaeology*, by Walter Johnson. (Cambridge University Press, 1912.) Chapter I, p. 23.

(105) *Londinium : Architecture and the Crafts*, by W. R. Lethaby. (London : Duckworth & Co., 1923.) Chapter XI, pp. 217–18.

(106) Described by Professor I. A. Richmond, of King's College, Newcastle-upon-Tyne, to the Society for the Promotion of Roman Studies, January 9th, 1951. (Reported in *The Times*, January 10th, 1951.)

(107) *The Transition from Roman Britain to Christian England*, by Gilbert Sheldon. (London : Macmillan & Co. Ltd., 1932.) Chapter III, p. 40. Also, *Roman Britain and the English Settlements*, by Collingwood and Myres. Section XVI, pp. 264–5.

(108) *Roman Britain and the English Settlements*, by R. G. Collingwood and J. N. L. Myres. Section XVI, p. 264.

(109) *Ibid.*, Section XVI, pp. 261 and 264.

(110) *The Philosophy of Witchcraft*, by Ian Ferguson. (London : Harrap & Co., 1924.) Chapter II, p. 50.

(111) *Chapters of Early English Church History*, by William Bright, D.D. Chapter I, p. 35. *England Before the Norman Conquest*, by Charles Oman. (London : Methuen, 4th edition, 1910.) Book III, Chapter XIV, pp. 260–1. *Councils and Ecclesiastical Documents relating to Great Britain and Ireland*, by Arthur Haddon and William Stubbs. (Oxford : Clarendon Press, 1869.) Vol. I, pp. 116–17.

(112) *Byways in British Archaeology*, by Walter Johnson. Chapter I, p. 5.

(113) *Ecclesiastical History of the English Nation*, by the Venerable Bede. Book III, Chapter IV.

(114) *Celtic Scotland : a History of Ancient Alban*, by William Skene, D.C.L., LL.D. (Edinburgh : Davis Douglas, 2nd edition, 1887.) Vol. II, Book II, Chapter I, p. 2. Chapter II, p. 46.

(115) Skene, *opus cit.* Chapter II, p. 46.

CHAPTER XIV

(116) *The Ecclesiastical History of the English Nation*, by the Venerable Bede. (Everyman Library edition.) Book I, Chapter XXVI.

(117) *The Architecture of Adventure*. A paper delivered by William Richard Lethaby before the Royal Institute of British Architects, April 18th, 1910, and reprinted in *Form in Civilization* (Oxford University Press, 1922).

BOOKS REFERRED TO IN THE TEXT

(118) *A Concise Glossary of Architecture*, by John Henry Parker. (Oxford and London : James Parker & Co. Fourth edition, 1875.) p. 191.

(119) *Social life in the days of Piers Plowman*, by D. Chadwick. (Cambridge University Press, 1922.) p. 55.

CHAPTER XV

(120) *Harrison's Description of England in Shakespere's Youth*, edited by Frederick J. Furnival. (Published for the New Shakespere Society by N. Trubner & Co., London, 1877.) Vol. I, Book II, Chapter V, p. 129.

(121) *Ibid.*, pp. 129–30.

(122) *Ibid.*, Vol. I, Book II, Chapter XII, p. 238.

(123) *Ibid.*, Book II, Chapter XII, pp. 239–40.

CHAPTER XVI

(124) *Harrison's Description of England in Shakespere's Youth*, edited by Frederick J. Furnival. (Published for the New Shakespere Society by N. Trubner & Co., London, 1877.) Vol. I, Book II, Chapter XII, p. 240.

(125) *Ibid.*, Vol. I, Book II, Chapter XII, pp. 238–9.

(126) *Five Hundred points of good husbandry united to as many of good huswiferie*, by Thomas Tusser (1573), p. 5, fol. 2.

(127) *Farm and Cottage Inventories of Mid-Essex, 1635–1749*. (Essex Record Office Publications, No. 8.) Inventory of the goods and chattels of John Draper of Writtle, yeoman. p. 124.

(128) Quoted in *England as Seen by Foreigners*, by William Brenchley Rye. (London : John Russell Smith, 1865.) pp. 77–80.

CHAPTER XVII

(129) *Farm and Cottage Inventories of Mid-Essex, 1635–1749*. (Essex Record Office Publications, No. 8.) p. 127.

(130) *Ibid.*, p. 149.

(131) *Diary*, April 30th, 1666.

(132) Quoted by Hubert Hall in *Society in the Elizabethan Age*. (Swan Sonnenschein & Co. Ltd. 4th edition, 1901.) p. 150.

(133) Published by Lawrence & Bullen.

(134) *Diary*, November 1st, 1660.

(135) *The World*, No. 12. March 22, 1753. (New edition, 1795. Printed for P. Dodsley, Pall-Mall.) pp. 68–9.

(136) *Ibid.*, p. 69.

(137) *The World*, No. 38. September 20, 1753. p. 241.

(138) *Ibid.*, p. 243.

CHAPTER XVIII

(139) *Harrison's Description of England in Shakespere's Youth*, edited by Frederick J. Furnival. (Published for the New Shakespere Society by N. Trubner & Co., London, 1877.) Book III, Chapter 16.

(140) *Joseph Andrews*, by Henry Fielding. Chapter XV.

(141) *Furniture and Furnishing*, by John C. Rogers, A.R.I.B.A. (Oxford University Press, 1932.) Chapter V, p. 53.

(142) *England as Seen by Foreigners*, by William Brenchley Rye. (London : John Russell Smith, 1865.) Note 134, pp. 272–3.

(143) *Harrison's Description of England in Shakespere's Youth*, edited by Frederick J. Furnival. Book III, Chapter 16.

(144) *Ibid.*, Book I, Chapter 18.

(145) *The Englishman's Food*, by J. C. Drummond and Anne Wilbraham. (London : Jonathan Cape, 1939.) Part One, Section 7.

(146) Some evidence is quoted by Ronald Duncan in *Tobacco Cultivation in England*. (London : The Falcon Press, 1951.) Chapter I, p. 16.

(147) "Elizabethan Overseas Trade", by Lawrence Stone. *Economic History Review*, second series, Vol. II, No. 1, p. 48.

(148) *Roman Britain and the English Settlements*, by R. G. Collingwood and J. N. L. Myres. (Oxford : The Clarendon Press, 1936.) Section IV, p. 71.

(149) *Ibid.*, Chapter XIII, p. 221.

(150) *An Encyclopaedia of Gardening*, by John Claudius Loudon. (London : Longman, Hurst, Rees, Orme & Brown, 1822.) Section 2132, p. 1224.

(151) *Domestic Life in England*, by the Editor of "The Family Manual and Servant's Guide". (London : Thomas Tegg & Son, 1835.) pp. 211, 212.

(152) *Cottage Economy*, by William Cobbett. (London : C. Clement, 1822.) Part I, p. 11.

(153) *Ibid.*, Part II, p. 44.

(154) *Ibid.*, Part VI, p. 207.

(155) *Domestic Life in England*, pp. 204, 205.

(156) *Cottage Economy*, by William Cobbett, Part I, p. 22.

(157) *Domestic Life in England*, p. 210.

(158) *A History of England in the Eighteenth Century*, by W. E. H. Lecky. (London : Longmans, Green & Co., 1878.) Vol. I, Chapter III, p. 479.

(159) *England as Seen by Foreigners*, by William Brenchley Rye. Note 20, p. 190.

(160) *Ibid.*, Note 20, p. 191.

(161) *Harrison's Description of England*, Book II, Chapter VI, p. 146.

(162) *Domestic Life in England*, p. 209.

(163) *Cottage Economy*, by William Cobbett. No. 7, pp. 197–8.

(164) *Tom Brown's Schooldays*, by Thomas Hughes. Chapter IV.

(165) *Farm and Cottage Inventories of Mid-Essex, 1635–1749*. (Essex Record Office Publication, No. 8.) p. 258.

(166) *The History of Signboards*, by Jacob Larwood and John Camden Hotten. (London : J. C. Hotten, Piccadilly, 1867.) Chapter XIII, p. 421.

(167) *Tobacco Cultivation in England*, by Ronald Duncan. Chapter II, p. 30.

(168) *Ibid.*, Chapter VI, p. 81.

BOOKS REFERRED TO IN THE TEXT

(169) *Diary*, October 22nd, 1658.

(170) *The Social History of Smoking*, by G. L. Apperson. (London : Martin Secker, 1914.) Chapter V, p. 89.

(171) *Daedalus, or Science and the Future*, by J. B. S. Haldane, F.R.S. (London : Kegan Paul, 1924.) p. 36.

(172) *The Journeys of Celia Fiennes*, edited by Christopher Morris. (London : The Cresset Press, 1947.) Part III, p. 257.

(173) *The Torrington Diaries*, edited by C. Bruyn Andrews. (London : Eyre & Spottiswoode, 1934.) Vol. I, p. 221.

(174) *The Social History of Smoking*, by G. L. Apperson. Chapter IX, p. 139.

(175) *Every Night Book ; or Life After Dark*, by the Author of " The Cigar ". (London : T. Richardson, 1827.) pp. 92–3.

(176) " An Ode to my Tea-Pot ", reprinted from John Bull, in *The Spirit of the Public Journals*. (London : Sherwood, Gilbert & Piper, 1826.) p. 460.

(177) *The Encyclopaedia of Cottage, Farm and Villa Architecture and Furniture*, by J. C. Loudon. (London : Longman, 1833.) Section 1431, p. 682.

(178) *Ibid.*, Section 1410, pp. 675–6.

CHAPTER XIX

(179) *Early Man in Britain*, by W. Boyd Dawkins. (London : Macmillan & Co., 1880.) pp. 431–3.

(180) *Ibid.*, pp. 431–3.

(181) *Dog and Duck*, by Arthur Machen. (London : Jonathan Cape, Travellers' Library edition, 1926.) Essay : " Why New Year ? " pp. 27–8.

(182) *Itinerary Through Wales*, by Giraldus Cambrensis. (Everyman Library edition.) Book I, Chapter V.

(183) *Diary*, July 16th, 1654.

(184) *Diary*, March 3rd, 1668.

(185) *A History of Cast Iron in Architecture*, by John Gloag and Derek Bridgwater, B.Arch., F.R.I.B.A. (London : George Allen & Unwin Ltd., 1948.) Section One, p. 41. *Grand Alliance*, by Basil H. Tripp. (Published for Allied Ironfounders Limited by Chantry Publications, 1951.) Section II, p. 18.

(186) Letter to Richard Bentley, from Tonbridge. (August 7th, 1752.)

(187) *The Builder's Director, or Bench-Mate : being a Pocket-Treasury of the Grecian, Roman, and Gothic Orders of Architecture*, by Batty Langley, Architect. (London : Printed for H. Piers, 1751.) pp. 160–84.

(188) *A Description of Fonthill Abbey*, by John Rutter. (London : Longman, Hurst & Co. Third edition, 1822.) p. 27.

(189) *Pugin : a mediaeval Victorian*, by Michael Trappes-Lomax. (London : Sheed & Ward, 1933.) Chapter VIII, p. 75.

(190) *Progress at Pelvis Bay*, by Osbert Lancaster. (London : John Murray, 1936.) *Drayneflete Revealed*. (Murray, 1949.)

(191) *A History of the Protestant " Reformation ", in England and Ireland,* by William Cobbett. (London : Charles Clement, 1824.) Letter II, paragraph 66. The pages of the book are not numbered.

(192) *Ibid.,* Letter V, paragraph 155.

(193) *Ibid.,* Letter VI, paragraph 183.

(194) *Lectures on Architecture and Painting,* by John Ruskin. Addenda to Lectures I and II.

(195) *The True Principles of Pointed or Christian Architecture,* by A. Welby Pugin. (London : John Weale, 1841.) p. 40.

(196) " How I Became a Socialist ", by William Morris. (From his Lectures and Essays.)

(197) " Art and Socialism ", by William Morris. (From his Essays and Lectures.)

(198) *New Bats in Old Belfries,* by John Betjeman. (London : John Murray, 1945.)

CHAPTER XX

(199) *Dog and Duck,* by Arthur Machen. (London : Jonathan Cape, Travellers' Library edition, 1926.) Essay : " St. George and the Dragon ". p. 133.

(200) *An Historical Account of Dunwich, Antiently a City, now a Borough ; Blithburgh, Formerly a Town of Note, and now a Village ; Southwold, Once a Village, and now a Town-Corporate,* by Thomas Gardener. (London : Printed for the author, and sold by him at Southwold, in Suffolk ; and also by W. Owen, at Homer's Head, near Temple Bar, 1754.) Southwold. Chapter IX, p. 256.

(201) *The Early English Tobacco Trade,* by C. M. MacInnes. (London : Kegan Paul, 1926.) Chapter V, p. 129.

(202) *Byways in British Archaeology,* by Walter Johnson. (Cambridge University Press, 1912.) Chapter II, p. 87.

(203) *London and its Environs Described.* (London : Printed for R & J. Dodsley, 1761.) Vol. V, p. 262.

(204) *A History of Richmond Park,* by C. L. Collenette. (London : Sidgwick & Jackson Ltd., 1937.) Part I, p. 37.

(205) *Ibid.,* p. 37.

(206) *Neolithic Man in North-East Surrey,* by Walter Johnson and William Wright. (London : Elliot Stock, 1903.) p. 68.

(207) *Gleanings in Natural History,* by Edward Jesse. (London : John Murray, Third series, 1835.) pp. 244–6.

(208) *Gleanings in Natural History,* by Edward Jesse. (First series, 1832.) pp. 158–9.

(209) *Ibid.* (Third series, 1835.) pp. 244–6.

(210) " Richmond Park ", by J. T. Beighton. I. Historical Associations. *The Leisure Hour,* 1887. p. 450.

(211) *A History of Richmond Park,* by C. L. Collenette. Part I, p. 37.

(212) *Historical Richmond,* by Edwin Beresford Chancellor. (London : George Bell & Sons, 1885.) Chapter VI, pp. 217–19.

INDEX

Figures in brackets denote a reference in a caption.

INDEX

Beau Nash, 16
Bebbington, Cheshire, 48
Becket, Thomas à, 78
Beckford, William, 260
Bede, the Venerable, 8, 34, 59, 121, 122, 124, 125, 134, 231, *quoted 126, 130, 131, 136, 137*
Bedrooms, 206, (182)
Beds, 181, (127), (189)
Beehive huts, 15, 30, (31)
Beer, 228, 232, 234, 238, (237)
Beighton, J. T., 289, *quoted 288*
Bell, Clive, *quoted 279*
Bennett, Arnold, 46
Bentley, Richard, 260
Betjeman, John, *quoted 282*
Bevis Marks, London, 29
Bidston, Cheshire, 48
Birkenhead, 48, 52, 55, 56, 61, 79, (49), (50), (51), (54)
— Park, 51
— Priory of, 48, 55
Birmingham, 99
Biscop, Benedict, 59, 124
Blenheim Palace, 164
Blithburgh, 284
Boadicea, 64
Boards, 186
Boleyn, Anne, 286, 288, 289
Bolingbroke, Lord, 85
Book of the Duchesse, The, 181
Borrow, George, *quoted 234*
Boudicca, 64
Brandon, Colonel, 243
Breasted, Professor, 21
Brewing machine, 232
Brickmaking, 124, 150
Bright, Dr. William, 131
Brighton, 179
Britain, Dark Ages in, 10, 11, 16, 17, 29
—, glass industry in, 10
—, industrial development in, 85
—, mediaeval, 34, 39, 78
—, —, building in, 13, 15, (14)
—, pre-Roman, 30–2, 35
—, Roman, Province of, 8, 10, 12, 13, 15, 29, 35, 36, 110–14
—, —, — —, remains in, 8–10, 60, 61
—, Saxon, 36, 37, 39, 116
—, —, building in, 9
Britannia, 10
British History, 8, 60
British Tobacco Growers' Society, 244

Broadway, New York, 70
Bromsash, Herefordshire, 12
Buchan, John, 8
Builder's Director or Bench-Mate, The, 260
Building for the People, 104
Building materials, 150, 159
Burlington, third Earl of, 205, 274, (204)
Butler, Dr. Alfred J., 23, 24
Byng, the Hon. John, 248
By-Ways in British Archaeology, 285

Cabinet Dictionary, The, 200
Cabinet-Maker and Upholsterer's Guide, The, 278
Cabinet-Maker's and Upholsterer's Drawing Book, The, 212
Cabinet making, 203
Caerleon, 60, 109, 255, 256
Caerwent, 61
Caister-next-Norwich, 12
Calleva Atrebatum, 12, 27, 132, (63)
Cambridge, 77, 98
Camden, William, 10, (33)
Camomile Street, London, 29, 65
Camps, Roman, 19
Canals, 99
Canterbury, 137, (69)
Capitol, Washington, 57
Caractacus, 30
Carlton House Terrace, 86, 179
Caroline, queen of George II, 5
Carrawburgh, 132
Cartographers, 32, 34, 35
Castor, Northants, 12
Castor ware, 13
Cathedrals, 139
Chair making, 193, 197, 200
Chairs, 184, 186, 193, 197, 200, 257, (194), (198), (199), (201), (209), (215), (277)
Chamber horse, 210, 212
Chapters of Early English Church History, 131
Charles I, 91, 243, 288
Charles II, 176, 203, 285
Charlesworth, Dr. M. P., 12
Charteris, Leslie, 42
Chatsworth, 51
Chaucer, 46, 181
Chelsea Hospital, 88
Cheltenham, 179
Chester, 19, 79

INDEX

INDEX